Theology, Political Theory, and Pluralism

How can we live together in the midst of our differences? This is one of the most pressing questions of our time. Tolerance has been the bedrock of political liberalism, while proponents of agonistic political thought and radical democracy have sought an answer that allows a deeper celebration of difference. Kristen Deede Johnson describes the move from tolerance to difference, and the accompanying move from epistemology to ontology, within recent political theory. Building on this "ontological turn," in search of a theological answer to the question, she puts Augustine into conversation with recent political theorists and theologians. This theological option enables the Church to envision a way to engage with contemporary political society without losing its own embodied story and practices. It contributes to our broader political imagination by offering a picture of rich engagement between the many different particularities that constitute a pluralist society.

KRISTEN DEEDE JOHNSON is Associate Director of The CrossRoads Project and Assistant Professor of Political Science at Hope College in Holland, Michigan.

Cambridge Studies in Christian Doctrine

Edited by
Professor DANIEL W. HARDY, *University of Cambridge*

Cambridge Studies in Christian Doctrine is an important series
which aims to engage critically with the traditional doctrines
of Christianity, and at the same time to locate and make sense
of them within a secular context. Without losing sight of the
authority of scripture and the traditions of the Church, the
books in this series subject pertinent dogmas and credal
statements to careful scrutiny, analysing them in light of the
insights of both church and society, and thereby practise
theology in the fullest sense of the word.

Theology, Political Theory, and Pluralism

Beyond Tolerance and Difference

KRISTEN DEEDE JOHNSON

CAMBRIDGE UNIVERSITY PRESS
Cambridge, New York, Melbourne, Madrid, Cape Town, Singapore, São Paulo

Cambridge University Press
The Edinburgh Building, Cambridge CB2 2RU, UK

Published in the United States of America by Cambridge University Press, New York

www.cambridge.org
Information on this title: www.cambridge.org/9780521870030

First published 2007

Printed in the United Kingdom at the University Press, Cambridge

A catalogue record for this publication is available from the British Library

ISBN-13 978-0-521-87003-0 hardback
ISBN-10 0-521-87003-8 hardback

And as this grain has been gathered from many fields into one loaf
and these grapes from many hills into one cup, grant, O Lord, that thy
whole Church may soon be gathered from the ends of the earth
into thy kingdom.
Even so, come, Lord Jesus.

Contents

Acknowledgments

The interdisciplinary nature of this work has provided me with a unique opportunity to see the potential that exists within the academy for different disciplines and scholars to work together, crossing the boundaries of subjects, institutions, and countries. Indeed, this project was only possible because of the generosity of people from different fields of study and institutions who gave unhesitatingly of their time and efforts, sharing their work, reading and discussing my writing, and meeting with me to discuss a variety of related interests. Though these meetings have probably long since disappeared from their memories, their impact is visible in small and large ways within this work. I think particularly of Chuck Mathewes of the University of Virginia and Ed Song, now of Louisiana State University, without whom I would never have found my way clearly through the sprawling terrain of Augustine and John Rawls, respectively. I have in mind as well, from the University of St. Andrews, N. J. Rengger, John Skorupski, Olivier Ruchet, and Emily Raudenbush, and, from elsewhere, William Connolly, John Milbank, Catherine Pickstock, Jean Bethke Elshtain, Stephen White, Jim Skillen, Jeanne Heffernan, Stanley Hauerwas, Jeff Polet, and Keith Starkenburg.

I would also like to acknowledge two authors whose books were published after this manuscript was written, but whose work would certainly have influenced the contours of my argument. The careful reader will find mention of these works within these pages, but the mention is small compared to the great ideas and vision cast by them. One is Jeffrey Stout and his *Democracy & Tradition*, the other Bill Connolly and his most recent book, *Pluralism*. In the case of the

latter, I now find much more overlap between our concerns and visions than I once did. In the case of the former, the resonances between the two are obvious, as are the differences.

I am grateful to the seminars, institutions, and people who graciously allowed me to present my work to them and furthered it through their own comments and concerns. I think particularly of the Institute for Theology, Imagination and the Arts and the theology seminar of St. Mary's College, Jim Skillen and the Civitas Scholars of the summer of 2002, and the Center for Religion and Democracy of the University of Virginia. The support that has been given to me through the Center for Religion and Democracy and the Institute for Advanced Studies in Culture, also of the University of Virginia – financially, intellectually, collegially, and otherwise – has made this project possible. I am especially thankful for the able leadership provided by James Davison Hunter, whose own work, vision, and life have been among the most shaping influences on my own.

To those who have been directly involved in this project, I owe a special word of thanks. First, a large thankyou goes to the Rotary Club of Bailey's CrossRoads and to Rotary International, for their generous financial support that enabled me to go to St. Andrews, find fruitful conversation partners and wise teachers, and begin this work. One of those wise teachers was Alan Torrance, whose approach to theology has influenced my own more than he knows. Another was Michael Partridge, who Michael Partridge valiantly stepped in to provide much-needed wisdom and knowledge in areas unfamiliar to me and, with his characteristic generosity, stayed on to walk alongside me through every stage of this work. When David Fergusson and Mark Elliott they raised important questions that, without a doubt, helped examined this as a doctoral thesis my argument to become more focused. Finally, to Trevor Hart, who through the Institute for Theology, Imagination and the Arts has created an intellectual conversation space that has fostered and sharpened the thinking of all who have been involved in it, I am particularly indebted. The shape of this work owes much to our conversations, and his concern for our Church and our culture has played no small part in directing mine.

From our initial contact all the way through to the final stages of manuscript preparation, Kate Brett of Cambridge University Press

has never failed to respond to my queries quickly and thoroughly, providing much-needed direction (and a few interesting family stories) along the way. I am very grateful for her patience, and that of the other editors with whom I communicated, as I found my way into the world of book publishing. Dan Hardy has likewise offered welcome support and constructive insight as this moved through its editorial stages, and I am deeply appreciative of his interest in making this book a part of his series. I have learned much from other books in this series, and I am honored to be a part of it. I would also like to thank my anonymous reader whose encouragement and comments both buoyed and directed me in the final revisions. I owe a great debt as well to Lisa Walcott, who valiantly and generously created my cover illustration at the eleventh hour.

A final word of thanksgiving goes to those who have lived and prayed with me throughout the research and writing that have gone into this piece of work. Much in my life has changed in the years since I began this project, but at each stage I have received unfailing support from family and friends near and far. To all those with whom I have shared homes, offices, conversations, and life, I am more grateful than words can express. To the one who has most recently shared with me not only his home and his life but also his family and his name, I am overwhelmingly thankful. Without Trygve's unfailing belief in and grace towards me, I cannot imagine how I would have come to the end of this journey. May we be only at the beginning of our own. And finally to my parents, Elka and Peter Deede, who have believed in me and supported me not only during this project but throughout my life. It is with thanksgiving for your love and faithfulness that I dedicate this to you.

1

Introduction

How do we live together in the midst of our differences? The time may well have come to let a new voice speak into this pivotal question, a new voice that is, in truth, an old voice. This question is once again inspiring fresh conversation, as it invariably does in societies faced with the realities of diversity and plurality in their midst. The intensity of the conversation ebbs and flows with changing religious, political, economic, cultural, and geographic tides. Today it can be heard in high volume, as virtual cornucopias of cultures, philosophies of life, communities of belief, and ways of being are trying to live together in single western political societies, and in an increasingly connected global world. How are we to live together in the midst of this tremendous and ever-increasing pluralism?[1] What shall be the basis of our common life, what guiding framework can we share, how do we acknowledge the differences in our midst, and what ethos will mark the interactions between those differences? These are among the most pressing questions involved in this most important conversation. And this conversation continues, with no signs of ending soon, because its current participants have yet to provide answers that fully or adequately resolve the tensions arising from today's pluralist situation.

One voice in the conversation, that which has been heard the loudest and has held the most sway in liberal democracies, offers an answer based in toleration: we live together by tolerating the differences we find around us. That is to say, we may disapprove of

---

1. In this context, "pluralism" is used descriptively to refer to the co-existence of distinct faiths, cultures, ethnicities, races, and ideologies within one society, rather than as a belief or ideology in and of itself.

others' beliefs and choices, we may have deep-seated reasons for thinking those beliefs and choices are morally deficient, but we nevertheless make the decision not to repress their differences. While various strands of contemporary liberal political thought provide different arguments in defense of toleration and different descriptions of what tolerance is and what it entails, the legacy of liberal toleration lies in the Enlightenment and certain beliefs about the nature of knowledge and reason. That is to say, liberal invocations of tolerance have their roots in a very distinct epistemology, which includes a belief that through the use of reason all people can be unified around a body of common truths and morals, regardless of their other differences. The goal is a unity that can stand despite and independent of differences, so that "public" life engages only with that which is held in common, while "divisive" differences are left in the "private" sphere.

Early liberalism sought this unity based on what, following political philosopher John Rawls, we will call a comprehensive philosophical doctrine. This doctrine held as a basic tenet that if all people accepted their duty to exercise reason, then all could be united around a body of moral truths, to which reason had led them, that would serve as the basis of public life. More recent liberalism, having recognized that such Enlightenment-based dreams have not come true and having accepted that the use of reason does not guarantee agreement on philosophy or way of life, seeks to find a new means of unity. This involves adapting liberal concepts to a genuinely pluralist society, seeking to find ways to agree on those concepts that do not require adherence to the fuller Enlightenment project. The quest, as taken up by John Rawls, the leading voice in the recent conversation, is for "freestanding" conceptions with which all people, regardless of their comprehensive doctrines, belief systems, or ways of life, can agree, so long as they are "reasonable." In the face of difference, through appeals to reason and tolerance, political liberals seek unity.

Some new voices have entered the conversation about plurality and diversity in recent years, bringing with them considerable questions about the sufficiency of political liberalism's approach to difference. For within political liberalism, as articulated by Rawls, difference is seen as a fact or a problem to be dealt with rather than a part of life and identity to be acknowledged, embraced, and

celebrated. In contrast to this view, more recent theorists argue that such differences are not incidental and that it is problematic to assume that they can and should be left in the private realm. The scholarship most commonly associated with such a position recommends what has come to be known variously as the politics of difference, the politics of recognition, and multiculturalism. Yet another group of political thinkers operating in the name of difference goes even further than what we commonly associate with multiculturalism; for these agonistic theorists or proponents of radical democracy, difference is to be celebrated because it lies at the very heart of the way the world is and the way our identities are constituted. They bring to the conversation a concern that liberal tolerance is not sufficient because it still, by definition, involves disapproval rather than embrace of difference and, to work, it requires that differences not be recognized in any public way. By assuming that it is possible to keep difference and conflict out of our common political life, political liberalism overlooks the conflictual, agonistic nature of reality. The presence of conflict and power in all aspects of life, relationships, institutions, and structures means that attempts to find unity or to develop political theories in the name of unity always suppress or do violence to difference. Unity cannot, according to these agonistic or post-Nietzschean political theorists, be the goal, nor tolerance the way to get there. Instead, these theorists search for a way to move beyond tolerance and unity to a deeper and richer embrace of difference. For the sake of diversity, they relinquish the hope of unity.

In short, when it comes to answering how we might live together in the midst of our pluralism, liberal tolerance emphasizes the quest for unity, while agonistic difference prioritizes diversity. Indeed, each can be accused of pursuing the one at the expense of the other, of pushing to unnecessary extremes the dichotomies of the universal and the particular, the one and the many. These two "schools" of political theory represent prominent attempts to use political and theoretical imagination to create pictures of what it could look like to live together in the midst of increasing recognition of difference. They also reflect recent changes in the cultural and intellectual climate of Western society. The theories and practices related to these "schools" of thought, however, have yet to provide sufficient or adequate pictures of what our collective life

can look like under conditions of extreme diversity. This is, of course, due in some measure to the complicated nature of these issues; both theoretically and practically, questions related to difference and tolerance, to the organization of political society in times of high levels of plurality, will have no easy answers.

But it may also be due to our own impoverished political imagination. Perhaps answers, or hints towards answers, may be found by welcoming into the conversation a voice that is no longer considered helpful or plausible from the perspective of political theory, indeed from one of the very quarters that is most often blamed for the rise and perpetuation of intolerance, namely Christianity. The voice of Christian theology may help provide an alternative picture to those given by either political liberalism or post-Nietzschean political thought that offers a glimpse of a way out of our current morass, by helping us to think more creatively about the mutually fulfilling relationship between the universal and the particular, between unity and diversity, that does not leave us stranded in unhelpful bifurcations. It may contribute to the reinvigoration of contemporary public discourse, which is not infrequently diagnosed as impoverished, as "too spare to contain the moral energies of democratic life,"[2] by offering a richer picture of conversation between those who constitute today's pluralist society than the truncated pictures offered by other political theorists. A Christian theological voice may, further, help religious identity be heard as an important difference that goes largely unrecognized within contemporary academic discussions of diversity.[3]

The Church, also, as it tries to navigate the tricky waters of tolerance, difference, liberalism, and pluralism, is in need of a theological investigation of recent political theory. Such an investigation could help the Church articulate how its Christian ontology, or beliefs about the nature of human being and reality, influences its understanding of diversity, unity, and the political realm. It might, indeed, help remind Christians that they have a crucial role to play in the development of communities in which unity and diversity can come together through participation in the reconciling work of

2. Michael J. Sandel, *Democracy's Discontent: America in Search of a Public Philosophy* (Cambridge, MA: Belknap Press, 1996), p. 323.
3. Cf. Jeff Spinner-Halev, *Surviving Diversity: Religion and Democratic Citizenship* (Baltimore, MD: The Johns Hopkins University Press, 2000), pp. 6–7.

the Triune God. And it might help Christians to see ways to love God and neighbor in the Church *and* in the "earthly city," by providing them with the theological resources to be engaged in the social and political structures and institutions of this world without compromising or forgetting that they are first and foremost citizens of the Heavenly City and members of God's family in the Church. These concerns for the Church provide much of the impetus for this work, so that while it is a sustained engagement with political theory, it is nevertheless primarily and unapologetically theological.

To say that this work is theological is not, I hope, to say that it has nothing to offer to those who do not share its Christian theological presuppositions. On the contrary, the project is undertaken because of the belief that theology and political theory have overlapping fields of interest and concern, and that genuine conversation between them needs to happen for the sake of both. Nevertheless, I do hope in this work to write theologically about issues far too long left to nontheologians and to explicate the implications of Christian theology for the situation of pluralism and "tolerance" in which we find ourselves today. This is indeed but to be faithful to the own inner themes of Christianity, which have to do with nothing if not with community, unity, diversity, difference, and harmony.[4] My goal in writing, therefore, is neither to convert to Christianity those who do not yet believe its story, nor to provide an apologetic for the ontology, political society, or "social usefulness" of Christianity. My goal is rather to think theologically and critically about tolerance and difference as currently proffered, and by so doing to help expand our current political imagination as we seek answers to contemporary problems; this should be of interest to all who share Western political arrangements.

Before moving on to introduce in more detail the contents of this book, it may prove helpful to step back to consider the concept of toleration, both in its own right and in terms of its relationship with liberalism. Toleration and liberalism are crucial characters in the intellectual story I am weaving and the theological critiques I am offering. The complexity of definition and discussion surrounding both prohibits the possibility of either one being covered sufficiently,

---

4. Cf. Oliver O'Donovan, *The Desire of the Nations: Rediscovering the Roots of Political Theology* (Cambridge: Cambridge University Press, 1996), p. 3.

but even a brief introduction to these complexities will help some of the key issues become clearer. After this brief introduction, the move within political theory from tolerance to difference, and the concomitant move from epistemology to ontology, is described a little more fully, along with the ways this ontological turn opens the door for a theological turn. Finally, a description of the contents of this book, chapter by chapter, is provided.

A brief introduction to tolerance and liberalism

As long ago as 1689, John Locke told the English readers of his letter concerning toleration that "there is no nation under heaven in which so much has already been said upon that subject as ours."[5] Yet more than three hundred years later, contribution after contribution continues to be made to the subject. Some contributions take as their starting assumption that tolerance is the rightful reigning "value" of our day; some view tolerance as the necessary culmination of centuries of liberal political thinking, theorizing, and implementation; others decry the intolerance and repression of difference that they see as veiled concomitants of so-called liberal tolerance; and others yet raise significant philosophical questions about the very definition of toleration, as well as how attainable or desirable it is as an ideal.

Toleration may, indeed, be among the more complicated "virtues" of our time, in terms of its origins, its conceptuality, its merits, and its entailments. Its complexity is increased because it is of relevance to both informal, "unregulated" life and legal and institutional aspects of political life. As a "virtue," it is certainly among the most controversial. Perhaps evaluations of toleration are best viewed along a spectrum. On one end are those who laud the accomplishment that tolerance represents, and who would agree with William Galston that, "in the real world, there is nothing 'mere' about toleration."[6] In the middle are those concerned with what toleration is and is not, the paradoxes it raises as a moral

5. John Locke, *A Letter Concerning Toleration*, ed. Mario Montuori (The Hague: Martinus Nijhoff, 1963), p. 3.
6. William A. Galston, *Liberal Pluralism: The Implications of Value Pluralism for Political Theory and Practice* (Cambridge: Cambridge University Press, 2002), p. 120.

concept, and the potential impossibility of its realization.[7] And at the other end are those who, for a variety of reasons that would keep them from being happily grouped together, regard tolerance as repressive, discriminatory, pretentious, and/or dangerous.[8] Regardless of the evaluation, one would be hard-pressed to deny the central role that toleration has played and continues to play in political theory and practice. This makes it all the more interesting that, as Andrew Murphy writes, "the meaning of the term continues to elude us."[9] David Heyd concurs on the elusive nature of this virtue:

> Tolerance is a philosophically elusive concept. Indeed, in the liberal ethos of the last three centuries, it has been hailed as one of the fundamental ethical and political values, and it still occupies a powerful position in contemporary legal and political rhetoric. However, our firm belief in the value of tolerance is not matched by analogous theoretical certitude.[10]

Others, such as Bernard Williams, are concerned that toleration is not only elusive but also impossible: "Toleration, we may say, is required only for the intolerable. That is its basic problem."[11]

Most scholars of the subject agree that toleration, by definition, involves disapproval, so that the object of toleration is viewed as morally wrong or undesirable even as those who offer toleration make the decision not to interfere with or repress that which they

7. See, for example, *Res Publica* 7, no. 3 (2001), containing the proceedings from the Annual Conference of the UK Association for Legal and Social Philosophy on "The Culture of Toleration;" Susan Mendus, ed., *The Politics of Toleration: Tolerance and Intolerance in Modern Life* (Edinburgh: Edinburgh University Press, 1999); Susan Mendus, *Toleration and the Limits of Liberalism* (Atlantic Highlands, NJ: Humanities, 1989); Susan Mendus, ed., *Justifying Toleration: Conceptual and Historical Perspectives* (Cambridge: Cambridge University Press, 1988); David Heyd, ed., *Toleration: An Elusive Virtue* (Princeton, NJ: Princeton University Press, 1996).
8. See, for example, Robert Paul Wolff, Barrington Moore, Jr., and Herbert Marcuse, *A Critique of Pure Tolerance* (Boston, MA: Beacon, 1969); J. Budziszewski, *True Tolerance: Liberalism and the Necessity of Judgement* (New Brunswick, NJ: Transaction Publishers, 1992); William E. Connolly, *The Ethos of Pluralization* (Minneapolis, MN: University of Minnesota Press, 1995); William T. Cavanaugh, "'A Fire Strong Enough to Consume the House:' The Wars of Religion and the Rise of the State," *Modern Theology* 11, no. 4 (October 1995), pp. 397–420; and A. J. Conyers, *The Long Truce: How Toleration Made the World Safe for Power and Profit* (Dallas, TX: Spence, 2001).
9. Andrew Murphy, "Tolerance, Toleration, and the Liberal Tradition," *Polity* 29 (1997), p. 594.
10. Heyd, *Toleration*, p. 3.
11. Bernard Williams, "Tolerance: An Impossible Virtue?" in *Toleration: An Elusive Virtue*, ed. David Heyd (Princeton, NJ: Princeton University Press, 1996), p. 18.

have deemed immoral or objectionable. Toleration is not, then, equivalent to indifference or skepticism. Tolerance can turn into indifference if one ceases to view a particular behavior or belief with disapproval, or into skepticism if one declines to pass any judgment on another's way of life or beliefs because one questions the existence of a right or a standard by which to pass such judgments. True tolerance, however, depends upon a situation of diversity marked by both difference and disapproval. And herein lies its paradox. As Susan Mendus asks, how can toleration be counted as a virtue when it is based on moral disapproval, with the implication that the thing tolerated is wrong and ought not to exist? Why is it good to tolerate?[12]

Different justifications have been offered, historically and more recently, for the good of toleration. The perceived need of tolerance arises, for obvious reasons, under conditions of pluralism and diversity within a given political society. The most commonly told story of the rise of tolerance links it directly and inextricably with the diversity of post-Reformation Europe that inspired the emergence of liberalism.[13] In this story, liberalism arises out of the wars of religion of the sixteenth and seventeenth centuries with tolerance playing a leading role as the answer to the antagonism and bloodshed that marked the prolonged religious conflicts of the day. And so we have Brian Barry's estimation that toleration is a defining feature and, perhaps, even the core of liberalism, and Judith Shklar's sense that toleration can be considered the core of the historical development of political liberalism, and William Galston's opinion that the virtue of tolerance is a core attribute of liberal pluralist citizenship.[14] Some recent scholarship attempts to expand current conceptions of tolerance, in which tolerance is almost exclusively linked to liberalism, by finding examples of tolerant political arrangements and principled defenses of toleration that pre-date the rise of liberalism or by drawing attention to the

12. Mendus, *Toleration and the Limits of Liberalism*, pp. 18–19.
13. See, for example, Andrew Heywood, *Political Theory: An Introduction*, 2d. ed. (Hampshire: Palgrave, 1999), p. 268; John Gray, *Two Faces of Liberalism* (New York: The New Press, 2000), p. 1; and John Rawls, *Justice as Fairness: A Restatement*, ed. Erin Kelly (Cambridge, MA: Belknap Press, 2001), p. 1.
14. Brian Barry, *Culture and Equality: An Egalitarian Critique of Multiculturalism* (Cambridge: Polity, 2001), p. 131; Judith N. Shklar, "The Liberalism of Fear," in *Liberalism and the Moral Life*, ed. Nancy L. Rosenblum (Cambridge, MA: Harvard University Press, 1989), p. 23; Galston, *Liberal Pluralism*, p. 126.

differences between the earliest so-called liberal arguments for religious toleration and the toleration of contemporary liberal theorists.[15] Although other forms of tolerance have existed and continue to exist, it nevertheless seems safe to say that the tolerance that predominates in contemporary Western society has its roots in liberalism and continues to be promulgated by liberal theorists today.

Liberalism approaches toleration in the complexity of defining and explaining it, in terms of either its historical origins or its contemporary articulations. The breadth of opinion on what liberalism has been and continues to be, even between those who consider themselves contemporary liberal political theorists, plays no small part in this seeming complexity. Indeed, the competing branches of liberalism try to convince others of their position by persuading them to accept their own version of liberalism's definition. As to the origins of liberalism, J. S. McClelland writes of the modern state that it "emerged from the feudal order. Beyond that nothing is certain. There is no agreement about how it happened or when it happened beyond saying that it happened at different times in different places."[16] This description applies equally well to liberalism. Although we may not be able to successfully identify liberalism with a particular date or site of emergence, we do have some hint of its origins. Here we again agree with McClelland that "what does not seem to be in doubt is that liberalism, as a set of ideas and as a first, tentative approach to the treatment of political and social problems, began in the Enlightenment."[17] To get a sense of what that means, we will look closely at the work of John Locke, who is commonly associated, although not without

---

15. For the former, see Michael Walzer *On Toleration* (New Haven, CT: Yale University Press, 1997); Cary J. Nederman, *Worlds of Difference: European Discourses of Toleration, C. 1100–C. 1550* (University Park, PA: The Pennsylvania State University Press, 2000); John Christian Laursen and Cary J. Nederman, eds., *Beyond the Persecuting Society: Religious Toleration Before the Enlightenment* (Philadelphia, PA: University of Pennsylvania Press, 1998); and Cary J. Nederman and John Christian Laursen, eds., *Difference and Dissent: Theories of Toleration in Medieval and Early Modern Europe* (Lanham, MD: Rowman & Littlefield, 1996). For the latter, see Andrew R. Murphy, *Conscience and Community: Revisiting Toleration and Religious Dissent in Early Modern England and America* (University Park, PA: The Pennsylvania State University Press, 2001).
16. J. S. McClelland, *A History of Western Political Thought* (London: Routledge, 1996), p. 278.
17. Ibid., p. 428.

exception, with the earliest articulations of both liberalism and toleration.[18]

John Locke plays a leading role in the story of toleration, due to the influential publication of *A Letter Concerning Toleration*. Written in 1685 and published in 1689 (in four different languages that very year), its enduring legacy stems not from it being the first work on toleration as such but instead from it being the first work to use toleration as the basis for a different, limited role for the nation-state. He was among the first to advocate tolerance on the political and ecclesiastical level on the basis of principled philosophical argument.[19] His justification for religious toleration is rooted in his understanding of the nature of salvation and the limits of human knowledge, and stems more from his case for the irrationality of forced belief than from a belief in the inherent goodness and desirability of difference.[20] This helps explain why he does not extend toleration to atheists and Roman Catholics: his concern for social cohesion allowed toleration at the private level so long as it did not disrupt order at the public level. Roman Catholics would be more faithful to the Bishop of Rome than the civil magistrate in their own land, while those who do not believe in God would not have reason to uphold the "promises, covenants, and oaths, which are the bonds of human society."[21]

If Locke does not make his argument for toleration from a conviction of the inherent desirability of religious diversity, what is it that prompts him to write of toleration as "the chief characteristic mark of the true church?"[22] Of utmost importance is his understanding of the nature of salvation as such that it cannot be forced or coerced but must stem from individual choice. His emphasis on the ineffectiveness of coercion stems largely from what he believes to be the nature of reason, knowledge, and faith. Though Locke retains a Christian belief in the necessity of salvation, his understanding of how one epistemologically acquires the faith that is

---

18. For examples of exceptions, see Murphy, *Conscience and Community*, pp. xiv–xv and Laursen and Nederman, *Beyond the Persecuting Society*, pp. 2–4.
19. Ian S. Markham, *Plurality and Christian Ethics* (Cambridge: Cambridge University Press, 1994), p. 13.
20. This latter position is most often associated in early modern political thought with John Stuart Mill.
21. Locke, *Letter Concerning Toleration*, p. 93.
22. Ibid., p. 7.

necessary for salvation is as important to him as the attainment of salvation itself. Religion is one of "those things that every man ought sincerely to inquire into himself, and by meditation study, search, and his own endeavors, attain the knowledge of;"[23] in such matters no one can go against the dictates of his own conscience or fail to use his own reason.[24] Locke argues for toleration in matters of religion not merely for pragmatic reasons, not merely, that is, to aid the attainment of a *modus vivendi* that would enable the overcoming of bloodshed and conflict (though he was certainly influenced by a desire to overcome the violence that he associated with "intolerance"), but because of his view of the nature of belief: exhortations and arguments are acceptable in matters of conversion where coercion and force are not because "nobody is obliged in that matter to yield obedience unto the admonitions or injunctions of another, further than he himself is persuaded. Every man in that has the supreme and absolute authority of judging for himself."[25] This is in keeping with Locke's thought more generally, specifically his belief that it is the duty of each person to examine all beliefs, religious, moral, and otherwise, thereby individually arriving at a rational morality and rational religion as opposed to depending upon moral and religious traditions.[26] This rational morality could, Locke hoped, provide a unified basis for political life that did not depend on revelation, religion, religious authority, or tradition.

Locke's support of toleration also depends upon drawing a clear distinction between the role of civil government and the role of religion: civil government must concern itself only with things temporal because the commonwealth is by (Locke's) definition a society constituted to secure civil interests, by which he means "life, liberty, health, and indolency of body; and the possession of

23. Ibid., p. 49.
24. Andrew R. Murphy argues that a transformation of the understanding of conscience, from an objective faculty that corresponded to God's law and a standard of right and wrong, and could therefore be sinned against, to a faculty that had a subjective element that called for individual assent, may be the most significant contribution of early modern tolerationists. See Murphy, *Conscience and Community*, pp. 227–233.
25. Locke, *Letter Concerning Toleration*, p. 81.
26. For more on this aspect of Locke's thought, as well as a critique of it, see Nicholas Wolterstorff, "The Role of Religion in Decision and Discussion of Political Issues," in Robert Audi and Nicholas Wolterstorff, *Religion in the Public Square: The Place of Religious Convictions in Political Debate* (Lanham, MD: Rowman & Littlefield, 1997), pp. 80–90.

outward things, such as money, lands, houses, furniture, and the like."[27] In other words, interests that have to do with this life, as opposed to "the care of souls," which is properly left to the church. Indeed, in Locke's view, the salvation of souls is the only business of the church.[28] As he writes, "the political society is instituted for no other end but only to secure every man's possession of the things of this life. The care of each man's soul, and of the things in heaven, which neither does belong to the commonwealth nor can be subjected to it, is left entirely to every man's self."[29] In Locke's view, an acceptance of the delineation between these two spheres is essential for the realization of toleration.

Contemporary questions related to what we now call the separation of church and state have clear resonances with this line of thinking in Locke's writings. One can begin to see what prompted Stanley Fish to write that Locke's "framing of the question, 'How do we settle the just bounds between church and state?' and the components of his answer ... still preside over the discussion he initiated so long ago."[30] Indeed, many aspects of the philosophical liberalism articulated by Locke in his account of toleration and his other works on political society continue to influence political philosophy. Yet in other ways we are far from where Locke was, certainly when it comes to presuppositions about the use of reason and the foundations of knowledge. Locke's defense of toleration is concomitant with certain ideas about the nature of knowledge, conscience, the individual, and reason; it is but one part of a larger, comprehensive doctrine that carries with it a distinctive, universalizing epistemology, anthropology, and ontology.[31] This comprehensive doctrine is generally associated with Enlightenment liberalism.

According to many recent liberal theorists, liberalism does not have to be associated with the Enlightenment, or with any comprehensive philosophy of life. More than that, such scholars argue, to the extent that contemporary formulations of liberalism are

---

27. Locke, *Letter Concerning Toleration*, p. 15.
28. Ibid., p. 59.
29. Ibid., p. 85.
30. Stanley Fish, *The Trouble with Principle* (Cambridge, MA: Harvard University Press, 1999), p. 175.
31. Throughout this work "ontology" is used to refer to an understanding of the nature of human being and "what there is" more generally.

linked to or based in Enlightenment ideals, they will fail.[32] The level of diversity and the breadth of difference within current society, a level and breadth that points to the vast heterogeneity of conceptions of the good, preclude the general acceptance of Enlightenment values or an Enlightenment conception of the good life. And yet many of the institutions and values still present within contemporary society – separation of church and state, and toleration, to name but two – have been inherited from the Enlightenment, having been undergirded by certain presuppositions about the nature of reason, knowledge, human being, and the world more generally. The question, while not original to this investigation, is nonetheless pressing: can these institutions and values be sustained if their original sources of sustenance have been largely discredited? That is to say, as J. Judd Owen writes,

> The liberal institutions concerning religion – the separation of church and state, religious pluralism, religious freedom – were originally justified on the basis of a revolutionary comprehensive philosophic doctrine, covering human nature, the purpose of political society, and the proper domain of religious faith. The liberal doctrines concerning religion were the product of the Age of Reason, or the Enlightenment. ... Today, belief in the comprehensive philosophic teaching of the Enlightenment appears to lie in ruins, and few hope that any other comprehensive philosophy could successfully replace it. This despair is, to a considerable extent, due to a radical critique of reason as such.[33]

To put this in terms of toleration, toleration is a plausible option in original conceptions of liberalism because reason and rationality are able to provide a natural, universal basis for public (political) life while religion, and other divisive differences, can peacefully remain in the private sphere. The question today is whether liberalism and its solution to the problem of tolerance remain viable options given recent critiques of Enlightenment rationalism and accusations of intolerance in the name of liberal ethnocentrism. That is to say, if, as Mendus writes, "historically, discussions of toleration have often placed faith in the possibility of reasoned resolutions to

---

32. See, for example, John Gray, *Enlightenment's Wake: Politics and Culture at the Close of the Modern Age* (London: Routledge, 1995), p. viii.
33. J. Judd Owen, *Religion and the Demise of Liberal Rationalism: The Foundational Crisis of the Separation of Church and State* (Chicago, IL: University of Chicago Press, 2001), p. 1.

intolerance," what support can liberalism give to toleration if that faith has been lost?[34]

We have come this far in our discussion without even attempting to define liberalism. The complexity of its definition is due in no small part to the question of the relationship between liberalism and the Enlightenment, so that some scholars, such as Gray, Galston, and Nancy Rosenblum, write of the two faces or concepts of liberalism. One face is liberalism as a universal regime, as a moral ideal that all in a given society could, theoretically, accept as the best way of life.[35] Galston links this face to the ideal of autonomy, by which he means individual self-direction connected with commitment to sustained rational examination of self, others, and social practices.[36] This, in turn, he links to an historical impulse associated with the Enlightenment: "liberation through reason from externally imposed authority."[37] (This form of liberalism should remind us of Locke; both Galston and Gray mention his name in connection with it.[38]) The other face of liberalism is more of a political *modus vivendi* that, rather than trying to promote one ideal way or philosophy of life, accepts a diversity of forms of life.[39] Galston associates this face with the principle of diversity; it has, he claims, more to do with recognizing legitimate differences between individuals and groups over questions of the good and the true than with promoting the ideal of liberal autonomy.[40] On this face, liberal toleration is, as Gray writes, "the belief that human beings can flourish in many ways of life."[41] For the other face of liberalism, liberalism as a universal regime or moral ideal, liberal toleration is, according to Gray, "the ideal of a rational consensus on the best way of life."[42]

34. Mendus, *Politics of Toleration*, p. 2.
35. Gray, *Two Faces*, pp. 1–5; Nancy L. Rosenblum, introduction to *Liberalism and the Moral Life*, ed. Nancy L. Rosenblum (Cambridge, MA: Harvard University Press, 1989), p. 5. Cf. John Gray, "Two Liberalisms of Fear," *The Hedgehog Review* 2, no. 1 (Spring 2000, pp. 9–23).
36. Of course other liberal theorists contest even this identification of liberalism with autonomy. See, for example, Barry, *Culture and Equality*, pp. 118–123.
37. Galston, *Liberal Pluralism*, p. 24.
38. See ibid., p. 21; Gray, *Two Faces*, p. 2.
39. Gray, *Two Faces*, pp. 5–6; Rosenblum, introduction to *Liberalism and the Moral Life*, p. 6.
40. Galston, *Liberal Pluralism*, p. 21.
41. Gray, *Two Faces*, p. 1.
42. Ibid.

Because of these two faces, it may be easier to speak of what liberalism opposes than what it promises, as Rosenblum suggests. Perhaps the most minimal description that can be offered of liberalism, in its "thin" version, is that it is a theory of limited government, concerned with protecting the personal liberty and private property of citizens from political absolutism and arbitrariness.[43] One of the most oft-cited recent prescriptions for liberalism is offered by Judith Shklar, whose "liberalism of fear" "has only one overriding aim: to secure the political conditions that are necessary for the exercise of personal freedom." In other words, "every adult should be able to make as many effective decisions without fear or favor about as many aspects of her or his life as is compatible with the like freedom of every other adult."[44] Shklar herself insists that liberalism is a "political doctrine, not a philosophy of life."[45] While recognizing the existence of other articulations of liberalism, the liberalism that she believes in is, she claims, independent of and compatible with all religious or philosophical systems of thought so long as they do not reject toleration or refuse to recognize a difference between the spheres of public and private. Her version of liberalism has no *summum bonum* of its own, though it begins with a *summum malum*, the evil of cruelty and the fear it inspires. This, she maintains, is the only universal claim that the liberalism of fear makes.[46] Gray and Galston are likewise concerned with limiting the universal claims of liberalism, for they object to the homogenizing tendencies they see within certain conceptions of liberalism and tolerance that are tied too closely to larger, Enlightenment-based ideals of autonomy or reason.[47] Galston, for example, believes that "to the extent that many liberals identify liberalism with the Enlightenment, they limit support for their cause and drive

43. I have borrowed here from the clear, concise definition that Rosenblum gives to liberalism in her introduction to *Liberalism and the Moral Life*, p. 5.
44. Shklar, "Liberalism of Fear," p. 21.
45. Ibid.
46. Ibid., pp. 24, 29.
47. And both propose solutions and adaptations to such conceptions of liberalism and tolerance through a reappropriation of "value pluralism," drawn from the thought of Isaiah Berlin. Despite certain kinships in their assessments of strands of liberalism and their appeal to value pluralism, in the end they reach different conclusions about what is necessary in our time. For Galston's own description of the differences between them, see Galston, *Liberal Pluralism*, pp. 48–64.

many citizens of goodwill – indeed, many potential allies – into opposition."[48]

No political philosopher is more famous for his efforts to move from a universal doctrine of liberalism to one that could be accepted by diverse constituents within a liberal political society than John Rawls. As Locke is widely considered the most influential political theorist of the seventeenth century, so is Rawls considered the most influential political theorist of the twentieth century. His *A Theory of Justice* (hereafter *Theory*) is argued by some to be the greatest contribution to liberal theory in the last hundred years.[49] In most estimations, his work in *Theory* brought life, vigor, and debate back to the discipline of political philosophy that had seen little or no innovative work in the preceding decades. Even those who most vehemently disagree with Rawls cannot deny that he sets the terms of the debate to which they must respond or try to alter. And yet Rawls himself significantly changed his approach to liberalism and tolerance in the years after the publication of *Theory*, in light of his growing sense of the pluralism of contemporary society. Whereas his earliest work articulated a comprehensive philosophical doctrine of liberalism, along the lines of that offered by Locke, his subsequent work attempts to limit the comprehensive nature of his ideas through the development of a liberalism that is, supposedly, "political, not metaphysical."[50] (Here we are reminded of Shklar's liberalism of fear that she describes as political rather than a way of life.) This is his effort to distance his version of liberalism from the Enlightenment so that it might stand despite the recent demise of belief in the unifying nature of reason. It is his way of coming to terms with the diversity of doctrines and ways of life that concurrently exist within contemporary liberal society. It exhibits his belief that the exercise of reason will not, as for Locke, lead us all to the same body of moral truths, but will instead result in "a plurality of reasonable yet incompatible comprehensive doctrines."[51] With

48. Galston, *Liberal Pluralism*, p. 26.
49. See, for example, Charles Larmore, *Patterns of Moral Complexity* (Cambridge: Cambridge University Press, 1987), p. 119.
50. "Political not Metaphysical" is the title of a lecture written by Rawls in 1985 that became Lecture I of *Political Liberalism*. See John Rawls, *Political Liberalism*, paperback ed. (New York: Columbia University Press, 1993), pp. 3–46, esp. p. 10.
51. Ibid., p. xviii.

this in mind, Rawls develops a theory that he believes can be neutral towards competing conceptions of the good and thereby allows the flourishing of a diversity of comprehensive doctrines and philosophies of life. Once Rawls acknowledges that such diversity will always be a part of liberal society, he must give toleration an ever-more central and important role within his political theory. As Galston notes, contemporary liberal theorists like Rawls "have dramatically expanded the scope of toleration."[52]

Yet, as noted earlier, tolerance itself has come under much scrutiny as of late, and not just because of its connection to the Enlightenment. Entire conferences, journals, books, and edited volumes have been dedicated to the question of tolerance, its justification, and its limits; so much so that one scholar writes, "the classical idea of toleration is now under fire from every party in our community,"[53] another that "toleration has lately fallen on hard times,"[54] and others that the theory of toleration "appears to have boxed itself into a corner."[55] Here, so that we have a feel for some of the difficulties surrounding this ideal, we raise a few of the questions that recent scholarship on tolerance is pondering.

The writings of the earliest defenders of toleration, Locke included, do not provide principled positive arguments for toleration, nor a case for why intolerance might be morally wrong. Such thinkers may support toleration because of a belief in rationality, as Locke does, or because of a commitment to skepticism that calls for the limitation of intolerance for pragmatic reasons,[56] but they do not provide reasons for the virtue of toleration in and of itself. In light of the extreme conditions of diversity that mark contemporary society, doesn't toleration need a stronger, more positive basis? If so, what sources can provide the support for such a virtue? Respect for persons, the greater good of freedom, and the inherent worth

52. William A. Galston, *Liberal Purposes: Goods, Virtues, and Diversity in the Liberal State* (Cambridge: Cambridge University Press, 1991), p. 7.

53. Steven Kautz, "Liberalism and the Idea of Toleration," *American Journal of Political Science* 37, no. 2 (May 1993), p. 610.

54. Gray, *Enlightenment's Wake*, p. 18.

55. Dario Castiglione and Catriona McKinnon, "Introduction: Beyond Toleration?" *Res Publica* 7, no. 3 (2001), p. 224.

56. For a discussion of the role of skepticism in early defenses of toleration, see Quentin Skinner, *The Foundations of Modern Political Thought*, vol. 2, The Age of Reformation (Cambridge: Cambridge University Press, 1978), pp. 246-249.

of diversity are common answers to be put forward, but each has its own problems when discussed in detail, and none avoids the question of what serves as its own source or grounding. Given the seeming incoherence of tolerance, namely that it calls people to allow to exist that of which they morally disapprove, it would seem particularly important to be able to provide a good justification for this virtue of all liberal virtues, a strong second-order reason that would provide sufficient motivation to not act upon a first-order moral evaluation.[57] Is it because of this lack of a strong positive support for toleration that it tends, at least on a popular level, to be conflated with indifference, so that people tolerate not because they have a commitment to toleration as a virtue but because they no longer hold their own beliefs and ways of life strongly enough to have reason to judge or repress those of others?

Even if a justification for toleration were to be found, reason still exists to question whether it is a worthy ideal. Is it perhaps better seen as a compromise, a best-case scenario in light of conditions of pluralism, rather than a good in its own right? By definition, tolerance implies moral disapproval, not acceptance. To live together under conditions of tolerance does not mean to accept others' beliefs and ways of life; it means, rather, to agree not to repress the beliefs and practices with which one disagrees. And yet surely, as Saladin Meckled-Garcia notes, "it is a valuable aim that citizens accept each other's ways of life." If this is so, then "tolerating each other does not represent political community, but a compromise."[58] This is further complicated by the relationship between the "tolerator" and the "tolerated": do certain relations of power emerge when one person chooses to tolerate another? Is the "tolerator" displaying arrogance or condescension towards the "tolerated" when he or she decides to tolerate rather than to accept a certain position or way of life? Is Anna Elisabetta Galeotti right to suggest that tolerance is based on a social asymmetry of power between "'virtuous' tolerators" and "'powerless' recipients"?[59] Does it, as Herbert Marcuse maintains, serve "the cause of oppression" as it

57. This language is drawn from Saladin Meckled-Garcia, "Toleration and Neutrality: Incompatible Ideals?" *Res Publica* 7, no. 3 (2001), pp. 296–297.
58. Ibid., p. 317.
59. Anna Elisabetta Galeotti, "Do We Need Toleration as a Moral Virtue?" *Res Publica* 7, no. 3 (2001), p. 290.

"favors and fortifies the conservation of the status quo of inequality and discrimination"?[60]

Or is it simply that tolerance, whatever its historical efficacy, is not able to sufficiently address the realities of pluralism and difference as they present themselves today? Kirstie McClure, writing on the limits of toleration, suggests that "it is not, perhaps, that we have no patterns for relating across our differences as equals so much as that the one we do have in the logic of toleration is inadequate to address their present articulation...."[61] This inadequacy, according to McClure, stems at least partially from the fact that toleration initially applied to expressions of religious "difference," whereas now the "difference" in question concerns gender, culture, and sexuality. Andrew Murphy likewise notes the difficulties involved in taking a concept initially developed for matters of religion and expanding it to apply to the differences of race, gender, and ethnicity with which contemporary society and "identity politics" are concerned. The toleration that developed in traditional liberalism had to do with matters of conscience, but conscience is a category that does not easily apply to the differences being emphasized today. Instead of assuming that today's liberalism expands the same notion of tolerance with which early liberals were operating, do we need to recognize that "identity politics poses new and different problems in political theory and practice" so that we do "not ask our concepts to perform impossible tasks"?[62]

Questions such as these help to highlight some of the conceptual difficulties surrounding toleration as a moral "virtue."[63] When combined with the challenges it faces in light of its historical connections with liberalism and the Enlightenment, it is no wonder that political theorists are trying to rethink and reshape how we approach tolerance and difference in liberal political societies.

60. Herbert Marcuse, "Repressive Toleration" and "Postcript," in Robert Paul Wolff, Barrington Moore, Jr., and Herbert Marcuse, *A Critique of Pure Tolerance* (Boston: Beacon Press, 1969), pp. 81, 123.
61. Kirstie M. McClure, "Difference, Diversity, and the Limits of Toleration," *Political Theory* 18, no. 3 (August 1990), pp. 386–387.
62. Murphy, *Conscience and Community*, p. 292; see also pp. 272–294.
63. These questions were inspired by the articles already cited in this section, as well as the discussions of tolerance found in Susan Mendus, introduction to *Justifying Toleration*, pp. 1–19; Castiglione and McKinnon, "Introduction: Beyond Toleration?" pp. 223–230; and Glen Newey, "Is Democratic Toleration a Rubber Duck?" *Res Publica* 7, no. 3 (2001), pp. 315–336.

From tolerance to difference

One such theorist is William Connolly, a leading agonistic political theorist, who tries to articulate a political theory that moves beyond tolerance in the name of difference. While tolerance may acknowledge difference, it does not go far enough, according to Connolly, in recognizing the degree to which all identities are impacted and indeed constituted by the differences they encounter. When one constituency tolerates another, it often does so from a position of hegemony within a culture, allowing the recipient of toleration to do nothing more than exist as an enclave within a dominant cultural identity. Toleration itself does nothing to break down barriers between differences and enable difference to be truly respected and embraced. In short, Connolly and other agonistic political theorists are in search of a way to move beyond liberal invocations of tolerance to a deeper celebration of difference. These theorists remain unconvinced that liberal tolerance can ever sufficiently respect the breadth and depth of diversity within contemporary political society. Their political thought is characterized by a belief that attempts to create and refine political societies that acknowledge difference and particularity need to engage much more explicitly with questions of ontology.

The primary motivation of such theorists is a concern for difference and a desire to see society rework and expand its pluralist imagination. In one sense, this concern for difference is merely a novel way of dealing with the same reality of diversity and plurality that motivates liberal tolerance. Yet the deeper ontological presuppositions entertained by these post-Nietzschean theorists and proponents of radical democracy as they consider the question of difference move them far beyond the invocation of tolerance in much contemporary liberal thought. These thinkers represent what has been referred to as the ontological turn within political theory. This turn to ontology is part of a larger story: in short, recent answers to the question of difference and diversity articulated within political theory are inextricably connected to an intellectual story in which ontology has replaced epistemology as the leading character. Theorists have come to recognize that procedures and methods of knowledge are not neutral and that theories of knowledge rest upon or invoke deeper sets of presuppositions about the

nature of human being and what there is more generally. This has been recognized to a limited degree within political liberalism, by John Rawls, as we have seen, and by Richard Rorty, who takes Rawls' project one step further with his "antifoundationalist" liberalism. Agonistic political theorists take a more fully developed ontological turn, recognizing that their theories invoke deep and controversial beliefs about the nature of human being and the world and explicitly articulating their political theories in terms of these beliefs. In each case, recognition of pluralism and difference is among the strongest motivating factors for the articulation of the theory in question.

Post-Nietzschean theorists argue persuasively for conversations about political life and difference to be moved to the ontological level, presenting powerful cases against the exclusionary nature of political liberalism in its many "neutral" guises. Their own ontologies, however, rooted in Friedrich Nietzsche and Michel Foucault, emphasize power, chaos, and conflict to such an extent that all hope for harmony or unity within political society must be relinquished, by their own admission. They desire deep ethical sensibilities that enable us to respect and celebrate ever-increasing difference, but significant questions must be asked of the ability of their vision to sustain the ethos they put forward. In other words, by so thoroughly ontologizing and naturalizing conflict, agonistic theorists may be guilty of the charge leveled against them by Charles T. Mathewes, namely that of "refusing all imaginative possibilities for some sort of ideal absolute harmony."[64] Theology may help open us to some different ways of picturing the relationship between unity and diversity, harmony and difference, the universal and the particular. If N. J. Rengger is right in his estimation of the importance of overcoming the strict dichotomization that seems to mark contemporary political theory, if negotiating the dichotomy of the universal and the particular is "a central 'task' for contemporary political theory," then the rich history of Christian theology in this area has much to offer in helping us expand our current political imagination.[65]

64. Charles T. Mathewes, "Faith, Hope, and Agony: Christian Political Participation Beyond Liberalism," *Annual of the Society of Christian Ethics* 21 (2001), p. 137.
65. N. J. Rengger, *Political Theory, Modernity and Postmodernity: Beyond Enlightenment and Critique* (Oxford: Blackwell, 1995), p. 225.

Indeed, the ontological turn in political theory opens the way for a theological turn: theology offers nothing if not accounts of human being and what there is more generally, while the questions of unity, diversity, and community with which political theory is engaged are questions that lie at the very heart of theology. In contrast to the ontology of conflict offered by post-Nietzschean, agonistic political theorists, Christianity offers, to borrow the language of John Milbank, a vision of "ontological peace" which provides us with hope for peace on earth, rooted in a divine, eternal source of plenitude. Christianity recognizes the tragic condition in which we live but refuses to "ontologize" it, viewing conflict as a (contingent) result of the fall while offering an ontology of peace that enables us, as Milbank writes, to "unthink the necessity of violence."[66] If Augustine is right that peace is both the true end and the precondition of justice, then it is of utmost importance that we think beyond the ontology with which our agonists remain content.

The deeper aim of this project is, then, to put theology into conversation with political theory in an attempt to expand our current political and pluralist imagination. Political theory is nothing if not an exercise of imagination, offering new or different pictures of collective life in the hopes of remolding, refashioning, or altogether altering contemporary political arrangements. Indeed, the success or popularity of a political theory could be said to depend upon the extent to which it offers a picture of political society and life that is more attractive and persuasive than that of the *status quo*. To take but one example, imagination was crucial in fostering the move to organize collective life into nations, for nations are, as Benedict Anderson shows, imagined political communities.[67] Yet today, the concept of nationhood is so entrenched that, according to Michael Hardt and Antonio Negri, "the nation becomes the only way to imagine community! Every imagination of a community becomes overcoded as a nation, and hence our conception of community is severely impoverished."[68] This is where

66. John Milbank, *Theology and Social Theory: Beyond Secular Reason* (Oxford: Blackwell, 1993), pp. 411, 390; John Milbank, "The Midwinter Sacrifice: A Sequel to 'Can Morality be Christian?'" *Studies in Christian Ethics* 10, no. 2 (1997), p. 25.
67. See Benedict Anderson, *Imagined Communities: Reflections on the Origin and Spread of Nationalism*, rev. ed. (London: Verso, 1983), p. 7.
68. Michael Hardt and Antonio Negri, *Empire* (Cambridge, MA.: Harvard University Press, 2000), p. 107.

theology can play a subversive role, challenging the givens of our current political situation by presenting an alternative picture of political community and social reality. This is to think of imagination as Walter Brueggemann defines it, as "the human capacity to picture, portray, receive, and practice the world in ways other than it appears to be at first glance when seen through a dominant, habitual, unexamined lens."[69] By applying a Christian imagination to the question of difference, we have an opportunity both to be critical of social reality and to undertake the ethical task of creating alternative pictures of communal and political life. By ensuring that this undertaking is primarily theological, we offer, as William Cavanaugh puts it, "a different kind of political imagination, one that is rooted in the Christian story,"[70] but one that can nevertheless help augment the political imagination of contemporary political theory and pluralist society.

An overview

This book tells the story of political theory's engagement in recent years with the question of how we are to live together in the midst of our diversity. We begin our story with the theory of John Rawls, whose political thought was deeply impacted, as we have seen, by contemporary conditions of pluralism. Because of the role of his theory in the resurgence of contemporary liberalism, and because most current liberal theorists base their thought on his, even if they write in reaction to it, we will look to Rawls and his "political liberalism" as the best starting point and representation of liberal thought.[71] The next chapter, therefore, begins with his earliest work before discussing his later articulations of political liberalism, highlighting, through the changes in his thought, the degree to which political liberalism recognizes that an Enlightenment-based comprehensive liberalism cannot be acceptable to the diverse components of contemporary political society. Rawls tries to articulate a liberalism that, by distancing itself from any

69. Walter Brueggemann, *The Bible and Postmodern Imagination: Texts Under Negotiation* (London: SCM, 1993), p. 13.
70. William T. Cavanaugh, *Theopolitical Imagination* (London: T & T Clark, 2002), p. 1.
71. For the remainder of this project, "liberalism" can be assumed to refer to Rawlsian political liberalism, unless explicitly stated otherwise.

controversial metaphysical and epistemological foundations, could appeal to a breadth of reasonable yet different constituents and comprehensive doctrines. This changed approach to political theory rooted in recognition of the inevitable fact of pluralism involves a concomitant prioritization of the value of tolerance. Richard Rorty shares this commitment to the primacy of tolerance as a liberal value, while moving one step further than Rawls in his quest to distance liberalism from the Enlightenment. Indeed, he claims that his "postmetaphysical liberalism," precisely because it is "post-metaphysical," is more tolerant than any liberalism to date. Rorty, then, represents the next step in this intellectual story in which concern for diversity, combined with changes in our under-standings of the nature of reason and knowledge, makes tolerance an ever more important liberal value. Yet the sufficiency of the accounts of tolerance provided by both Rawls and Rorty needs to be questioned, as significant queries are raised about the degree to which difference is actually recognized, respected, and included in their supposedly tolerant pictures of political society.

The third chapter continues this line of questioning through a discussion of agonistic political theory and radical democracy. Dri-ven by a concern for difference, but with a more developed sense of the degree to which all theory is impacted by ontological pre-suppositions, these theorists move the conversation on tolerance and difference to the ontological level. The interests that these theorists bring to political theory are introduced through a brief engagement with the thought of Bonnie Honig and William Corlett before this theory is investigated more fully through a discussion of the writings of Chantal Mouffe and William Connolly. This inves-tigation reveals the degree to which difference comes to replace tolerance as the leading character in the story of recent political theory, while, concomitantly, ontology replaces epistemology. Many of the critiques of these theorists very helpfully point to problematic aspects of political liberalism, while much of their ontological engagement opens our minds to more creatively ima-gine how we might welcome and publicly acknowledge the differ-ences in our midst and on the horizon. At the same time, we must question the degree to which the ontology of post-Nietzschean political theorists can sustain the strong ethos towards difference that they commend, as well as the desirability of making the

celebration of difference our greatest good, over all other ideals, virtues, and ends.

With the ontological turn of recent political theory in mind, as well as the inadequacies that have been uncovered in the ontologies openly articulated in post-Nietzschean thought and thinly disguised in political liberalism when it comes to finding ways to sustain pluralistic communities, the next chapter considers what a Christian ontology might contribute to discussions of diversity and unity. To this end, the fourth chapter is an immersion into the thought of St. Augustine of Hippo, as we look to Augustine's writings, and the relationship between his theology and political theory and practice, to see what theological resources he offers for an engagement with difference. As one who lived in a time of considerable plurality and was keenly aware of dynamics of power and domination, while operating with a vastly different ontology than that which has predominance in contemporary political thought, his picture of reality and human being might helpfully augment some of the deficiencies in prevailing attempts to imagine and live into communities in which differences are recognized and reconciled.

This encounter with Augustine's ontology represents the theological turn of political theory, for Augustine's ontology suggests that it is only in the *polis* of the Heavenly City that differences can come together in loving harmony through participation in the Triune God. Citizens of the Heavenly City come from all nations, speak all languages, adorn different dress and adhere to different manners of life, they are unrestrained by conformity of customs, laws, and institutions, and are free to have "their innumerable variety of desires and thoughts and everything else which makes human beings different from one another."[72] And yet they are unified through Jesus Christ, bound together in a fellowship of love. Their differences remain and are significant, even as they are woven together and directed towards a greater and more significant *telos*, namely love of God and one another.

This ontological picture and its implications for political theory in the "earthly city" are explored in the fifth chapter, in which Augustine's ontology is placed into conversation with contemporary

---

72. St. Augustine, *The Augustine Catechism: The Enchiridion on Faith, Hope, and Love* (hereafter *Enchiridion*) XXVII, 103, trans. Bruce Harbert, ed. John E. Rotelle, O.S.A. (Hyde Park, NY: New City Press, 1999).

theologians and with the ontologies of political liberals and post-Nietzscheans as the different strands of this project are drawn together. The chapter begins with an attempt to discern what sort of ontological commitments and community could sustain a move beyond liberal tolerance and agonistic difference. If the ideal goal is a rich celebration of difference in a *polis* in which diversity and unity can be mutually reinforcing, then its realization may only be possible in the Heavenly City. Yet this does not mean that the Heavenly City is to take over the earthly city or that Christianity offers a blueprint for the organization of our (earthly) political societies; the political realm is, rather, a providential provision for life in a fallen, divided world. This is explored in the next section of the chapter, as the discussion moves to an examination of the relationship between the Church and the political realm. This is done largely in conversation with John Milbank and Karl Barth. The discussion then moves from this more general exploration of the relationship between the Church and the political to a more focused consideration of what it is about the contemporary political realm that might be problematic for the particularity of Christianity. That is to say, if contemporary liberalism is critiqued for its inability to acknowledge difference and particularity, this impacts and hinders the particularity of the Church as well as that of other faith communities in our midst. Drawing on the recent work of William Cavanaugh and others, we discuss ways in which the Church has problematically redefined itself in terms of liberalism so that it is unable to exist within our pluralist society as its own public, social, embodied reality. Finally, we move from this consideration of the Church's particularity to how the many particularities of contemporary society might come together more honestly and openly from within their differences through a picture of rich and deep, sincere and humble conversation.

The hope is that this work of political imagination will contribute something to the creation of a picture in which Christianity and the other constituencies of Western society live and converse together in ways that are more true to their identities and differences than either political liberalism or post-Nietzschean political thought currently allows. Following Jean Bethke Elshtain, the goal is not a theory of collective, political life that is "an overarching *Weltanschauung* which, as Freud observed, 'leaves no question unanswered and no stone

unturned.' "[73] Following Seyla Benhabib, the concern is more for
"the public manifestation of cultural identities in civic spaces" than
for "classifying and naming groups and then ... developing a normative theory on the basis of classificatory taxonomies."[74] That is to
say, the end result will not be a comprehensive political theory that
can provide the foundation for our pluralist society nor a legislative
plan to identify and give particular legal, educational, and geo-
graphical rights to each of the existent and newly emerging groups
and cultures of our political society. We are more concerned with
recovering a hope that our pluralist society can be marked by an
ethos of rich, hospitable, and loving interaction among its differences. It will be enough if our picture points towards ways that these
differences can come together and find space for genuine conversation, conversation in which neither individual nor communal beliefs,
stories, and practices are curtailed by the tolerance of political liberalism or the difference of agonistic thought.

73. Jean Bethke Elshtain, *Public Man, Private Woman: Women in Social and Political Thought* (Oxford: Martin Robertson, 1981), p. 300.
74. Seyla Benhabib, *The Claims of Culture: Equality and Diversity in the Global Era* (Princeton, NJ: Princeton University Press, 2002), p. 18.

2

The recent journey of liberal toleration

Introduction

A political society composed of residents who do not agree on matters of faith, ways of belief, or manners of custom and life needs to find a way for those who live within it to be unified enough that they can coexist without ongoing violence and adhere to the same overarching rule of law. Liberalism, as a political theory, tries to articulate what the basis of this unity can be and how the basis can be found. Liberal thinkers have, in fact, proffered a number of different visions of life together in their search for a plausible, unifying political theory. In each vision, tolerance of those with whom one disagrees is an essential part of the proposed solution, just as tolerance is considered one of the indispensable values of liberal political societies today.

Liberalism and toleration have a decidedly close relationship, although each can exist and has existed without the other. John Locke is generally agreed to be the earliest thinker to make explicit the connection between them, while today one would be hard-pressed to find a liberal theorist in whose thought toleration did not feature strongly. This may, indeed, be one of the few commonalities that links contemporary liberal writers, for though in such writings toleration and liberalism seem to go hand in hand, no general consensus exists as to what either one means or entails. Perhaps this is why the political liberalism of John Rawls serves as the benchmark of most current political thought, providing a common basis for discussion and dissent. For liberalism itself has undergone significant changes through the decades and the centuries as intellectual and

political climates have shifted and the breadth of diversity and difference within society has increased. This has led to significant changes in Rawls' own versions of liberalism, as he attempts to move away from a theory that resembles a universal or comprehensive, Enlightenment-based liberalism to one that is compatible with what he calls the fact of reasonable pluralism. And it has contributed to the development of other political theories that attempt to move further than Rawls in terms of both distance from Enlightenment liberalism and engagement with and recognition of the particularity of difference. Richard Rorty, for example, articulates a "postmetaphysical liberalism"; others call for a "politics of difference" or multiculturalism that gives public recognition to different cultural and group identities; and others yet long to move altogether beyond the ontological presuppositions of liberalism that hinder its ability to adequately engage with the depth of difference within our midst.

Each step along this recent journey within political theory, a journey that begins, for our purposes, with Rawlsian liberalism, involves a concomitant move for toleration. It is the story of the changes within liberalism and the journey that this has involved for toleration that this chapter tells, beginning with Rawlsian liberalism, moving to Rorty's "redescriptive" liberal project, and touching briefly on the politics of difference. By the time we reach the end of the chapter, we shall begin to see why agonistic political theorists want this journey to move beyond toleration altogether.

Rawlsian liberalism: from comprehensive doctrine to political toleration

John Rawls was without doubt the most influential political theorist of the twentieth century. His *A Theory of Justice* (hereafter *Theory*) renewed the ailing discipline of political philosophy, sparking the conversations and debates over contemporary liberalism that have come to mark the past thirty years of political philosophy and show no signs of abating in the near future.[1] Yet in Rawls himself we see an interesting development since the publication of *Theory*, a development that has prompted some to speak of the new

---

1. Meaning the thirty or so years since the publication of *Theory*. See John Rawls, *A Theory of Justice* (Oxford: Oxford University Press, 1972).

Rawls over against the old Rawls. Indeed, certain scholars have been left in the strange position of defending the old Rawls against the changes he himself has made to his political theory, while others remain unconvinced that his alterations address any of the significant problems that, in their estimation, undermined his original argument. Of what does the change consist and whence did it arise? It appears to have stemmed from Rawls' realization that his original theory overlooked "the fact of reasonable pluralism."

In *Theory*, Rawls presented an ideal well-ordered society in which all citizens accept his idea of justice as fairness as a comprehensive philosophical doctrine. He now identifies a "serious problem" with this attempt, namely that "a modern democratic society is characterized not simply by a pluralism of comprehensive religious, philosophical, and moral doctrines but by a pluralism of incompatible yet reasonable comprehensive doctrines."[2] The lectures and writings of Rawls since the publication of *Theory* try to limit the comprehensive nature of his original ideas by presenting them as political conceptions, and political liberalism is the name he gives to this effort. Political liberalism reflects the distinction he draws between his earlier work of moral philosophy and his more developed work concerned with the strictly political realm.[3] The main problem with which political liberalism is concerned is, according to Rawls:

> How is it possible that there may exist over time a stable and just society of free and equal citizens profoundly divided by reasonable though incompatible religious, philosophical, and moral doctrines? Put another way: How is it possible that deeply opposed though reasonable comprehensive doctrines may live together and all affirm the political conception of a constitutional regime? What is the structure and content of a political conception that can gain the support of such an overlapping consensus?[4]

This does not initially seem that far removed from Locke's concern for attaining and maintaining a political situation of toleration in the midst of religious diversity some three hundred years ago. Rawls himself traces the historical origin of political liberalism to the Reformation and the controversies over religion that followed it.[5] At

2. Rawls, *Political Liberalism*, p. xviii.
3. Ibid., pp. xviii–xix.
4. Ibid., p. xx.
5. Ibid., p. xxvi.

the same time, he tries to distance himself from any connections one might draw between his philosophy and "the so-called Enlightenment project of finding a philosophical secular doctrine, one founded on reason and yet comprehensive."[6] His version of political liberalism has no such ambitions, and therefore should be able to stand despite the recent demise of Enlightenment rationalism. One is tempted to wonder how much Rawls' reworking of the ideas of *Theory* is in fact a response to that very demise. At the least it appears to reflect a move away from autonomy towards toleration as the fundamental value of liberal theory.[7]

A theory of justice

In spite of the differences between the old and new Rawls, enough continuity between the two exists that the ideas involved in Rawls' version of political liberalism are better understood in light of their initial conception and use in *Theory*. Rawls wrote *Theory* against the backdrop of utilitarianism in an attempt to reconceptualize the traditional theory of social contract found in Locke, Jean Jacques Rousseau, and Immanuel Kant as a counter to the predominance of utilitarianism within modern moral philosophy. What this means conceptually is that Rawls uses the idea of an "original position," a hypothetical initial situation into which people are placed in order to generate fair principles of justice for the basic structure of society.[8] Underlying and motivating the use of the original position is a belief in the primacy of social justice and the need to derive a theory of justice that is fair to all participants in a social system. The original position should ensure that the principles of justice people would agree to would be the fairest possible principles, which requires that certain conditions and restraints be put on the original position and on those who find themselves in that position. In other words, only under certain conditions will the initial situation be fair and yield principles that will result in

6. Ibid., p. xx.
7. See Will Kymlicka, *Contemporary Political Philosophy: An Introduction*, 2d. ed. (Oxford: Oxford University Press, 2002), p. 229.
8. Rawls defines the basic structure of society as "the way in which the major social institutions [i.e., the political constitution and the principal economic and social arrangements] distribute fundamental rights and duties and determine the division of advantages from social cooperation" (*Theory*, p. 6).

justice as fairness, the crucial idea that remains central throughout Rawls' work.

The idea, then, is that the way to determine fair principles of justice, given justice's role as the primary virtue of social institutions, is to hypothesize what principles would be agreed to by people within an original situation that is itself fair. The way to ensure the fairness of the original position is to insist that the principles of justice be chosen behind a "veil of ignorance," which means that no knowledge is allowed of one's place in society, social or class status, natural assets and abilities, intelligence, strength, psychological propensities, or conceptions of the good. In this way no one will be influenced to choose principles that would favor his or her particular position, talents, or beliefs. Persons in the original position know themselves and each other as nothing but free, equal, and rational. As Rawls writes, "this initial situation is fair between individuals as moral persons, that is, as rational beings with their own ends and capable, I shall assume, of a sense of justice."[9] The result? That "the original position is, one might say, the appropriate initial status quo, and thus the fundamental agreements reached in it are fair. This explains the propriety of the name 'justice as fairness.' "[10]

Rawls' assumption of rationality on the part of those in the original position also involves mutual disinterest between persons, which results in each person choosing principles that he or she thinks will best advance his or her own system of ends, meaning the attainment of the most primary social goods. Primary goods are understood to be goods that all rational people desire regardless of their particular life plans, and they consist of such things as rights, liberties, opportunities, income, and wealth.[11] Self-respect is defined as the most important primary good, with implications that will be drawn out in more detail below. For now it is enough to note that Rawls' definition of a person's good as "the successful execution of a rational plan of life" is connected with these primary goods since such goods are deemed necessary for the realization of one's rational plan. Furthermore, those in the original position are assumed to determine the fairest principles of justice with this

9. Ibid., p. 11.
10. Ibid.
11. Ibid., p. 54.

definition of the good, and the concomitant desire for the max-
imization of primary goods, in mind.[12]

What, then, are the principles of justice that emerge as "everyone's
best reply" and serve to make this a theory not merely of justice but
of justice as fairness? Through *Theory* Rawls identifies two principles:

> First Principle
> Each person is to have an equal right to the most extensive total
> system of equal basic liberties compatible with a similar system of
> liberty for all.
> Second Principle
> Social and economic inequalities are to be arranged so that they
> are both:
> (a) to the greatest benefit of the least advantaged, consistent with
>   the just savings principle, and
> (b) attached to offices and positions open to all under conditions of
>   fair equality of opportunity.

These principles also involve what Rawls terms priority rules, such
that the first principle is lexically prior to the second principle and,
within the second principle, (b) is lexically prior to (a). This is to
ensure, in the first instance, that liberty always has priority, meaning
that basic liberties can be restricted for the sake of greater liberty but
not for the sake of, for example, greater economic equality. Likewise,
within the second principle it ensures that fair equality of opportunity retains priority over what Rawls calls the difference principle, or
the principle that inequalities must benefit the least advantaged.

We can now see how these principles relate to the veil of ignorance
of the original position. If people are not aware of their own conception of the good, they will surely be concerned to choose the first
principle that provides equal basic liberties so that they have the
freedom to pursue, and change, whatever conception of the good they
have once they emerge from the original position. Likewise, given
their lack of knowledge regarding their economic and social status,
Rawls assumes that it is most rational for those in the original position to choose the second principle as it ensures that even the worst
position in society benefits from the inequalities that are in place.

The details of this theory are not as important as the principal
concepts that emerge, both because these principal concepts are

---

12. Ibid., p. 380.

enough to enable us to perceive why some of the major criticisms of *Theory* have arisen and because many of them continue to play a role in his more developed political liberalism. For much the same reason, a few further ideas contained in *Theory* should be identified. Though Rawls does not initially mention this when he depicts the original position, he later writes that "equal liberty of conscience is the only principle that the persons in the original position can acknowledge."[13] Rawls, while viewing the question of the equal liberty of conscience as a fixed point in judgments of justice, believes that it is generated naturally by the conception of justice that results from the original position rather than needing to be brought in to the theory as a natural right or as part of a larger metaphysical system. Again, because of the veil of ignorance, the only way persons in the original position can guarantee that their own belief system will not be suppressed or persecuted is to ensure equal liberty of conscience for all. This likewise applies to toleration:

> Toleration is not derived from practical necessities or reasons of state. Moral and religious freedom follows from the principle of equal liberty; and assuming the priority of this principle, the only ground for denying the equal liberties is to avoid an even greater injustice, an even greater loss of liberty. Moreover, the argument does not rely on any special metaphysical or philosophical doctrine. ... The appeal is indeed to common sense, to generally shared ways of reasoning and plain facts accessible to all, but it is framed in such a way as to avoid these larger presumptions.[14]

Whether or not this is an accurate interpretation by Rawls is a matter to which we will return shortly.

Elsewhere in *Theory*, Rawls is more explicit about his reliance on broader philosophical doctrines, particular the philosophy of Kant. He admits that the principle of equal liberty can also have its source in Kant's interpretation of justice and his notion of autonomy. He writes that "the original position may be viewed, then, as a procedural interpretation of Kant's conception of autonomy and the categorical imperative within the framework of an empirical theory."[15] This recognition, which implicates his moral philosophy as part of a wider comprehensive doctrine with its roots in Kant and its

13. Ibid., p. 181.
14. Ibid., p. 188.
15. Ibid., p. 226.

affirmation of the primacy of the autonomy of persons, is part of what Rawls is trying to back away from in *Political Liberalism*, as we shall see below.

The final aspect of Rawls' *Theory* worth noting before we move into more explicit criticisms is the distinction Rawls makes between the public and private realms. We see in his theory a continuation of the distinction of spheres suggested by Locke, though Rawls certainly has a much broader view of which comprehensive doctrines are allowed in the private realm without undermining social cohesion. Rawls believes that society has no greater collective goal than the realization of the principles of justice, which enables individuals to pursue their private plans and be involved in various associations within the larger framework established by a just constitutional order. "Everyone's more private life is so to speak a plan within a plan, this superordinate plan being realized in the public institutions of society. But this larger plan does not establish a dominant end, such as that of religious unity or the greatest excellence of culture, much less national power and prestige, to which the aims of all individuals and associations are subordinate. The regulative public intention is rather that the constitutional order should realize the principles of justice."[16] The strict demarcation between the public and the private realms comes to the forefront in his later work, while his view of the "common good" remains restricted to the idea of justice. Rawls has come under much attack on both of these counts.

The main criticisms: metaphysics and ontology revealed

The importance of Rawls' *Theory* is reflected in the vast number of works written in response to it, some sympathetically and others rather critically. Many of the criticisms leveled against *Theory* arose out of concern for its metaphysical and "comprehensive" nature. The most well known response to the liberalism articulated in *Theory* has come to be known as "communitarianism." The four thinkers most often associated with communitarianism are Michael Sandel, Alasdair MacIntyre, Charles Taylor, and Michael Walzer, though these thinkers do not write under or all accept the label.[17]

16. Ibid., p. 463.
17. The "essential" communitarian texts are usually identified as Michael Sandel, *Liberalism and the Limits of Justice* (Cambridge: Cambridge University

Despite the differences in the emphases and nuances of their thought, what unites them is the common belief that liberalism in its classical and its Rawlsian expression inadequately accounts for the role of community and society in constituting human beings and their conceptions of the good. The degree to which these communitarian critiques have influenced the direction of Rawls' writing since *Theory* is a matter of some dispute.[18] Rawls himself more explicitly acknowledges a desire to move away from his theory as a comprehensive doctrine than he does that his work is a response to such criticism, though the vigor and quantity of communitarian writing spawned by *Theory* could not but have impacted him. Many of the concerns of the so-called communitarians have to do with the metaphysical and ontological presuppositions upon which Rawls' *Theory* depends, so regardless of their direct impact upon him, their thought helpfully illuminates the "comprehensive" nature of Rawls' earlier theory. Because Walzer's critique is less relevant to this discussion than those of Sandel, MacIntyre, and Taylor, the latter three will collectively provide the lens through which we can begin to see more clearly the large liberal suppositions upon which *Theory* is based.

Sandel's *Liberalism and the Limits of Justice*, often considered the most important critique raised of Rawls' *Theory*, is particularly concerned with what he identifies as the metaphysical conception of the person that underlies Rawls' writings. His work is meant to be a challenge to "deontological liberalism," a specific doctrine of liberalism with its roots in Kant that is concerned with the primacy of justice and individual rights. This form of liberalism prioritizes the right over the good, meaning that the principles by which a society should be ordered and governed do not rest upon a particular conception of the good but supposedly conform to the morally independent category of the right. And the right that has primacy is

Press, 1982); Alasdair MacIntyre, *After Virtue: A Study in Moral Theory*, 2d. ed. (Notre Dame, IN: University of Notre Dame Press, 1984); Michael Walzer, *Spheres of Justice: A Defense of Pluralism and Equality* (Oxford: Blackwell, 1983); and Charles Taylor, *Philosophy and the Human Sciences: Philosophical Papers*, vol. 2 (Cambridge: Cambridge University Press, 1985).
18. Rawls himself denies that his work is a response to the communitarian critique (see *Political Liberalism*, p. xix, fn. 6), while others remain unconvinced by his denials. See, for example, Stephen Mulhall and Adam Swift, *Liberals and Communitarians* (Oxford: Blackwell, 1992), pp. 167–226 and Kymlicka, *Contemporary Political Philosophy*, p. 229.

justice, understood as an end in itself, serving to regulate all other ends and setting the boundaries of conceptions of the good. Sandel locates the origins of the priority of the right in Kant's thought and notes how it is concomitant with a particular conception of the human being as a subject given prior to his or her ends. Moreover, this understanding of the person as subject forms the basis for this entire branch of political theory: a society that prioritizes the right over the good is a necessary result of defining human beings as autonomous individuals with freedom of choice. Were it to be otherwise, were a society dependent upon principles that presuppose a particular conception of the good, its subjects would not be free to make autonomous choices about their own conceptions of the good. Indeed, they would be treated as means to some greater good rather than ends in themselves.[19]

This Kantian belief in the importance of treating people as ends rather than means undergirds contemporary expressions of deontological liberalism, particularly that of Rawls. Sandel, however, identifies a crucial difference between the projects of Rawls and Kant. Whereas Kant's theory was openly dependent upon a metaphysical framework, Rawls aims to maintain the priority of the right and the priority of the self without relying upon a metaphysical or transcendental conception of the subject. Rawls instead believes that the original position can itself establish the necessary perspective and objectives without reference to transcendental deductions or presuppositions, that the original position can provide the Archimedean point that in turn provides a foundation for Rawls' liberalism without recourse to Kant's metaphysics.[20] Throughout the remainder of the book, Sandel attempts to demonstrate why Rawls fails to distance himself from certain metaphysical and metaethical claims that serve as the foundation of his thought and are ultimately mistaken, inadequate, and ultimately inconsistent. Perhaps the single largest inadequacy Sandel finds in Rawls' thought is the idea that a person's identity is formed independent of his or her conception of the good and certain ends to which he or she is attached. As Sandel writes,

> If the deontological ethics fails to redeem its own liberating promise, it also fails plausibly to account for certain indispensable

19. Sandel, *Limits of Justice*, pp. 1, 9.
20. Ibid., pp. 23–28.

aspects of our moral experience. For deontology insists that we view ourselves as independent selves, independent in the sense that our identity is never tied to our aims and attachments ... But we cannot regard ourselves as independent in this way without great cost to those loyalties and convictions whose moral force consist partly in the fact that living by them is inseparable from understanding ourselves as the particular persons we are – as members of this family or community or nation or people[21]

What ultimately results from the Rawlsian conception of the self as independent and incapable of constitutive attachments is not, in Sandel's view, "an ideally free and rational agent," but instead "a person wholly without character, without moral depth."[22] In other words, Sandel believes that Rawls' conception of the person as an independent, autonomous individual does not allow for the possibility that the identity of a person may be partially defined by his or her ends and attachments, which therefore excludes the possibility that any communal good might be integral to a person's identity.

This line of critique is somewhat similar to that raised by MacIntyre and Taylor, who argue in different ways for the primacy of the community and conceptions of the good in a person's life. MacIntyre perhaps goes further than Sandel in his emphasis on the role of the community, arguing not just that it can play some role in constituting a person's identity but that community is both essential to human identity and provides the framework and origin for all human goods and ends. In this respect, Rawls' form of liberalism with its asocial individualism reflects the more general modern failure to recognize that human goods are inseparable from the communal practices and traditions in which they have their origin. Rawls' original position therefore excludes the possibility that society is not based on rational individuals deciding what social contract they should reasonably enter into but instead consists of a community united by shared understandings of individual and collective goods.[23] In later works, MacIntyre further critiques liberalism for embodying its own particular conception of the good, based on the Enlightenment attempt to establish a tradition-transcending, universal morality. This liberalism, carried forward by Rawls, has

21. Ibid., p. 179.
22. Ibid.
23. MacIntyre, *After Virtue*, pp. 246–252.

not transcended tradition but has itself become a tradition, "the articulation of an historically developed and developing set of social institutions and forms of activity."[24] To put it differently, liberalism claims to provide the framework for a political society in which members with different conceptions of the good life derived from whatever theory or tradition to which they adhere could coexist, with one significant qualification, namely that these conceptions of the good cannot be applied to the community as a whole. "And this qualification," MacIntyre writes, "of course entails not only that liberal individualism does indeed have its own broad conception of the good, which is engaged in imposing politically, legally, socially, and culturally wherever it has the power to do so, but also that in so doing its toleration of rival conceptions of the good in the public arena is severely limited."[25]

The conclusions reached in Taylor's writings result in critiques very much in the same vein as those of MacIntyre and Sandel, though the works from which his "communitarianism" is drawn tend to be more broadly philosophical in nature rather than explicitly directed against liberalism. Taylor's philosophical arguments lead him to conclude, among other things, that orientations toward the good are integral to the identity of the self and that every moral and political theory embodies a conception of the good and of the self, regardless of whether or not such theories recognize these conceptions. Taylor believes that human identity cannot do without an orientation to the good, which involves not only a person's stand on moral and spiritual matters but also reference to a defining community. Further, according to Taylor, a person's sense of the good is inextricably connected to the frameworks of meaning within which that person lives his or her life. Such frameworks are derived from the narrative that informs a person's life, even if implicitly, for Taylor believes that life is best considered as narrative in nature. This narrative and the frameworks that help constitute it are and must be communal in nature, just as they must inevitably involve "hypergoods." By "hypergoods" Taylor means higher order goods which are incomparably more important than the other goods of a person's life and therefore provide a standpoint from

24. Alasdair MacIntyre, *Whose Justice? Which Rationality?* (Notre Dame, IN: University of Notre Dame Press, 1988), p. 345.
25. Ibid., p. 336.

which these other goods are weighed and judged.[26] With this in mind, Taylor critiques Rawls' prioritization of the right over the good, arguing that Rawlsian liberalism rests upon autonomy as a hypergood and is thus not as neutral between different conceptions of the good as it appears to be.[27]

These three thinkers, then, draw attention to the relationship of Rawls' theory to conceptions of the person and of goods that are generally associated with a Kantian metaphysics, which, in turn, is usually linked to the Enlightenment. As Stephen Mulhall and Adam Swift write, summarizing the communitarian critique, "in order to defend its claim about the right way to organize the sphere of political life ... , liberalism must draw upon the conceptions of human good and the general ontology of the human that make up the broad liberal ethical tradition of which this conception of politics is merely a part."[28] Rawls himself recognized the "comprehensive" and therefore controversial nature of his articulation of liberalism in *Theory*. This acknowledgement prompted him to considerably rework his initial presentation of justice as fairness under the term political liberalism. His concern is to present justice as a political conception, freed from any metaphysical or epistemological presuppositions. It is to the motivations behind and the substance of political liberalism that we now turn.

Political liberalism

We can now begin to see why "political" is such an important qualifier, as Rawls employs it in his attempt to delimit *political* liberalism over against liberalism as a comprehensive doctrine. Writing in the introduction to *Political Liberalism*, a compilation of lectures and articles written since the publication of *Theory* in attempts to clarify and address problems in that work, he empha-sizes the fundamental distinction "between comprehensive philo-sophical and moral doctrines and conceptions limited to the domain of the political."[29] This distinction, he admits, was not made in

26. These ideas are found in Charles Taylor, *Sources of the Self: The Making of the Modern Identity*, Part One (Cambridge: Cambridge University Press, 1989), pp. 3–107.
27. Ibid., pp. 88–89.
28. Mulhall and Swift, *Liberals and Communitarians*, p. 124.
29. Rawls, *Political Liberalism*, p. xvii.

Theory, in which he presented an unrealistic idea of a well-ordered society in which all citizens were expected to accept the concept of justice as fairness and its concomitant principles as part of a comprehensive philosophical doctrine. Rawls now identifies a "serious problem" intrinsic to this effort, namely that

> A modern democratic society is characterized not simply by a pluralism of comprehensive religious, philosophical, and moral doctrines but by a pluralism of incompatible yet comprehensive doctrines. No one of these doctrines is affirmed by citizens generally. Nor should one expect that in the foreseeable future one of them, or some other reasonable doctrine, will ever be affirmed by all, or nearly all, citizens. Political liberalism assumes that, for political purposes, a plurality of reasonable yet incompatible comprehensive doctrines is the normal result of the exercise of human reason within the framework of the free institutions of a constitutional democratic regime.[30]

His thought as presented in *Political Liberalism* recognizes this fact of inevitable plurality and recasts justice as fairness as a political conception of justice rather than necessarily concomitant with a larger comprehensive doctrine.[31] This change requires the articulation of a new family of ideas to make this political conception comprehensible and consistent, and to distance it from the metaphysical and epistemological foundations upon which it was originally conceived, tasks to which the writings contained in *Political Liberalism* are devoted.[32]

Rawls is concerned to distance himself intentionally from any perceived attempt to replace comprehensive religious doctrines with a comprehensive secular doctrine associated with the Enlightenment, a concern that leads J. Judd Owen to call Rawls' political liberalism "an antifoundationalist theory of liberalism."[33] In other words, Rawls' aim is not to supplant other comprehensive views with liberalism, nor to find a "true foundation" for liberal doctrines, but rather to develop a conception of political justice that

30. Ibid., p. xviii.
31. Rawls is not alone in this attempt to articulate a "political liberalism" that is not comprehensive and is therefore supposedly more inclusive. See, for example, Larmore, *Patterns of Moral Complexity* and "Political Liberalism," *Political Theory* 18, no. 3 (August 1990), pp. 339–360.
32. This new family of ideas is also helpfully discussed in Rawls, *Justice as Fairness* esp. pp. 1–38.
33. Owen, *Demise of Liberal Rationalism*, p. 105.

can be endorsed by the plurality of reasonable comprehensive doctrines that do, and will inevitably, exist within a given society. He is concerned to answer the question "how is it possible for there to exist over time a just and stable society of free and equal citizens, who remain profoundly divided by reasonable religious, philosophical, and moral doctrines?"[34] Here we begin to see why the issue of toleration is integrally connected to political liberalism, gaining much more prominence than it had in his earlier writings. If the existence of a diversity of incompatible and irreconcilable comprehensive doctrines is the inevitable outcome of human reason at work, then for obvious reasons the question of the grounds of toleration between these doctrines is a fundamental issue that needs to be addressed. Without toleration, how would a political society characterized by reasonable pluralism be sustainable as a just and stable democracy? We can see why Rawls considers toleration one of the two fundamental questions which political liberalism seeks to answer.[35]

We can likewise understand why Rawls is concerned to emphasize the practical goal of justice as fairness. It must be presented as a conception of justice that can be shared by citizens regardless of the different religious and philosophical doctrines to which they adhere. That is to say, it must express their shared and public political reason. This is what leads Rawls to assert that

> in formulating such a conception, political liberalism applies the principle of toleration to philosophy itself. The religious doctrines that in previous centuries were the professed basis of society have gradually given way to principles of constitutional government that all citizens, whatever their religious views, can endorse. ... Thus, political liberalism looks for a political conception of justice that we hope can gain the support of an overlapping consensus of reasonable religious, philosophical, and moral doctrines in a society regulated by it.[36]

This overlapping consensus is how Rawls resolves the question of toleration. It serves as the basis of public reason, defined by Rawls as the reasoning of citizens in the public forum about constitutional essentials and basic questions of justice, and the means whereby

34. Rawls, *Political Liberalism*, p. 4.
35. Ibid., pp. 3–4.
36. Ibid., p. 10.

justice can be seen as a freestanding, political conception that can be endorsed by all citizens. In short, this political conception of justice is "political not metaphysical."[37]

What does Rawls' overlapping consensus involve? It is based in the idea that reasonable comprehensive doctrines, though marked by differences and disagreements on fundamental matters, can nevertheless agree on a public conception of justice that is independent of any particular comprehensive doctrine. This political conception can be supported by and fit into various comprehensive doctrines, each of which affirms the conception on the basis of its own religious, moral, and philosophical beliefs. To put it differently, a consensus on a political conception of justice exists throughout the reasonable comprehensive doctrines found within society, but this consensus does not require that the grounds each doctrine has for supporting this conception be the same. Whereas the criterion used in *Theory* to devise a conception of justice was fairness, here the concern is to develop a conception of justice that can gain an overlapping consensus in light of the fact of reasonable pluralism, and Rawls presents his conception of justice as fairness as the best candidate to gain such a consensus.

A political conception of justice is not, then, the same as justice as fairness. It is used in a broader sense, with justice as fairness understood as one candidate among many different, competing conceptions of justice found within liberal society. The content of these conceptions is marked by three main features: first, the content specifies certain rights, liberties, and freedoms; second, it assigns a priority to these freedoms; and third, it provides measures that assure that all citizens, regardless of their social position, have the means to make effective use of their liberties and opportunities.[38] Different ways of defining and specifying these conditions result in different liberal conceptions of justice. When it comes to explaining the meaning of the term "political conception of justice," Rawls identifies three characteristic features. The first is the subject with which a political conception of justice is concerned, which Rawls refers to as the basic structure of society. The basic structure includes a society's main political, social, and economic

---

37. "Political not Metaphysical" was written by Rawls in 1985 and became Lecture I of *Political Liberalism*. See especially p. 10 on this point.
38. Ibid., pp. xlviii, 6.

institutions, as well as how they fit together into a unified system of social cooperation that moves from one generation to the next. A political conception of justice is thus developed to deal with the basic institutions of a society. Also of integral importance to a political conception of justice is its mode of presentation, which we have heretofore referred to as a freestanding view, meaning that a political conception must be presented as independent of any particular comprehensive doctrine. Although Rawls' hope is that it could be derived from, justified by, and a part of a range of reasonable comprehensive doctrines, Rawls is careful to distinguish between how a conception is derived and how it is presented. In short, such a conception must not be presented as part of a larger doctrine but as its own freestanding view. The third and final characteristic of a political conception of justice identified by Rawls is that its content is expressed in terms of the fundamental ideas found within the public political culture of a democratic society. The tradition of democratic thought and the main institutions of a democratic society are thought to serve as "a fund of implicitly shared ideas and principles" which are familiar to the citizens of that society (or at least to their "educated common sense") and in terms of which a political conception of justice should be framed.[39] Rawls hopes that this public political culture will provide the source for a public justification for justice that would be impossible to establish on the basis of one particular comprehensive doctrine given the plurality of such doctrines within a society.[40]

From here Rawls goes on to elucidate justice as fairness as a political conception of justice in terms of the fundamental ideas he identifies in a certain democratic tradition, namely society as a fair system of cooperation over time, from one generation to the next, with the two companion ideas of citizens, referring to those who undertake that system of cooperation, as free and equal persons and well-ordered society as a society effectively regulated by a political conception of justice.[41] The ideas of the original position and the veil of ignorance that were initially presented in *Theory* as part of justice as fairness are discussed again in light of political liberalism and reasonable pluralism. Rawls continues to maintain that the

39. Ibid., p. 14; pp. 11–15.
40. Ibid., pp. 150–151.
41. Ibid., pp. 14–46.

original position is the best device to create an adequate political conception of justice, though he is careful to specify that it is only a device of representation and, as such, does not presuppose a metaphysical conception of the person.[42] Instead, he emphasizes, in a now familiar refrain, the political rather than metaphysical conception of the person upon which his theory relies,[43] a claim to which we shall return below.

Once Rawls has presented justice as fairness, and its principles of justice, as a freestanding political conception concerned with the basic structure of society, he turns to the question of the stability of justice as fairness. Stability is a necessary criterion for a political conception of justice to be satisfactory so this question is of great importance in Rawls' investigation of justice as fairness. The first part of the question of stability concerns whether citizens growing up under just institutions, as defined by the political conception in question, acquire a sense of justice that is sufficient for them to comply with those institutions (i.e., to render those institutions stable over time by inculcating an adequate conception of justice and allegiance to those institutions), and it is answered by looking at the moral psychology by which people acquire a normally sufficient sense of justice. The second part of stability involves the over-lapping consensus mentioned previously, as it raises the question of whether, given the fact of reasonable pluralism, the political conception can be the focus of an overlapping consensus of reasonable comprehensive doctrines. Rawls notes that this kind of stability is based "on its being a liberal political view, one that aims at being acceptable to citizens as reasonable and rational, as well as free and equal, and so as addressed to their public reason."[44] The terms used by Rawls in this sentence refer to very particular ideas that are at the heart of Rawls' theory; a more focused look at how he uses these terms will aid our understanding of his liberalism, as well as our later critiques of it.

Rawls identifies the "reasonable" and the "rational" as independent but complementary ideas. Rather than defining them, he has

---

42. Note that here he appears to be responding to the criticisms of Sandel, not by changing his position but by arguing that understood as a device of representation, the original position has no metaphysical implications. See ibid., p. 27.
43. For specifics of this conception, see ibid., pp. 29–35.
44. Ibid., p. 143.

his readers gather their meaning from how they are used and the contrast between them.[45] The rational refers to single, unified agents as they seek, adopt, and prioritize their own interests and ends, as well as the means to meet those ends. The reasonable, by contrast, is more of a public conception because it is related to the idea of society as a system of fair cooperation. When persons are concerned that the standards and propositions of society be fair terms of cooperation that it is reasonable for everyone to accept, then these persons are reasonable. Reasonable persons "desire for its own sake a social world in which they, as free and equal, can cooperate with others on terms all can accept."[46] Integral to this is what Rawls calls the idea or criterion of reciprocity, namely that all who are involved in social cooperation and do their part guided by the necessary rules and procedure should benefit in an appropriate way as assessed by a suitable benchmark of comparison.[47] People who are reasonable, then, should desire the establishment of a framework for the public social world that it is reasonable to expect everyone to endorse.[48] Because of the public role of the reasonable, it is, in political liberalism, of more importance to the matter of toleration than the rational.

Rawls acknowledges another important aspect to the concept of the reasonable, namely recognition of "the burdens of judgment" as the source of reasonable disagreement.[49] The burdens of judgment are Rawls' attempt to explain the fact of reasonable pluralism by identifying some of the obstacles that prevent the clear and con-scientious use of reason and judgment.[50] They represent his way of explaining how disagreements between people exist even if all persons conscientiously attempt to be reasonable, that is to employ fair terms of cooperation and to be fully cooperating members of society. He mentions six sources of this reasonable disagreement, including, to give two examples, that the evidence bearing on a case may be conflicting and complex and that because all concepts are vague and subject to hard cases we must rely on judgment and

45. Rawls, *Justice as Fairness*, p. 82.
46. Rawls, *Political Liberalism*, p. 50.
47. Ibid., p. 16.
48. Ibid., pp. 48–58.
49. For a description of these burdens of judgment see ibid., pp. 54–57 and *Justice as Fairness*, pp. 35–36.
50. Rawls, *Justice as Fairness*, p. 34.

interpretation, which may lead reasonable people to differ, and concludes that "many of our most important judgments are made under conditions where it is not to be expected that conscientious persons with full powers of reason, even after free discussion, will all arrive at the same conclusion." Rawls believes that "these burdens of judgement are of first significance for a democratic idea of toleration."[51]

Rawls reaches this conclusion based on the idea that reasonable people who recognize the implications of the burdens of judgment will inevitably endorse liberty of conscience and freedom of thought. Of crucial importance here is Rawls' application of the reasonable to comprehensive doctrines, based on the assumption that reasonable people will affirm only reasonable comprehensive doctrines. A reasonable comprehensive doctrine is an exercise of theoretical and practical reason, meaning that "it covers the major religious, philosophical, and moral aspects of human life in a more or less consistent and coherent manner" and determines which values and aspects should have significance and priority.[52] A reasonable comprehensive doctrine will usually draw upon a tradition of thought and doctrine, though it also changes and evolves over time. The implications of the burdens of judgment are that reasonable people adhere to a variety of comprehensive doctrines, while others who affirm comprehensive doctrines that differ from our own are still reasonable, and it is therefore unreasonable to use political power to repress comprehensive doctrines merely because they are not the same as ours. In other words, "reasonable persons see that the burdens of judgment set limits on what can be reasonably justified to others, and so they endorse some form of liberty of conscience and freedom of thought. It is unreasonable for us to use political power, should we possess it, or share it with others, to repress comprehensive views that are not unreasonable."[53] Thus we have the necessity behind and basis for toleration.

Rawls is careful to distance his understanding of the burdens of judgment and the concomitant need for toleration from skepticism on matters of truth. This stems at least partially from the practical need to avoid controversial claims that would prevent

51. Rawls, *Political Liberalism*, p. 58.
52. Ibid., p. 59.
53. Ibid., p. 61.

the possibility of an overlapping consensus. That is to say, because
many reasonable comprehensive doctrines would not affirm a
political conception that involved skepticism about or indifference
to truth, Rawls recognizes the need to distance himself from such
skepticism if the goal of finding an overlapping consensus is to be
attained.[54] Political liberalism, according to Rawls, does not question the possibility of truth-claims, nor does it desire that adherents
of different comprehensive doctrines will relinquish their convictions in the name of skepticism. Instead, it affirms that political and
moral judgments can be held up to different criteria of correctness
and reasonableness and recognizes that people within varying
comprehensive doctrines will hold to their own beliefs as true, or at
least reasonable. Indeed, the goal of the overlapping consensus is to
find a political conception of justice that can be accepted as reasonable or true by a variety of reasonable comprehensive doctrines
that exist within a given society.

Rawls identifies overlapping consensus as one of the two key ideas
that are not presented in *Theory* that are needed to meet the fact of
reasonable pluralism.[55] Public reason is the other, and it may be this
idea more than any other that Rawls has returned to and refined
since the initial publication of *Political Liberalism*. In the introduction
to the paperback edition, he makes considerable revisions to some
of the main ideas of his original articulation of public reason, while
three years later he includes "The Idea of Public Reason Revisited"
in his publication of *The Law of Peoples*.[56] In this latter work, Rawls
identifies public reason as a basic feature of democracy that is
necessary because of the fact of reasonable pluralism. When reasonable citizens recognize that they cannot reach agreement on the
basis of their comprehensive doctrines, they turn instead to reasons
that they might reasonably assume others could adhere to, which is
to say reasons that are independent of any particular comprehensive
doctrine. Rawls' proposal is "that in public reason comprehensive
doctrines of truth or right be replaced by an idea of the politically
reasonable addressed to citizens as citizens."[57] This conception of

54. Ibid., pp. 62–63, 150–151.
55. Ibid., p. xlvii.
56. John Rawls, "The Idea of Public Reason Revisited," in *The Law of Peoples*
(Cambridge, MA: Harvard University Press, 1999), pp. 129–180.
57. Ibid., p. 132.

reason is deemed public in three ways: first, because it is the reason of free and equal citizens, it is to be considered the reason of the public; second, it applies to questions of the public good concerning matters of fundamental political justice (meaning questions of constitutional essentials and basic justice); and, third, as the expression of public reasoning through a family of reasonable conceptions of political justice that satisfy the criterion of reciprocity, its nature and content are public.[58]

It is important to note, as Rawls is careful to, that public reason applies only to discussions that take place in the public political forum, which is separate from what Rawls terms the background culture. The public political forum consists of the discourse of judges, government officials, and candidates for public office and their campaign managers (although Rawls applies the idea of public reason differently in each of these three realms), while the background culture is the culture of civil society. Rawls defines this as "the culture of the social, not of the political," and it consists of such agencies and associations as churches, universities, clubs, teams, and scientific societies that make up daily life.[59] Public reason, then, applies to matters of the public political forum rather than to discussions and arguments that might take place in the background culture or personal deliberations about political questions. Furthermore, it does not apply to all matters that arise in the public political forum but only those involving constitutional essentials and questions of basic justice, which involve fundamental principles that specify the general structure of government and the political process, and the equal basic rights and liberties of citizens that are to be respected.[60]

Despite these limits on the application of public reason, it still has relevancy for the average citizen, meaning the citizen who is not a judge, legislator, or political candidate. This is because "ideally citizens are to think of themselves *as if* they were legislators and ask themselves what statutes, supported by what reasons satisfying the criterion of reciprocity, they would think it most reasonable to

58. Ibid., p. 133.
59. Rawls, *Political Liberalism*, p. 14. Note that in a footnote in his later essay Rawls also recognizes the media as nonpublic political culture, serving to mediate between the public political culture and the background culture (Rawls, "Public Reason Revisited," p. 134).
60. Rawls, *Political Liberalism*, p. 227.

enact."[61] That is to say, when citizens are involved in political activities in the public forum and vote in elections in which matters of basic justice and constitutional essentials are at stake, the ideal of public reason rather than personal or private convictions alone should govern them. Rawls bases this in the duty of civility, which requires that citizens be able to explain to one another their decisions on matters of principles, policies, and elections in terms of the political values of public reason, as well as the willingness to listen to others and accommodate to their views when this is reasonable.[62] This moral duty is vital, Rawls believes, to the enduring strength and vigor of democracy.[63] In Rawls' initial articulation of the ideal of public reason, he insisted that it required that citizens be able to explain their political decisions in terms of reasonable public political values, though citizens recognize that each other's political values are undergirded by different reasonable comprehensive doctrines. In other words, when engaged in public reasoning, citizens could not offer reasons or arguments based in their comprehensive doctrines but had to appeal to reasons to which all reasonable people could reasonably be assumed to adhere. This is the site of one of Rawls' considerable revisions. He now believes in what he calls a wide view of public reason as specified by the "proviso," namely that reasons based in reasonable comprehensive doctrines may be introduced in public reason provided that at some point public reasons supported by a reasonable political conception are offered as support to the initial reasons given.[64] Though the details of the proviso are not worked out, this represents a rather significant change to his initial conception of public reason. Rawls now believes that positive reasons exist for the introduction of comprehensive doctrines into public debate, based on the acknowledgement that the political conceptions upon which democratic society relies find their basis and strength within various comprehensive doctrines.[65] Nevertheless, either at the beginning or along the way citizens must "present to one another publicly

61. Rawls, "Public Reason Revisited," p. 135.
62. Rawls, Political Liberalism, p. 217.
63. Rawls, "Public Reason Revisited," p. 136.
64. Rawls, Political Liberalism, pp. li–lii.
65. Rawls, "Public Reason Revisited," pp. 153–154.

acceptable reasons for their political views in cases raising fundamental political questions. This means that our reasons should fall
under the political values expressed by a political conception of
justice."[66]

We saw above that Rawls appeals to the *moral* duty of civility in
his advocacy of public reason. A moral element is also involved in
the overlapping consensus. Rawls is careful to articulate this to
distinguish his conception of an overlapping consensus from a
modus vivendi. Rawls borrows the term *modus vivendi* from international relations, in which context it refers to a treaty between two
countries that have competing interests and adhere to the treaty
only because it is to the advantage of each to do so. While recognizing that the hope of a political community based on a unifying
comprehensive doctrine is not a possibility under conditions of
reasonable pluralism, at least when the use of coercive state power
on such matters has been rejected, Rawls wants to maintain that
more can be attained within a society than a mere *modus vivendi*
between competing comprehensive doctrines. This is because the
political conception of justice which serves as the object of an
overlapping consensus is a moral conception that is affirmed on
moral grounds, by which Rawls means that its content contains
ideals, principles, and standards that articulate certain (political)
values.[67] To be more specific, the political conception of justice that
Rawls hopes persons can affirm from within their own comprehensive doctrines includes conceptions of society and citizens as
persons, principles of justice, and an account of political virtues by
which those principles can be embodied and expressed. The overlapping consensus, then, is deeper than a *modus vivendi*, containing a
moral conception which persons from within a number of competing comprehensive views can affirm for its own merit. As such, it
is a political conception that can be supported regardless of shifts in
political power related to comprehensive doctrines, which means
that it is a much more stable concept than the one a mere *modus
vivendi* would provide.[68]

---

66. Rawls, *Justice as Fairness*, p. 91.
67. Rawls, *Political Liberalism*, pp. 11, 147.
68. Ibid., pp. 146–148. It is worth noting that Rawls' insistence that liberalism
be more than a *modus vivendi* creates a significant distinction between him and
other liberal theorists, a matter to which we will return below. See, for

Rawls, in fact, has high hopes for what the discovery of an over-lapping consensus would accomplish:

> Were justice as fairness to make an overlapping consensus possible it would complete and extend the movement of thought that began three centuries ago with the gradual acceptance of the principle of toleration and led to the nonconfessional state and equal liberty of conscience. This extension is required for an agreement on a political conception of justice given the historical and social circumstances of a democratic society. To apply the principles of toleration to philosophy itself is to leave to citizens themselves to settle the questions of religion, philosophy, and morals in accordance with views they freely affirm.[69]

As much as, according to Rawls, "political liberalism is sharply different from and rejects Enlightenment Liberalism," we see here that links continue to exist between earlier articulations of liberalism and Rawls' political liberalism, particularly when it comes to the centrality of liberty of conscience and toleration.[70] Rawls' ruling assumption is that every reasonable comprehensive doctrine accepts some form of the political idea of toleration. With "reasonable toleration" in place, it is possible for those adhering to competing comprehensive doctrines to coexist within a well-ordered constitutional democratic society.[71]

Rawls' toleration questioned

Rawls' conclusion would lead us to believe the above, yet the reasons for questioning Rawls' political liberalism in the name of toleration itself are manifold. Of course, criticisms have been leveled against Rawls' formulation of political liberalism on a number of different issues, but for the purposes of this project we restrict ourselves to looking only at those that are most relevant for the question of toleration. Certain admissions and assumptions overtly made by Rawls leave one wondering how much legitimacy can be given to his supposed concern that comprehensive religious, moral, and philosophical doctrines thrive within democratic

example, Larmore, *Patterns of Moral Complexity*, p. 123; Gray, *Two Faces*, pp. 5–7, 139; and Galston, *Liberal Pluralism*, pp. 6–9.
69. Rawls, *Political Liberalism*, p. 154.
70. Rawls, "Public Reason Revisited," pp. 176, 151–152.
71. Ibid., pp. 176–180.

society. Rawls openly admits that political liberalism depends upon the values of the political domain outweighing whatever values might conflict with them.[72] This is possible because the values of the political are "very great values," governing the basic framework of our social lives.[73] They even, he writes, serve as "the very groundwork of our existence."[74] For those who strive to make their own religious or philosophical views the framework of their lives, these claims for the primacy of political values may be rather problematic. John Gray and William Galston both pick up on this area as a matter of concern, based on their own accounts of liberalism that are rooted in value pluralism. Galston believes that Rawls has a "monistic" account of value that fails to recognize the genuine heterogeneity of value that will preclude any one account of value, even a "political" account, from being broadly accepted.[75] Gray argues that Rawls' belief in the possibility of finding one set of common values around which all people can be united reveals links to the universal liberal regimes of John Locke and Immanuel Kant, whereas real acceptance of pluralism would result in the relinquishment of attempts to associate liberalism with particular values, even those found in theories of justice.[76] So, where Gray believes that a *modus vivendi* between competing values and ways of life is the only way forward for a liberalism that recognizes pluralism, Rawls maintains that a consensus of value is needed to provide the necessary stability for a political liberal society marked by pluralism. And here, in the search for this "stable and enduring overlapping consensus," is where Rawls admits that his theory is significantly helped by the fact that most of the comprehensive views found in society are not fully but only partially comprehensive.[77]

According to Rawls, many citizens will not even think about how their political and comprehensive values relate to each other because most people do not actually view their philosophical, moral, and religious doctrines as comprehensive. As a result, "there is lots of slippage, so to speak, many ways for liberal principles

72. See Rawls, *Political Liberalism*, p. 139. Cf. Rawls, *Justice as Fairness*, p. 37, in which he appears to say the exact opposite.
73. Rawls, *Political Liberalism*, p. 139.
74. Ibid. Here he is using a phrase from J. S. Mill's *Utilitarianism*.
75. See Galston, *Liberal Pluralism*, pp. 6–8.
76. Gray, *Two Faces*, pp. 5–6, 138–139.
77. Rawls, *Justice as Fairness*, p. 193.

of justice to cohere loosely with those (partially) comprehensive views. . . ."[78] Indeed, the success of political liberalism is to some degree dependent upon this assumption of slippage. Because citizens have not usually worked out fully comprehensive doctrines, political principles are able to win their primary allegiance. If a conflict later emerges between political principles and their (partially) comprehensive doctrines, "then they might very well adjust or revise these doctrines rather than reject those principles."[79] Further, "these adjustments or revisions we may suppose to take place slowly over time as the political conception shapes comprehensive views to cohere with it."[80] Rawls admits that many doctrines view such comprehensiveness as an ideal to be attained,[81] but, according to his own thinking on the matter, political liberalism might well be at risk if such comprehensiveness occurred with some regularity. In other words, the success of political liberalism is utterly reliant on comprehensive doctrines not actually being comprehensive so that political liberalism can take priority over and even shape the comprehensive doctrines found within political liberal society.

Rawls speaks further about the revisions that should be made to comprehensive doctrines in the name of liberalism when writing on the attainment of constitutional consensus. He openly admits that liberal principles of justice can and should alter citizens' comprehensive doctrines so that they can accept a liberal constitution. The existence of reasonable rather than simple pluralism may actually depend upon the alteration of comprehensive doctrines into a reasonable (i.e., liberal) form.[82] His willingness to see comprehensive doctrines adapted so that political liberalism can be attained leads to some obvious questions. How much respect does Rawls extend to comprehensive doctrines in their own right? How much space does his political liberalism have for a genuine diversity of doctrines, values, and way of life? How well does political liberalism tolerate comprehensive doctrines that do not already prioritize liberal principles of justice? Before turning to this latter question more directly through a consideration of how Rawls treats comprehensive

---

78. Rawls, *Political Liberalism*, p. 160.
79. Ibid.
80. Rawls, *Justice as Fairness*, p. 193.
81. Rawls, *Political Liberalism*, p. 175.
82. Ibid., pp. 163–164.

doctrines that he does not consider reasonable, let us refer once more to Rawls' own words to make sure we understand his position:

> many if not most citizens come to affirm the public political conception without seeing any particular connection, one way or the other, between it and their other views. Hence it is possible for them first to affirm that conception on its own and to appreciate the public good it accomplishes in a democratic society. Should an incompatibility later be recognized between the political conception and their comprehensive doctrines, then they might very well adjust or revise the latter rather than reject the public conception.[83]

Based on this line of thinking in Rawls, it is easy for us to see how Owen concludes that, in Rawls' form, "liberalism depends on religion being substantively transformed."[84] Indeed, not just religious but all types of reasonable comprehensive doctrines should be concerned about how welcome they are in a liberal regime that hopes they will prioritize liberal views and values over their own.

The use of "reasonable" to qualify the comprehensive doctrines that Rawls' theory admits raises even more questions along this line. Rawls finds no space within liberal democratic society for comprehensive doctrines that are not reasonable. When Rawls uses the term "reasonable," he relates it to the idea of fair social cooperation, the use of terms that all citizens regardless of their comprehensive doctrines can be expected to accept, and satisfaction of the criterion of reciprocity. Reasonable doctrines, by definition, support political conceptions of justice and constitutional democracies, while those that do not support such principles or democratic society are not considered reasonable. Furthermore, though comprehensive doctrines may contain principles that they consider higher than political values, a reasonable comprehensive doctrine will not override political values in favor of its, for example, transcendent principles. If, however, a comprehensive doctrine does override these political values, then it is, again by definition, unreasonable. Rawls gives fundamentalist religious doctrines, the doctrine of the divine right of monarchs, forms of aristocracy, and autocracy and dictatorship as examples of unreasonable comprehensive doctrines.[85] The

83. Rawls, *Justice as Fairness*, p. 193. See also Rawls, *Political Liberalism*, pp. 208–209.
84. Owen, *Demise of Liberal Rationalism*, p. 117.
85. Rawls, "Public Reason Revisited," pp. 172–173.

public reason of political liberalism "does not trespass upon religious beliefs and injunctions insofar as these are consistent with the essential constitutional liberties, including the freedom of religion and liberty of conscience."[86] Doctrines that do not affirm these constitutional liberties, doctrines that prioritize the philosophically or religiously true over toleration or liberty of conscience, are "simply" labeled "politically unreasonable. Within political liberalism nothing more need be said."[87]

Rawls' treatment of unreasonable comprehensive doctrines does not depend upon his appraisal of how many such doctrines exist within a given society. He openly admits that every actual society contains numerous unreasonable doctrines, but his identification of such doctrines as a threat to democracy and the realization of the ideal of public reason are, to him, sufficient grounds for their exclusion from consideration. Rawls is careful to clarify that this does not mean that those who adhere to such doctrines are not to be tolerated (in his most extended discussion of the question of "toleration of the intolerant," in his earlier *Theory*, Rawls writes that the intolerant should be curbed only when the security of the tolerant and the institutions of liberty are in danger[88]), but it does mean that they are unable to participate in the democratic society his theory seeks to design. Owen notices that "the capacity of people to come to an agreement despite their supposedly profound differences is not so amazing, since Rawls has from the outset included as parties only those liberals who do not differ on the crucial political question at issue."[89] Indeed, many scholars view this exclusion as evidence of intolerance within political liberalism itself.

Heidi Hurd wonders at the nature of Rawls' project when he excludes from consideration those very people who most need convincing. While she recognizes the difficulty Rawls may see in trying to reason with the unreasonable, she also points out that his definition of the unreasonable includes a striking portion of the population, including classical liberals, libertarians, act consequentialists and utilitarians, egoists, altruists, Catholics, Protestants, hedonists, perfectionists, communists, socialists, feminists,

86. Ibid., pp. 175–176.
87. Ibid., p. 178.
88. Rawls, *Theory*, pp. 190–194. Cf. Rawls, *Political Liberalism*, pp. 178–179.
89. Owen, *Demise of Liberal Rationalism*, p. 113.

and communitarians. She is, in fact, led to the conclusion that the purpose of *Political Liberalism* can only be descriptive, aimed at describing the liberal principles of justice as fairness to those who, as liberals, already adhere to those principles.[90] Placing his investigation of political liberalism within the context of the historical development of toleration within political theory, Andrew Murphy reaches an even stronger conclusion. He believes that the requirements of public reason, and the concomitant exclusion of arguments based in comprehensive doctrines and unreasonable doctrines themselves, serve to restrict rather than protect liberty of conscience. He notes the irony of Rawls' claim that political liberalism represents the "completion and extension" of liberty of conscience when it actually involves the constriction of what citizens are allowed to publicly affirm and abide by, whereas "historically, the expansion of liberty of conscience has resulted in a steadily increasing sphere in which religious and conscientious concerns were removed as bases for punishment or the denial of public benefits and citizenship rights."[91] In short, he accuses Rawls of having developed a theory that, in its exclusion of unreasonable comprehensive doctrines, is far more repressive than many legal prohibitions of the past.

This discussion of the role of reason and the reasonable within Rawls' theory leads to the obvious question of how Rawls defines and uses these concepts. The observant reader will have noticed that we used the word reasonable even as we tried to define what Rawls meant by the term, implying, perhaps, a certain level of vagueness in his description. As Jean Hampton notices, one might think that Rawls uses "reasonable" as an adjective to describe that which is consistent with public reason, yet the fact that the overlapping consensus of public reason must develop out of reasonable comprehensive doctrines suggests that the "reasonable" is somehow conceptually prior to public reason. In an interesting exposition of the burdens of judgment, Hampton discloses how Rawls' use of the reasonable implies the existence of "a fact of the matter about what is reasonable and what is not."[92] Though Rawls' theory

90. Heidi M. Hurd, "*Political Liberalism* (book review)," *Yale Law Journal* 105, no. 3 (December 1995), pp. 795–824.
91. Andrew Murphy, "Rawls and a Shrinking Liberty of Conscience," *Review of Politics* 60, no. 2 (1998), p. 274.
92. Jean Hampton, "The Common Faith of Liberalism," *Pacific Philosophical Quarterly* 75 (1994), p. 203. For a different but likewise interesting discussion of

acknowledges that in certain matters the use of reasoning leads to a plurality of ideas, when it comes to the reasonableness of disagreement and a concomitant policy of toleration, they are seen as reasonable conclusions that all reasonable people should recognize. This reliance on reason to reveal certain politically-relevant truths that can serve as the basis of social harmony shows, according to Hampton, that Rawls is just as committed to an Enlightenment understanding of reason as any traditional liberal thinker.[93]

Hampton is not alone in accusing Rawls of smuggling Enlightenment conceptions into his theory. Nicholas Wolterstorff, in a similar vein to Hampton, argues that Rawls' reliance on common human reason is a carry-over from the Enlightenment ideal of removing ourselves from our comprehensive doctrines and uniting ourselves through the use of our common reason, a notion which fails to recognize the degree to which human reason is always shaped by what we already believe.[94] He further maintains that precisely because of the influence of our particular belief systems on our reason and rationality, it is more reasonable to expect that dissensus will be the result of the use of reason when it comes to political conceptions of justice just as, as Rawls admits, dissensus is the inevitable result of the use of reason when it comes to comprehensive doctrines.[95] Gray follows a similar line of thinking, asking "when society contains not one but many ways of life, each with its own conception of the good, will there not be as much divergence in views of fairness as there is in understandings of the good? When ways of life differ widely in their view of the good, will they not support different views of justice?"[96] Whence, we might ask, comes Rawls' belief that we can be divided in our comprehensive doctrines with their competing conceptions of the good and yet be united around a political conception of justice? Part of the

Rawls' burdens of judgment, see Leif Wenar, "*Political Liberalism*: An Internal Critique," *Ethics* 106, no. 1 (1995), pp. 43–48. For a related critique directed at Rawls' public reason, see Benjamin Gregg, *Thick Moralities, Thin Politics: Social Integration Across Communities of Belief* (Durham, NC: Duke University Press, 2003), p. 7.

93. Ibid., pp. 186–216.

94. Nicholas Wolterstorff, "The Role of Religion in Decision and Discussion of Political Issues," in Audi and Wolterstorff, *Religion in the Public Square*, pp. 98–99.

95. Nicholas Wolterstorff, "Religious Reasons, Liberal Theory and Coercion," unpublished paper, pp. 27–29.

96. Gray, *Two Faces*, p. 19.

answer lies in his understanding of and belief in reason, while another part lies in a classic liberal idea, namely a distinction between "public" and "private."[97]

This distinction between public and private serves as the major emphasis of Jürgen Habermas' critique of Rawls' political liberalism.[98] In short, Habermas accuses Rawls of making a neo-Kantian distinction between the sphere of the political and other cultural value spheres which results in a divide within moral persons between their public identity as citizens and their nonpublic identity as private persons shaped by particular conceptions of the good.

> But such an a priori boundary between public and private not only contradicts the republican intuition that popular sovereignty and human rights are nourished by the same root. It also conflicts with historical experience, above all with the fact that the historically shifting boundary between the private and public spheres has always been problematic from a normative point of view.[99]

Wolterstorff likewise disagrees with the strict demarcation between public and private advocated by Rawls. He points out that the necessary reliance on public reason which Rawls posits goes against the religious convictions of many people within democratic society that their decisions on such fundamental issues as justice should be based upon their religious convictions. Though Rawls' addition of the proviso, which allows citizens to introduce reasons on political matters based in their comprehensive doctrines provided that they later introduce reasons based in public reason, may appear to ameliorate some of the requirements of the strict division between one's private and public reasoning, in actuality it does not go very far towards allowing comprehensive doctrines into the public sphere (as Murphy writes, "the 'proviso' makes Rawls' exclusion of comprehensive doctrines from public life kinder and gentler, but no less real"[100]). Furthermore, Wolterstorff argues, recognition of citizens in the particularity of their identities as adherents to

---

97. See, for example, Rawls, "Public Reason Revisited," pp. 160–161.
98. The details of the differences between the liberalisms of Habermas and Rawls are beyond the scope of this investigation. See Jürgen Habermas, "Reconciliation Through the Public Use of Reason: Remarks on John Rawls's *Political Liberalism*," *The Journal of Philosophy* 92, no. 3 (March 1995), pp. 109–131. Rawls' response, originally published as pp. 132–180 of the same issue, is included in the paperback edition of *Political Liberalism*, pp. 372–434.
99. Habermas, "Reconciliation," p. 129.
100. Murphy, "Shrinking Liberty of Conscience," p. 269.

particular comprehensive doctrines is what amounts to true respect, respect that is more substantive than that based merely on citizens as free and equal.[101] Michael Sandel argues similarly that the toleration advocated by Rawlsian liberalism cultivates respect for persons rather than for the convictions or ways of life of those persons. Such toleration "may afford a kind of social peace, but it is unlikely to realize the higher pluralism of persons and communities who appreciate and affirm the distinctive goods their different lives express."[102]

These are important and worthwhile points, ones to which we will have occasion to return in more detail below. As we raise these criticisms related to public and private, however, we must be fair to Rawls by pointing out that he does not believe his theory necessarily requires a sharp split between what citizens affirm in their political and their nonpolitical lives.[103] Rather, he hopes that each reasonable comprehensive doctrine will furnish its own support for conceptions of justice and society that can serve as the basis of an overlapping consensus between different comprehensive doctrines, even if the foundations of those conceptions differ. In other words, he hopes for convergence between citizens' comprehensive doctrines and society's reasonable political conceptions. Indeed, in his development of the wide view of public political culture, of which the proviso is an integral part, he goes so far as to recognize that citizens' comprehensive doctrines provide the vital social basis for these political conceptions.[104] We must remember, however, the priority that Rawls places upon these political conceptions and his willingness to see comprehensive doctrines adapted and altered so that they can accommodate the political conceptions necessary for a liberal society.

We must also remember that Rawls' understanding of the relation between public and private depends upon a particular conception of the person, for, as Jean Bethke Elshtain elucidates in relation to John Locke, one's view of the individual is of significant importance for how one articulates the relationship between public and

---

101. Wolterstorff, "Role of Religion," pp. 105, 110–111.
102. Sandel, *Democracy's Discontent*, p. 116.
103. In this respect Larmore may be more honest in his recognition of what political liberalism requires, namely the abandonment of "the cult of wholeness" (Larmore, "Political Liberalism," p. 351).
104. Rawls, "Public Reason Revisited," pp. 153–154.

private.[105] Rawls' understanding of the person may not adequately account for the degree to which people's comprehensive doctrines are intimately related to their identity or sense of self and are therefore not easily separable from their political views.[106] Rawls is careful, once again, to emphasize that the conception of the person upon which his theory relies is political rather than metaphysical, and that the moral psychology upon which his theory rests is likewise drawn from a political rather than psychological conception.[107] He recognizes that a political conception of justice necessarily presupposes a theory of human nature because it has to take into account the feasibility of the ideas it presents in terms of the capacities of human nature and the potential instability of democratic institutions.[108] At the same time, he believes that a political conception of the person must be distinct from a conception of the person found in a personal, associational, religious, or moral ideal, arguing that the basis of toleration is at stake when this distinction is not recognized. This is because the conception of the person that applies to the political realm needs to be one which ensures the basis of fair social cooperation, meaning one that could serve within an overlapping consensus, one that is independent of and compatible with a variety of comprehensive doctrines' conceptions of the person.[109] Yet Rawls himself openly relies upon a Kantian view of persons as free and equal moral persons, and it is this view of citizens, as free and equal, that forms the basis of the political conception of the person that he puts forward in his political liberalism.[110] Leif Wenar points out a number of places in which Rawls is explicitly defending a Kantian moral psychology against other philosophical conceptions, and then goes on to list a range of philosophical positions that are excluded from the overlapping consensus on the basis of their non-Kantian moral psychologies.[111] Rawls also relies heavily upon a developmental theory of moral psychology that has its roots in Lawrence Kohlberg, Jean Piaget, and William McDougall; an extensive account of his theory of moral

105. Elshtain, *Public Man, Private Woman*, pp. 116–120.
106. See Murphy, "Shrinking Liberty of Conscience," pp. 260–261, 254–255.
107. Rawls, *Political Liberalism*, pp. 29–35, 86–88.
108. Ibid., pp. 346–347.
109. Ibid., p. 369.
110. Ibid., pp. 280–281.
111. Wenar, "*Political Liberalism*," pp. 49–51.

development is found in *Theory*, and, rather than distancing himself from it in *Political Liberalism*, he instead refers the reader to it.[112] Such developmental psychological theories as those of Kohlberg and Piaget are not without their own substantive moral conceptions and secular psychological assumptions that adherents of many comprehensive doctrines would be loathe to accept.[113] Once again we find evidence that Rawls' political theory contains many assumptions and components that maintain his link to Enlightenment thought and that serve to exclude rather than include a considerable number of comprehensive doctrines.

The same could be said of the importance that Rawls attributes to what he calls the primary good of self-respect. Primary goods are understood to be goods that all rational people desire regardless of their particular conceptions of the good and they are, according to Rawls, necessary for the advancement of all reasonable conceptions of the good. Of all the primary goods, Rawls assigns fundamental importance to that of self-respect, and he argues, in his earlier *Theory* as in *Political Liberalism*, that the principles of justice as fairness provide the best basis for ensuring self-respect for all citizens.[114] How does Rawls define self-respect? "Self-respect is rooted in our self-confidence as a fully cooperating member of society capable of pursuing a worthwhile conception of the good over a complete life."[115] Its importance lies in the fact that "it provides a secure sense of our own value, a firm conviction that our determinate conception of the good is worth carrying out. Without self-respect nothing may seem worth doing . . . ."[116] The upshot of the definition and role that Rawls assigns to self-respect is that public principles of justice must not allow citizens to question each other's conceptions of the good. Because an essential element of self-respect is a "secure sense of our own value rooted in the conviction that we can carry out a worthwhile plan of life," and because "our sense of our own value, as well as our self-confidence, depends on the respect and mutuality shown us by others," citizens must

112. Rawls, *Political Liberalism*, p. lxii; *Theory*, pp. 397–449.
113. This is a point well argued and documented by James Davison Hunter, *The Death of Character: Moral Education in an Age Without Good or Evil* (New York: BasicBooks, 2000). See esp. pp. 83–84, 187–188.
114. Rawls, *Theory*, pp. 386–391, 477–480; *Political Liberalism*, pp. 318–320.
115. Rawls, *Political Liberalism*, p. 318.
116. Ibid.

recognize the worth each citizen attaches to his or her way of life.[117] By defining self-respect in terms of life plans and comprehensive doctrines, Rawls eliminates the possibility that self-respect might be based on, for example, an innate human dignity or the *imago Dei* rather than one's sense that one holds a worthwhile conception of the good. Further, the link that Rawls draws between self-respect and the need to see one's own plan of life as worthy and valuable has tremendous implications for the ability of citizens to question and discuss with each other their different, often incompatible comprehensive doctrines and ways of life. Will not such discussions, rooted in one comprehensive doctrine rather than another, be seen as questioning the worth of the other's way of life and thereby as undermining the primary good of self-respect? Does that mean that any genuine discussion that seeks to probe and question, understand and perhaps critique other conceptions of the good is ruled out *a priori* by Rawls' liberalism?

If such discussion is not ruled out by his conception of self-respect as a primary good, then it is by other aspects of his liberalism. For the entire point of his theory is to find conceptions of justice upon which all people can agree, that form the basis of a consensus, so that disagreement and dissensus can be kept out of the political realm. Not even the principles of justice themselves are the result of dialogue, as Seyla Benhabib and Romand Coles both note, for the "rational selves" of the original position are prior to and uninterested in dialogue or each others' differences when they choose these first principles.[118] The emphasis throughout Rawls' political liberalism is not on what can be achieved as different comprehensive doctrines come together, but what can unify them despite their differences. The differences themselves are not considered appropriate material for the public realm, nor is the public realm particularly known as a site of deliberation. As citizens reason together, they are best guided, according to Rawls, by a political conception of justice that they can all endorse and by public reason, which

---

117. Ibid., p. 319.
118. Seyla Benhabib, "Liberal Dialogue Versus a Critical Theory of Discursive Legitimation," in *Liberalism and the Moral Life*, ed. Nancy L. Rosenblum (Cambridge, MA: Harvard University Press, 1989), p. 144; Romand Coles, *Self/Power/Other: Political Theory and Dialogical Ethics* (Ithaca, NY: Cornell University Press, 1992), p. 5.

ensures that they only present ideas, concepts and reasons with which other people can agree. If they try to introduce reasons that are based in their own comprehensive doctrines, parts of which will not be translatable into reasons to which people outside of those comprehensive doctrines would adhere, then they are likely to be labeled "unreasonable" and excluded from debate. Whereas, according to Hampton, a liberal following in the tradition of Mill could argue that a view was wrong but not unreasonable, and then proceed to offer arguments in favor of his or her position, a liberal following Rawls seems able to dismiss the viewpoint as unreasonable and thereby dismiss it altogether in a rather illiberal fashion.[119] Rawls seems to have no hope that anything positive or constructive could result from conversations that occur as people speak from within their different doctrines and ways of life; he seems to leave no space for what people can learn from each other and how they might be persuaded by the merits of another's position, even if they are not presented in terms with which they already have reason to agree. For this reason, his liberalism has little room for genuine political deliberation. As Gray writes, "in 'political liberalism' nothing of importance is left to political decision. ... The central institution of Rawls's 'political liberalism' is not a deliberative assembly such as a parliament. It is a court of law. All fundamental issues are removed from political deliberation in order to be adjudicated by a Supreme Court."[120] This desire to limit the realm of political discussion, and to constrain whatever public discourse does occur by the parameters of public reason, reveals a fundamental pessimism about what can be accomplished through conversation. It also discloses the inability of Rawls' theory to publicly recognize the different comprehensive doctrines and ways of life of which the citizens of a liberal political society are constituted. Further, it brings to light a certain optimism regarding the possibility of attaining unity in and banishing disagreement from the public realm;[121] the hope of this unity, based on "political" values that supposedly stand

---

119. Hampton, "Common Faith," pp. 186–216, esp. pp. 203–214.
120. Gray, *Two Faces*, p. 16.
121. As Newey writes, "Disagreement about public affairs is what constitutes politics and gives rise to it in the first place, so it is quixotic to think (as Rawls does) that 'political' principles are derivable from agreement or 'overlapping consensus' " ("Is Democratic Toleration a Rubber Duck?" p. 333).

apart from any one tradition or doctrine, is surely reminiscent of certain Enlightenment dreams and ideals.

Indeed, this investigation seems to hint at the conclusion reached by Will Kymlicka, namely that "the entire distinction between political and comprehensive liberalism is overstated."[122] Wenar likewise accuses Rawls of incorporating into political liberalism a partially comprehensive doctrine with a decidedly Kantian emphasis, thereby undermining the very overlapping consensus Rawls' theory was designed to create, for all recognizable comprehensive doctrines except a comprehensive Kantianism are, according to Wenar, excluded from his conception of justice.[123] Owen offers a similar conclusion, drawing attention to the comprehensive and even theological nature of the liberalism Rawls is presenting. The "political" of political liberalism does nothing to limit its comprehensive nature. Instead of finding an overlapping consensus that leaves competing comprehensive doctrines intact, we find that "toleration displaces all other doctrines as the core of the true religion."[124]

Rawls rightly recognizes the existence of competing religious, philosophical, and moral doctrines that makes the well-ordered society he depicted in *A Theory of Justice* unattainable. He deserves much respect for seeking to revise and limit his theory of justice as fairness so that it would adequately accommodate the deep pluralism found in democratic society. He acknowledges that the solution to the problem of pluralism will not be found by "confronting religious and nonliberal doctrines with a comprehensive liberal philosophical doctrine," which leads him to try to formulate a freestanding liberal political conception that nonliberal doctrines can endorse as the basis of a reasonable overlapping consensus.[125] He limits the place of final ends and aims within political society so that the competing ends and aims that are concomitant with a variety of comprehensive doctrines will not result in unnecessary exclusion, recasting the common good of society as the pursuit of justice for all citizens in the hope that it is an end upon which all

122. Kymlicka, *Contemporary Political Philosophy*, p. 239.
123. Wenar, "Political Liberalism," pp. 58, 59.
124. Owen, *Demise of Liberal Rationalism*, p. 122; see also pp. 121–128.
125. Rawls, *Political Liberalism*, p. xlvii.

citizens can agree.[126] And he is surely sincere when he says, "I make a point in *Political Liberalism* of really not discussing anything, as far as I can help it, that will put me at odds with any theologian, or any philosopher."[127]

Yet we have also seen the many ways in which Rawls explicitly and implicitly prioritizes the values of political liberalism over those of any comprehensive doctrine and the degree to which he smuggles in again and again assumptions and conceptions that are deeply inimical to many, even "reasonable," religious, moral, and philosophical doctrines found in democratic society today. Ample evidence, beyond that which has been presented here, seems to support the conclusion that Rawls' political doctrine is much more comprehensive than he realizes, while the parameters he establishes for inclusion in his political society in the name of toleration serve to exclude a vast number of comprehensive doctrines. For this reason, liberal theorists such as Gray and Galston continue to group Rawlsian liberalism and its view of toleration with universal liberal regimes that hope for rational consensus, fail to recognize the (controversial and comprehensive) goods involved in their theories, and, therefore, limit both the breadth of diversity and the recognition of particularity within contemporary society. Though Rawls recognizes the inevitable existence of pluralism in contemporary society, though, with this recognition in mind, he tries to move away from a comprehensive or universal doctrine of liberalism, and though through this move he comes to give toleration ever-increasing prominence in order to protect this pluralism, we have uncovered considerable reason to question the success of his efforts. Rawls' liberalism is neither as uncontroversial nor as tolerant as he would like it to be, as it continues to prioritize the universal over the particular. Is it possible to develop an account of either liberalism or liberal toleration that more successfully leaves behind liberalism's "universal" Enlightenment roots and simultaneously allows space for the presence of difference in its particularity? Richard Rorty hopes to articulate just such a liberalism.

---

126. Ibid., pp. 41, 109. See also Bernard G. Prusak, "Politics, Religion & the Public Good: An Interview with Philosopher John Rawls," *Commonweal* 125, no. 16 (1998), pp. 12–18.
127. Prusak, "Politics, Religion & the Public Good," p. 16.

Towards the recognition of difference: from the universal to the particular

Richard Rorty's postmetaphysical liberalism

Richard Rorty shares John Rawls' concern to distance liberalism from any sort of comprehensive doctrine or "foundationalism." Like Rawls, he also places primacy on toleration, drawing explicit links between the realization of this liberal ideal and the restriction of truth-claims and conceptions of the good in the public sphere. Yet where Rawls is careful to distinguish his theory of liberalism from indifference or skepticism towards matters of truth, recognizing that the controversial nature of such positions would inhibit an overlapping consensus, Rorty views indifference as a necessary component of toleration. Indeed, Rorty believes we would all be better off if we would cease asking what is true or what is universally valid and focus instead on what is most helpful. Where Rawls' project aims to establish *political* liberalism, Rorty hopes for a *postmetaphysical* liberalism (or, to use his term, a postmodernist bourgeois liberalism[128]) that, precisely because it is postmetaphysical, is more tolerant than any liberalism to date.

Rorty is explicit about his rejection of foundationalism, viewing his own project as one of "redescription," or "trying to reformulate the hopes of liberal society in a nonrationalist and nonuniversalist way."[129] The need for this redescription comes from Rorty's belief that "Enlightenment rationalism, although it was essential to the beginnings of liberal democracy, has become an impediment to the preservation and progress of democratic societies."[130] To put it differently, Rorty wants to preserve and build upon the liberal tradition without retaining its commitment to such universal truths as reason, rationality, morality, or innate human dignity. This would be the culmination of the liberation from religion and freedom from authority that the Enlightenment project began but only partially

128. For his explanation of this term, see Richard Rorty, "Postmodernist Bourgeois Liberalism," in *Objectivity, Relativism, and Truth: Philosophical Papers*, vol. 1 (Cambridge: Cambridge University Press, 1991), pp. 198–199.
129. Richard Rorty, *Contingency, Irony, and Solidarity* (Cambridge: Cambridge University Press, 1989), p. 44.
130. Ibid.

attained. The resultant culture of liberalism, or what he refers to as the "liberal utopia,"

> would be one which was enlightened, secular, through and through. It would be one in which no trace of divinity remained, either in the form of a divinized world or a divinized self. ... The process of de-divinization ... would, ideally, culminate in our no longer being able to see any use for the notion that finite, mortal, contingently existing human beings might derive the meaning of their lives from anything except other finite, mortal, contingently existing human beings. In such a culture, warnings of "relativism," queries whether social institutions had become increasingly "rational" in modern times, and doubts about whether the aims of liberal society were "objective moral values" would seem merely quaint.[131]

According to Rorty, the search for absolute truth or universal knowledge is futile and serves only to distract us from matters that should be of concern, such as the reduction of cruelty and suffering. More important than determining whether our beliefs are true in the sense of corresponding to a greater or transcendent reality is determining whether or not they are useful. His critique of absolutism and religious truth is offered not in the name of an alternate truth or epistemology but rather on the basis that religion often serves as a "conversation-stopper," preventing consensus with those who do not share the religious beliefs in question and at times encouraging, as Owen puts it, "a spirit of absolutism that lends itself easily to intolerance and even cruelty, the opposition to which almost entirely defines liberalism ... for Rorty."[132] Likewise, the redescription of liberalism offered by Rorty is not given because it more adequately corresponds to a truth or reality which liberalism seeks to express but because a newer vocabulary will be more helpful to the realization of liberalism's values. Now that science and rationalism have lost their primacy, liberalism will be more successful if it moves beyond the vocabularies associated with them and instead associates itself with the cultural developments and vocabularies that are replacing them (he identifies art and utopian

---

131. Ibid., p. 45.
132. Owen, *Demise of Liberal Rationalism*, pp. 45, 73 (Owen draws the term "conversation-stopper" from Richard Rorty, "Religion as Conversation-Stopper," *Common Knowledge* 3 [1], pp. 1–6).

politics as the two main replacements[133]). In short, "truth" should be fashioned around whatever will be most useful for reaching liberalism's goals.[134]

What are the goals of liberalism that Rorty identifies and retains? Borrowing his definition from Judith Shklar, he thinks of liberals as "people who think that cruelty is the worst thing we do."[135] He is concerned, however, not merely with a description of liberals but with sketching a figure of the "liberal ironist," one who recognizes the contingency of his or her central beliefs and desires while including among those desires the "hope that suffering will be diminished, that the humiliation of human beings by other human beings may cease."[136] In Rorty's liberal utopia, ironism is universal and Freedom has replaced Truth as the goal and purpose of society.[137] Liberal ironists, recognizing the variety of vocabularies that exist and the power of redescription to change the appearance of these vocabularies, hold their own final vocabulary, and thus themselves, with a sense of contingency and fragility.[138] This sense that our final vocabulary does not correspond to a universal reality or truth decreases our need to impose our vocabularies on others, thereby increasing our toleration.

While Rorty's liberal utopia would consist entirely of liberal ironists, he does not intend to impose the inculcation of irony onto today's liberals, or even to argue for it. Instead of providing arguments, he posits the increased usefulness such irony has for realizing the liberal goals of tolerance, justice, and the reduction of suffering. And instead of advocating imposition, he thinks that integral to the definition of "liberal" is a fundamental distinction between public and private that ensures that citizens have the freedom to be ironists or Kantians or Christians within the private realm. Indeed, one of the motivations behind Rorty's work seems to

---

133. Rorty, *Contingency*, p. 52. As he writes elsewhere, in postmetaphysical liberalism it is the poet, the novelist, and the journalist who are more effective than the philosopher or theologian in expanding our moral imagination to increase our willingness "to use the term 'we' to include more and more different sorts of people" (Rorty, "On Ethnocentrism: A Reply to Clifford Geertz," in *Objectivity, Relativism, and Truth: Philosophical Papers*, vol. 1 [Cambridge: Cambridge University Press, 1991], p. 207).
134. Rorty, *Contingency*, pp. 51–53.
135. Ibid., p. xv.
136. Ibid.
137. Ibid., pp. xv, xiii.
138. Ibid., pp. 73–74.

be the desire to correct the mistaken assumptions of such ironists as Friedrich Nietzsche, Martin Heidegger, and Michel Foucault that irony must play out at a public as well as a private level. Irony, when applied to the self, leads to a conception of "self-creation": because the self is a product of contingency and social construction, the individual ironist can work towards redescribing and recreating him- or herself. Yet, Rorty argues, instead of looking for a comprehensive doctrine that can allow self-creation and justice to be combined within a single vision, we need to recognize that self-creation is necessarily private while justice is necessary public, and the two are combined only to the extent that the aim of a just society "is to let everybody have a chance at self-creation to the best of his or her abilities."[139] The public and private coexist and their concerns for solidarity and self-creation, respectively, have equal validity, but they are not commensurable within a single theory or vision. No consensus on conceptions of the good or the true is necessary, or even desirable, within liberal society. Instead, public affairs need only be concerned with two matters:

1 how to balance the needs for peace, wealth, and freedom when conditions require that one of these goals be sacrificed to one of the others and
2 how to equalize opportunities for self-creation and then leave people alone to use, or neglect, their opportunities.[140]

In Rorty's emphasis on the distinction between public and private, we see definite continuity with liberal political theories of the past, including those of Rawls and Locke. Indeed, Rorty views himself as building upon and bringing to maturation the liberal democratic tradition of which he is a part. Of course, in this aspect, as in others we have been discussing, Rorty seems to go well beyond either Locke's classical liberalism or Rawls' political liberalism.

If one is tempted to ask what justification Rorty has for continuing on in the liberal tradition or what defense he offers for such liberal values as the reduction of suffering and cruelty, one will find no answer in Rorty beyond what was just mentioned, namely that Rorty finds himself in a culture based in the liberal tradition. For Rorty, that is enough. As Mulhall and Swift write, "for Rorty,

139. Ibid., p. 84; pp. xiii–xv.
140. Ibid., p. 85.

liberalism is now simply a part of our cultural weather system ...
and we should simply get on with the business of developing and
refining the political vocabulary with which we find ourselves
equipped, in accordance with the standards that are internal to that
vocabulary and culture."[141] We work towards justice because we are
the heirs of the Enlightenment for whom justice was a primary
concern, we aim for the reduction of suffering because liberalism
has traditionally been concerned with such a reduction; because we
find ourselves in this culture, we have no other option. This is part
of Rorty's understanding of the contingency of acculturation and
the inevitability of ethnocentrism. His denial of transcendent truths
or reality, his antirepresentationalism, is concomitant with the
recognition that what we know and our options for how we live are
utterly dependent upon the culture in which we find ourselves. No
"skyhook" based in a greater reality, whether it be God or science,
can rescue us from the cultural socialization of which we are a part.
The only hope for transcending our acculturation lies in "splits" or
tensions that arise in one of two ways. Either these tensions are
already present in our culture or they result from an internal or
external revolt that brings forth new initiatives and ideas to try to
overcome the tensions that already exist. In short, standards, values,
and options are based only in the traditions and consensus of particular communities and cultures; they, and consequently those
who hold them, are inescapably ethnocentric.[142]

   This ethnocentricism does not have the last word, however. Liberals
today are convinced that nothing is worse than cruelty because that
is where the processes of socialization have led and "*we* have to start
from where *we* are," but the progress and processes of liberal society
embody another idea that "takes the curse off this ethnocentrism."[143]
This is a dedication to "enlarging itself, to creating an even larger and
more variegated *ethnos*;" the people who make up the "we" are people
"who have been brought up to distrust ethnocentrism."[144] Part of

141. Mulhall and Swift, *Liberals and Communitarians*, p. 245.
142. Richard Rorty, introduction to *Objectivity, Relativism, and Truth: Philosophical
Papers*, vol. 1 (Cambridge: Cambridge University Press, 1991), pp. 13–15; "The
Priority of Democracy to Philosophy," in *Objectivity, Relativism, and Truth:
Philosophical Papers*, vol. 1 (Cambridge: Cambridge University Press, 1991),
pp. 176–177.
143. Rorty, *Contingency*, p. 198; author's emphasis.
144. Ibid.

the liberal project, then, is the expansion of who is included in that project, the move to include as many people in that "we" as possible. Human solidarity is a legacy of the Enlightenment that is taken over but detached from its larger metaphysical attachments. This solidarity comes not from an innate human dignity or rational power or basis in divine creation that serves to unite us, but rather from a recognition that all traditional differences of religion, race, class, etc. are unimportant compared to the similarities we have in terms of pain and humiliation (humiliation being of particular importance because it is a type of pain experienced only by humans).[145] Furthermore, in this expanded solidarity lies our hope for overcoming our ethnocentrism and acculturation: "our best chance for transcending our acculturation is to be brought up in a culture which prides itself on *not* being monolithic – on its tolerance for a plurality of subcultures and its willingness to listen to neighboring cultures."[146]

We see here the emergence of a second reason for the importance of toleration within Rorty's liberalism. The first reason is that tolerance is a legacy of liberalism and part of the liberal culture in which we find ourselves; the second is that it is only as we encounter difference and diversity and embrace it as part of our own culture that we are able to transcend our radical ethnocentrism. For this toleration to be realized, Rorty's project calls for an end to absolute truth claims because, according to Rorty, they inevitably result in exclusion, intolerance, and presumably pain and humiliation, the opposite of what our liberal culture should be seeking to attain. Rorty himself tries to avoid appealing to absolute claims as he puts forward his political thought. He denies the claim that he is relying on a set of philosophical first principles by maintaining that his concern is rather to change the very questions that philosophy is asking, to get away from questions of metaphysics and epistemology because "the very idea of a 'fact of the matter' is one we would be better off without."[147] Yet he does admit a moral purpose behind his "light-minded aestheticism" towards traditional philosophical questions: "such philosophical superficiality and light-mindedness helps along the disenchantment of the world. It helps make the world's inhabitants more pragmatic, more tolerant, more liberal,

145. Ibid., pp. 192, 92.
146. Rorty, introduction to *Objectivity, Relativism, and Truth*, p. 14.
147. Rorty, "Priority of Democracy," p. 193.

more receptive to the appeal of instrumental rationality."[148] For Rorty, the more disenchanted we are, the more we recognize the contingency of the world in which we live, of the vocabularies that we hold, and of the selves that we are, the more we let go of questions pertaining to truth and reality, in short, the more ironic we are, the more useful we will be in helping to fulfill the liberal, tolerant purposes of society.

Rorty may well be right that part of the liberal culture we have inherited is a desire to be ever more inclusive of those who are different. At the least, we can say that Rorty's move towards the embrace of diversity is shared by a wide range of contemporary political and philosophical thought that has come to be increasingly characterized by concern for difference. Rorty is likewise not alone in attempting to discern how this espousal of difference interacts with the public, political life of a society in which confidence in the unifying, universalistic notions of Reason, Truth, and God has been lost. If we are indeed living "amid the debris of Reason," and if it was "on the twin pillars of 'Reason' and 'Revelation' that the unique balance between public and private, universal and particular interests that defined civil society was maintained," then it is no wonder that so many today are seeking to understand, define, or reimagine the proper relationship between public and private, between the universal and the particular.[149] Rorty's redescription calls for leaving behind questions of the universal and focusing on the particular while fostering a public realm in which suffering is decreased and tolerance increased.

Yet to what does this "tolerance" amount? Rorty's use of the word is clearly different than that of Rawls, bordering on indifference towards competing subcultures, religions, and worldviews. According to Rorty, we tolerate diversity in the sense that we are not particularly bothered by the competing truth-claims or worldviews that are concomitant with diversity; this indifference is based on recognition of the contingency of all beliefs and cultures, the limitations of absolutism, and the need to include other cultures so that we can somehow move beyond our own ethnocentrism. None of

148. Ibid.
149. Adam Seligman, *The Idea of Civil Society* (Princeton, NJ: Princeton University Press, 1992), pp. 1, 11. Civil society is generally understood to be the realm between individuals and the state where citizens pursue social and individual ends.

this suggests that the particularity of the subcultures or individuals that come to be included in this ever-expanding "we" is respected in its own right, nor does it leave open the possibility that the ideals or values that they embody are of some enduring worth. If everything and everyone is a product of contingency and acculturation, how much respect can anything or anyone really be given? Furthermore, Rorty has no place for a toleration that involves both diversity *and* disapproval. Surely, if the implications of Rorty's recognition of contingency are anything, they are that no standard exists by which to judge others, no basis can be found by which to form disapproval, indeed no blame can really be placed upon those who hold the final vocabularies they do because such vocabularies are merely a result of time, chance, and acculturation.

Yet Rorty himself seems to express a disapproval of sorts, a disapproval that results not in toleration for the object of which he disapproves but in calls for limits to tolerance and for dismissal. This dismissal applies to anyone who raises questions or issues that cannot be taken seriously by those who have been brought up in our particular historical situation, for our upbringing sets the limits of sanity and those who break these limits can be labeled "crazy" and thereby dismissed. If we recognize that human beings are centerless selves with contingent vocabularies and histories, then we will realize that no guarantee of common ground exists between those inside and those outside liberal society. So such mad fanatics as Nietzsche or Loyola, to use Rorty's examples, such "enemies of liberal democracy," may well be beyond the point of engagement with those living within a culture of liberal democracy and can therefore be dismissed from consideration and inclusion. This has everything to do with Rorty's understanding of the contingency of truth, and, according to Rorty, "this short way of dealing with Nietzsche and Loyola seems shockingly ethnocentric" only to those who are still relying on the idea that "anybody who is willing to listen to reason – to hear out all the arguments – can be brought around to the truth."[150] Instead of listening to the arguments or questions that someone like Nietzsche or Loyola might raise, we need to recognize that

> accommodation and tolerance must stop short of a willingness to work within any vocabulary that one's interlocutor wishes to use, to

150. Rorty, "Priority of Democracy," p. 188.

take seriously any topic that he puts forward for discussion. To take this view is of a piece with dropping the idea that a single moral vocabulary and a single set of moral beliefs are appropriate for every human community everywhere, and to grant that historical developments may lead us to simply *drop* questions and the vocabulary in which those questions are posed.[151]

We see in Rorty's writing, as we saw in that of Rawls, a willingness to exclude those with whom an "overlapping consensus" cannot be reached. Indeed, these ideas of Rorty's emerge in an exposition of Rawls' work in which he attempts to identify Rawls as a fellow interpreter or "redescriber" of liberalism after metaphysics (an identification that has not been convincing to all). The propensity for exclusion that Rorty shares with Rawls results in the same problem we identified in Rawls, namely the exclusion of many who are already a part of our liberal democratic culture. In Rawls' case this exclusion applies to those who adhere to comprehensive doctrines that are not reasonable by the standards he applies; in Rorty's case this exclusion seems to apply to any who hold comprehensive doctrines at all.

Among those excluded from the conversation and community which Rorty depicts are, as Thomas Pangle identifies, such "sophisticated and intelligent nonliberals" as Nietzsche, Heidegger, Calvin, Thomas Aquinas, Rousseau, Aristotle, Marx, and Gandhi.[152] Pangle notes that Rorty's response to such people, to those who would advocate the relevance of their thought to the development of a richer public sphere, would be that they should privatize their ideas and rest content with that. This returns us to the question of whether such discrete distinctions between our public and private lives are possible. This possibility is addressed by David Hollenbach, who argues to the contrary that

> there are no airtight compartments in human consciousness, but rather a rich interweaving of its diverse elements. This implies that religious convictions can be transformed by social experience and the new emergence of new political ideas, just as politics can be transformed by moral and religious belief. The interaction is reciprocal, a two-way street. The effort to isolate

151. Ibid., p. 190.
152. Thomas L. Pangle, *The Ennobling of Democracy: The Challenge of the Postmodern Age* (Baltimore, MD: The Johns Hopkins University Press, 1992), p. 58.

religion from politics is impossible given this view of human
understanding.[153]

He goes on to suggest that the desire to restrict the interaction
between religion and politics undermines the interplay and inter-
connections necessary for beliefs to be developed and changed,
which in turn "risks precipitating the sort of fundamentalism,
intolerance, and conflict that it seeks to prevent."[154] Furthermore,
religion will be untrue to itself and theologically self-contradictory
if it accepts such relegation to the private sphere. In Hollenbach's
estimation, Rorty recognizes this and therefore ultimately pushes
for secularism, or what can be called universal irony. The result, as
Owen notes, is that despite the integral role tolerance plays in
Rorty's project of redescription as one of the core values of liberalism, "the place of believers among Rorty's 'we' seems to be ten-
uous at best."[155]

Rorty's liberalism does indeed move well beyond universalizing
notions of reason and truth associated with the Enlightenment,
while he retains a commitment to certain liberal ideas whose
heritage lies in the Enlightenment. Increased diversity and inclusivity are chief among the liberal ideas that Rorty claims, making
tolerance essential to his liberal society. Because of his understanding of contingency and the need to overcome ethnocentrism
through the embrace of difference, tolerance takes on even more
importance in his thought than it does in other versions of liberalism. Yet this is tolerance understood as indifference, which
thereby encourages members of liberal society not to be bothered
about the particulars of the differences they encounter. When all
persons, cultures, and beliefs are seen according to Rorty's view of
contingency, without any enduring value, it is hard to find a basis
for treating a particular person, culture, or belief as worthy of
respect or engagement. The lack of common ground between people means that no room exists for discussion between those who
disagree because no hope exists that such disagreements can be
overcome. The lack of anything universal connecting humanity
means, rather ironically, that Rorty can offer no basis for the

153. David Hollenbach, "Religion and Political Life," *Theological Studies* 52, no. 1
(March 1991), p. 104.
154. Ibid.
155. Owen, *Demise of Liberal Rationalism*, p. 92.

engagement of particularity. Not only is interaction between differences severely restricted, but all those who do not readily fit into Rorty's liberal utopia are automatically excluded from membership. If this is the result of Rorty's attempts to redescribe liberalism for a post-Enlightenment and post-metaphysical age, then we may do well to wonder what other options exist, for his "inclusivity" seems to have more to do with exclusion while his "tolerance" overlooks rather than recognizes difference.

Such a call for recognition of difference has been clearly sounded through the multifaceted movement known variously as the politics of difference, politics of recognition, identity politics, and multiculturalism. Though this movement consists of a number of disparate issues, the underlying concern is that the deep diversity and cultural pluralism of modern societies is ignored or stifled by most liberal thought.[156] Advocates of this politics believe that instead of abstracting from the particular identities of groups within contemporary society in the name of universal rights or liberal values, the identities and differences of each group should be recognized and accommodated. The fact that they seek this recognition in the public as well as the private sphere moves them well beyond the liberalisms of Rawls and Rorty.

Difference and multiculturalism: a brief description and critique

The politics of difference, or multiculturalism, represents another recent attempt to address the fact of pluralism and the breadth of diversity within contemporary Western society. It has not been without effect, nor has it escaped criticism. Though in some ways it moves beyond the minimal engagement with difference we found in political liberalism, in other ways it continues to fail to engage with differences and identities in their own right. For this reason, another group of thinkers operating in the name of difference articulates its own view of what is needed for difference

---

156. Kymlicka identifies some of these separate issues as: immigration, minority nationalism, racism, indigenous peoples, religious groups, and gender equality. For a list of recent writings in each area, as well as recent attempts to develop a more general theory, see Kymlicka, *Contemporary Political Philosophy*, pp. 370–372.

to be genuinely recognized and celebrated. These agonistic or post-Nietzschean political theorists are the next main character in the story of political theory and difference, but before turning to them we will look briefly at what has come to be known as the politics of difference. The critique of Stanley Fish will provide a way into the distinctions between this politics of difference and agonistic political thought, while also raising questions about the viability of tolerance within a strongly multiculturalist political theory.

Charles Taylor offers one of the most oft-cited descriptions of the politics of difference, which he generally refers to as the politics of recognition in contrast to a politics of universalism.[157] From the viewpoint of a politics of universalism, it is essential that citizens only be recognized *qua* human and not by the differences that characterize them in order for their equal rights to be protected. When attention is paid to citizens on the basis of individual rather than universal identities, or to the different collective goals that various groups within society might have, the potential for bias and discrimination enters in. Rawls, with his emphasis on political liberalism's concern for persons only as free and equal citizens, represents an example of this type of politics. Indeed, it is precisely conceptions of liberalism such as his that have brought forth accusations of forced homogeneity and inhospitability to difference.[158] In contrast to this, the politics of recognition asks that the unique identities of individuals and groups be recognized because, from this perspective, equal respect requires that particularity be acknowledged rather than "homogenized" into a universal mould. Furthermore, proponents of the politics of difference accuse the politics of universalism of reflecting and imposing a hegemonic culture under the guise of neutrality, thereby discriminating against other cultures in the name of equal dignity and universal rights.[159]

With this latter point in mind it may become clear why the politics of difference often manifests itself in "multiculturalism," or the desire to recognize, support, and foster interest in many cultures within political society rather than only one mainstream

---

157. Charles Taylor, "The Politics of Recognition," in *Multiculturalism: Examining the Politics of Recognition*, edited and introduced by Amy Gutmann (Princeton, NJ: Princeton University Press, 1994), pp. 25–73.
158. Ibid., pp. 37–42, 56–61.
159. Ibid., pp. 28–39, 42–43.

culture. Yet this move towards multiculturalism has not been without major critique. As Taylor notes, multiculturalism is often concomitant with the demand that all cultures be accorded equal value, so that respect is given and value accorded to all cultures *a priori*, without genuine consideration of the specifics or the merits of the culture in question. In other words, positive judgments of worth are granted across the board without actual engagement with or recognition of the specificity of different group or cultural identities. Not only does this fail to give genuine respect to the particularity of cultures (here we are reminded of our critique of Rorty's liberalism), but it also presupposes that those outside of the cultures and groups in question already have the necessary standards and norms for evaluating other cultures (that is to say, as Slavoj Zizek does, that multiculturalists seem to retain a privileged point of universality from which to appreciate other particular cultures properly[160]). Stanley Fish, coming from a very different perspective, likewise finds this presupposition problematic. In his estimation, this reveals a problem with both multiculturalism and toleration.

"Strong multiculturalism," as Fish calls it, is marked by indiscriminatory respect for all cultures and valuation of difference in and of itself. This respect and valuation are connected with tolerance, which is, according to Fish, the first principle of multiculturalism. Yet the multicultural understanding of tolerance has to do with acceptance and embrace rather than either disapproval or indifference, resulting in what Zizek calls a "multiculturalist universe of tolerance of difference, in which nobody is excluded."[161] This is inherently problematic, according to Fish, because at some point the culture of the values being tolerated will reveal itself to be intolerant, forcing strong multiculturalists to decide whether to extend their toleration to include the intolerance within the culture in question or to condemn that intolerance.[162] If they decide for the former and allow intolerance to be present, tolerance will no longer be their guiding principle, but if they opt for the latter, then they

160. And, he continues, thereby assert their own superiority. See Slavoj Zizek, *The Ticklish Subject: The Absent Centre of Political Ontology* (London: Verso, 1999), p. 216. For more on Zizek's critique of multiculturalism, see pp. 201–205, 215–221.
161. Ibid., p. 201.
162. Fish, *Trouble with Principle*, pp. 60–61.

deny the very distinctiveness of the culture they were so keen to respect. Either way, toleration is undermined.[163]

According to Fish, the inability of multiculturalism to live up to its ideal of toleration is a reflection of the incoherence of tolerance itself. All proponents of toleration come to a point at which they must draw limits to its scope, begging the question of the justification behind these limits. Fish believes that no justification exists "apart from the act of power performed by those who determine the boundaries, and that therefore any regime of tolerance will be founded on an intolerant gesture of exclusion."[164] This critique is not offered because Fish himself values toleration and wants to fault liberalism for its intolerance, nor because he adheres to liberal ideals and views liberalism's failure as a matter that needs to be corrected. Instead he is criticizing liberalism's claims because liberalism fails to recognize that conflict is our inevitable condition. Fish believes that democracy is meant to be an attempt to maintain difference in the face of inevitable conflict, not to force its citizens to release the particularity of their truth-claims in the name of substantive notions of toleration or in the hope of harmonization and cooperation.[165] Fish calls for the recognition that politics goes "all the way down," that partisan agendas inform every political decision, and that the political process itself is inherently normative. We can then see that such liberal concepts as toleration and the division between the public and private spheres embody substantive views, and that the extent to which these views are accepted may be the extent to which those who hold them are in positions of power and authority.

If Fish is right, diversity and difference inevitably result in conflict because, ontologically, conflict is what there is. This represents a marked difference from the other theories we have considered in this chapter, and if right has significant implications for how we think about how to live together in the midst of our differences.

---

163. Fish believes that most people opt for the latter, or what he refers to as "boutique multiculturalism," which claims to respect and appreciate other cultures but does not extend such respect or appreciation when those cultures contradict its own values and assumptions (Fish, *Trouble with Principle*, p. 56). See also Zizek, *Ticklish Subject*, pp. 219–220 and Alain Badiou, *Ethics: An Essay on the Understanding of Evil*, trans. Peter Hallward (London: Verso, 2001), p. 24.
164. Fish, *Trouble with Principle*, p. 167.
165. Ibid., p. 301.

Rawls and Rorty respond to the fact of pluralism by articulating versions of political liberalism that, supposedly, allow particularity to flourish in the private sphere while restricting it in the public realm. As we have seen, many comprehensive doctrines have to be altered, excluded, or dismissed for toleration to be attained within their different conceptions of liberalism, while neither version respects the integrity or particularity of religious or philosophical belief systems that cannot be neatly relegated to the private sphere. The politics of difference fares little better when it comes to recognizing the actual particularity of individual and cultural identities; with its unconditional acceptance of difference, it leaves little room for cultures to be recognized in their own right or to be held up to standards of evaluation that lead to meaningful approval or tolerant disapproval. Given the intractable difference upon which so much political theory is predicated, and the growing sense that such difference should be recognized in its particularity, what conceptions of political theory or tolerance are viable in our current context? Fish points the way towards a political theory that moves beyond tolerance in the name of difference while recognizing that discussions of tolerance, difference, and political theory more generally are deeply impacted by the nature of conflict and power. It is to more fully developed articulations of this agonistic political theory that we now turn.

3
_____

Beyond tolerance to difference

Introduction

The conversation about how to live together in the midst of our diversity continues, and the voices we will listen to in this chapter are not satisfied with the contributions liberal theorists have made to the discussion. They find themselves questioning the desirability of tolerance and the feasibility of unity. More than that, they query the very approach that political liberalism takes to political theory, offering their own visions of life together, openly rooted in their beliefs about the nature of human being and reality, as a way to more fully celebrate difference and radicalize democracy.

In Richard Rorty's political theory, we saw one attempt to critique the more typical approaches of recent liberal thought. Rorty tried to move beyond the epistemological concerns and ambitions of the so-called Enlightenment project while retaining the legacy of certain liberal ideals and values that can form the basis of a "postmodernist bourgeois liberalism." Stanley Fish questions the very ideals that Rorty embraces, trying to persuade his readers that the recognition that politics goes all the way down precludes hope for a simple or lasting harmony in the midst of our diversity. Fish's emphasis on the pervasiveness of conflict and its relation to democratic society opens a window into the role of ontology within political theory more generally. While Rorty and John Rawls want to avoid questions related to the nature of human being and "what there is" more generally, William E. Connolly argues that "every political interpretation invokes a set of fundamentals about necessity and possibilities of human being, about, for instance, the forms into

which humans may be composed and the possible relations humans can establish with nature."[1] The ontological dimension of political theory is not often explicitly recognized by contemporary political theorists and their critics, as evidenced by Rawls' claim that his political liberalism is "political, not metaphysical," with metaphysics understood as "what there is."[2] There is, however, as Stephen K. White notes, "a curious commonality ... emerging across a wide variety of contributions in contemporary political theory. Increasingly there is a turn to ontology."[3] This ontological turn, marked by open reflection on the nature of human being and reality, is especially visible in a number of political theorists operating explicitly in the post-Nietzschean legacy. In contrast to and in critique of contemporary political theorists who think their work avoids the realm of ontology by remaining with epistemological matters of legislative and juridical procedure, these theorists believe in the need to engage with ontological concerns as we attempt to create and refine political societies that acknowledge difference and particularity.

Difference is a concern common to these theorists, motivating their work in much the same way that the recognition of the fact of pluralism led Rawls to give tolerance such a primary place in his later theory. This concern for difference is to some degree simply a novel way of engaging with the diversity and plurality that the varieties of liberal tolerance which we have considered thus far are trying to address. Yet the deeper ontological presuppositions held by these theorists motivate them to search for an engagement with difference that moves beyond the tolerance found in most strands of current liberal theory. In following such thinkers as Friedrich Nietzsche, Michel Foucault, and Jacques Derrida, these theorists, in varying degrees, stress that no political theory or society can fully include or incorporate all that there is to "life" and "identity," that "remainders" that exceed our ability to capture them will always exist, that a certain amount of chaos and conflict is irreducible, and that power permeates every realm of political society and every articulation of political theory. This means that at every point a particular configuration of identities or institutions within society

1. Connolly, *Ethos*, p. 1.
2. Rawls, *Political Liberalism*, p. 379.
3. Stephen K. White, *Sustaining Affirmation: The Strengths of Weak Ontology in Political Theory* (Princeton, NJ: Princeton University Press, 2000), p. 3.

based on contingent arrangements of power could be unnecessarily excluding and doing violence to "difference."

In the name of difference, then, these theorists attempt to draw our attention to the ontological dimensions of all political theory, to be forthright about their own ontologies and the ways in which these ontologies affect their theories and their concern for difference, to open our eyes to the role of power and the presence of conflict within all political and social arrangements, and to search for ways to expand our pluralist imagination so that difference can be engaged with more honestly and publicly. Such agonistic theory, with its belief in the all-pervasive nature of conflict and its concern for diversity, is anxious about too much emphasis on "harmony" within political theory and society. It follows Foucault and Nietzsche who, in Connolly's words, "think that the more compelling the drive to closure or unity is in a state the more likely it is either to constitute a repressive regime or to foment the very fragmentation it purports to fear the most. For the world is not amenable to such unity."[4] In contrast, then, to liberal theorists, who are concerned to find ways to fit difference into a unified political community, these theorists prioritize diversity over unity. As we turn to look at this theory in more detail, we shall begin to understand the reasons behind this prioritization.

Towards the recognition of difference: agonistic political theory

Agonistic or post-Nietzschean political theorists are concerned that as we think about our pluralistic political societies we acknowledge the inevitability of conflict and the all-pervasive nature of power within them. This involves expanding the concern for the "big powers" of state, sovereignty, and law that have historically and generally been the objects of consideration by liberal thinkers to include the more subtle power relations involved in institutions, discipline, and knowledge. Such thinkers as Bonnie Honig, William Corlett, Stephen K. White, Chantal Mouffe, and William E. Connolly represent these agonistic political theories. As White's discussion of the ontological turn within some of these political theorists

---

4. Connolly, *Ethos*, p. 26.

concludes, a concern common to their thought seems to be the development of an ethic or ethos that is more sensitive and attentive to others and otherness than the liberal values of tolerance and respect generally foster. This does not entail wholesale rejection or distrust of liberal democracy and its basic constitutional structures, but it does at least involve rethinking or reimagining ways of thinking about and living out certain liberal principles and ideals.[5]

To begin with one example of agonistic political theory, Bonnie Honig's *Political Theory and the Displacement of Politics* attempts, as the title suggests, to argue that "politics," understood as conflict and contestation between alternative perspectives, beliefs, and forms of life, has been inappropriately and indeed dangerously displaced from contemporary political theory. Instead of recognizing the inevitability of conflict, such political theory presupposes that its goal is the elimination of conflict and dissonance. It conflates politics with administration and pursues ways to build consensus and find stability through administrative and juridical settlements. The underlying assumption of these theories is that conflict, and therefore true politics, can and should be displaced. In contrast to these "virtue theories," as Honig calls them, stand *virtù* theories of politics. These theories recognize the perpetuity of political conflict and do not believe that politics can be maintained or overcome through a particular arrangement of administrative and juridical institutions or regulations.[6]

Virtue theorists (of whom Immanuel Kant, John Rawls, and Michael Sandel are her exemplary examples[7]) fail to see that political theory cannot involve overcoming dissonances and finding closure because subjectivity (i.e., the formation of a self into a subject) and political systems always have remainders – excess – which cannot be contained within one particular moral or political order. Drawing on Nietzsche and Hannah Arendt, "with Machiavelli in a minor, supporting role,"[8] Honig develops her understanding of *virtù* as the view that institutions can never adequately accommodate the identities of those whom they claim to represent because politics always has

---

5. White, *Sustaining Affirmation*, p. 152.
6. Bonnie Honig, *Political Theory and the Displacement of Politics* (Ithaca, NY: Cornell University Press, 1993), pp. 2–3.
7. Ibid., p. 2.
8. Ibid., p. 3.

remainders. This recognition of remainders exposes the extent to which moral and political orders have to work to conceal or overcome resistance to their system. As we saw with Rawls, to create his ordered political society, he has to exclude from participation all of those who disagree with its presuppositions. Based on his diagnosis of their "unreasonableness," he feels justified in occluding their place in his system. In Honig's estimation, there will be people in every political system who do not fit (i.e., remainders). We need to recognize this as an indication of the perpetuity of political contest, instead of stifling it under the false pretence that all people can and will fit perfectly into a given system, if only that system can be more perfectly designed and articulated. It is the latter that leads to unrecognized and indeed unnecessary exclusion.

The recognition of remainders serves another function, namely to create new spaces of possibility for our moral and political systems that more adequately allow for disagreement and difference. This stems partly from the attitude of *virtù* towards these remainders, which is one of celebration because "there is vitality in a self that exceeds all orderings."[9] This excessive vitality exposes the extent to which existing arrangements are not natural, inevitable, or "rational," and opens the space for alternative ethical and political ideals. The *virtù* perspective is related to, if not dependent upon, a vision of the self as multiple and plural. Both Arendt and Nietzsche believe that this multiplicity is the source of the self's power, energy, and action. The implication of this understanding of multiplicity as one of the conditions for action is, according to Arendt, that the public realm depends upon inner multiplicity. Autonomy cannot, therefore, be accepted as a value or ideal because it would impose a false unity on a self that is inevitability plural and erase the source of energy and action necessary for the existence of the public realm.[10] For the *virtù* theorist, "the inner multiplicity of the self and the plurality of the republic are conditions of action and politics. Both evidence space and belie, indeed resist, systematization."[11]

Honig wonders if, by acknowledging the inevitability of remainders and dropping the demand that all subjects fit into one system, we might decrease the propensity for self-loathing, vengeance, and

9. Ibid., p. 39.
10. Ibid., p. 83.
11. Ibid., p. 117.

violence that often result in and towards those who do not fit into that system. Similar concerns mark the work of William Corlett, who advocates "a supplementary approach" to politics through recognition of "the remainder, the difference that cannot be reduced to opposition."[12] He thinks that current political theory and discourse, dominated by the debate between political liberalism and communitarianism, are characterized by binary oppositions, such as black–white and man–woman, that fail to take into account both power differentials and the play or excess that cannot be fully captured in simple polarities. Drawing from the work of Foucault and Derrida, he argues that both sides of the communitarian-liberal debate fail to recognize the remainder that is not captured through their theories and, therefore, do not know the cost of the exclusion of this excess. As he writes, "the Foucauldian critique of ignoring what is left out in order to produce intelligible arguments within discourse has changed political theory."[13] Critics operating in Foucault's legacy "draw attention to the scraps, the fringe, the recalcitrant material that resists the production of reasonable discourse."[14] This leads to Corlett's proposal of community without unity: unity is impossible if there is always excess, if difference is irreducible to binary opposition, if one recognizes that underlying the diversity we encounter in everyday life are not order and unity but "forces of madness, oblivion, delusion, accident, or chaos."[15]

We can begin to see certain common themes emerging, particularly the desire to question the terms and sufficiency of the current debate within political theory. The recognition of chaos and conflict at the ontological level, among other things, seems to lead these theorists to wonder whether the theories submitted by political liberal or communitarian thinkers are inevitably closed to the possibility of real tolerance of or engagement with difference. We can appreciate Honig's desire to draw attention to "remainders" in order to facilitate more honesty about how we deal with those who do not fit into a given political theory or system. Instead of labeling such remainders "unreasonable," as Rawls is wont to do, or

12. William Corlett, *Community without Unity: A Politics of Derridian Extravagance* (Durham, NC: Duke University Press, 1989), pp. xvi, xvii.
13. Ibid., p. 37.
14. Ibid.
15. Ibid., p. 71.

"crazy," as Rorty does, thereby excluding many people from inclusion in political society, even many who are already part of our liberal democratic culture, Honig is seeking a way to recognize and be more open to the excesses that will always exist within a given society. We can also appreciate her concern that ignoring the inevitably and perpetually conflictual nature of politics and naïvely assuming that the agonistic element can be overcome within a political arrangement may result in dangerous, because unexpected, eruptions of the agon. Furthermore, as N. J. Rengger points out, when politics is displaced and its conflictual nature obscured from view in the manner described by Honig, we are prone to accept arrangements as they are; this puts us in danger of losing the ability to question or rethink the nature, convictions, identities, and symbols of our society and its political and social institutions as they currently stand.[16] Corlett's desire to move beyond the polarities that dominate contemporary political theory and society offers one way of helping us rethink some of those symbols and ideas, and of working towards moving beyond the communitarian–liberal polarity that provides the accepted conceptual framework for most understandings of democratic theory and citizenship.

And yet some preliminary questions raised by these approaches to political theory also emerge. Does Corlett, in seeking to overcome certain polarities, not simply replace them with other polarities, assuming, for example, that unity and diversity must always be held in polar opposition? Or is he right, and perhaps more honest than most, that if chaos and conflict reign at the ontological level then any hope for unity within a community is lost? If we take seriously the idea that the self and the republic exceed all attempts at ordering and systematization, what level of stability in a political society is really attainable? Honig assures us that points of stability are available and that political order is still possible, but the unexpected, unpredictable nature of the disruptions provided by the remainders and excess surely renders our attempts to foster order and stability problematic. Further, does Honig "ontologize" chaos and contingency to such an extent that those who have different ontologies, who presuppose a level of order and flexibility at the ontological level and concomitantly desire order and flexibility at

16. Rengger, *Political Theory, Modernity and Postmodernity*, p. 8.

the political level, would end up being excluded remainders within her political society?[17]

The issues raised in these questions will be drawn to our attention again, as will areas that we can appreciate for their help in expanding our political and pluralist imagination, as we look in more detail at two further agonistic political theorists, Chantal Mouffe and William Connolly.

Chantal Mouffe's return of the political

Similar to Honig's concern over the displacement of politics, the radical democracy advocated by Chantal Mouffe recognizes the "political" as the irreducible antagonism inherent in human relations, and the extent to which contemporary political theory fails to recognize it and therefore unsuccessfully, and dangerously, seeks to eliminate it.[18] In Mouffe's usage the political does not concern only a certain sphere of society or particular institutions within that sphere, but refers more broadly to the dimension of antagonism "that is inherent to every human society and that determines our very ontological condition."[19] The illusion of most contemporary variants of liberalism is that within conditions of pluralism a consensus can be attained without some degree of exclusion and antagonism (Rawls' overlapping consensus being one obvious example). However, the very concept of a democracy implies the existence of a people that belong to that *demos* (i.e., friends) as opposed to those who are excluded from it (i.e., enemies). This understanding of the political as connected to the creation of relations of friend and enemy, the establishment of an "us" versus "them," is drawn from Carl Schmitt.[20] According to Mouffe, he was concerned, among other things, to correct the (over)emphasis of certain strands of liberalism

17. Cf. Fish, *Trouble with Principle*, p. 235.
18. Chantal Mouffe uses the "political" where Honig uses "politics," namely to refer to the dimension of conflict within relations. She uses "politics" in reference to the "the ensemble of practices, discourses and institutions which seek to establish a certain order and organize human coexistence in conditions that are always potentially conflictual because they are affected by the dimension of 'the political' " (*The Democratic Paradox* [London: Verso, 2000], p. 101).
19. Chantal Mouffe, *The Return of the Political* (London: Verso, 1993), p. 3.
20. Mouffe engages with Carl Schmitt's work throughout her writings (and has edited *The Challenge of Carl Schmitt* [London: Verso, 1999]). She acknowledges his unfortunate political evolution (he joined the Nazi party in 1933) while maintaining that we can learn from his earlier insights.

on the struggle between individuals and the power of the state by drawing attention to the importance of the power at work within the formation of collective identities. In constructing collective identities an "us" has to be identified and delimited from a "them." This helps explain Mouffe's insistence on the irreducible antagonism involved in politics. As she writes, "when we accept that every identity is relational and that the condition of existence of every identity is the affirmation of a difference, the determination of an 'other' that is going to play the role of a 'constitutive outside,' it is possible to understand how antagonisms arise."[21] The very constitution of a given identity happens as a pattern of power relations establishes what will be included and what excluded in that identity; this means that every identity is constituted by both the "other" in contrast to which its own identity was formed and the acts of power which determined that relationship. This is why power has to be recognized in its place at the heart of our attempts to create and sustain a political order.[22]

With this understanding of the constitutive nature of power, politics becomes the attempt to create order and find unity within a context marked by exclusion and conflict. The goal is to find ways of organizing power and relations of power that are most compatible with democratic values, especially the values of liberty and equality. It is the creation of an agonistic pluralism, one that has converted antagonism to "agonism" by channeling passions in ways that allow for collective expression and identification and for "a vibrant clash of democratic political positions" that marks a well-functioning democracy.[23] It likewise enables enemies to be converted to "adversaries" who share the same symbolic space but disagree over how that space should be organized. Mouffe identifies this understanding of adversaries, as "friendly enemies" with whom we disagree while acknowledging their right to put forward their ideas, with "the real meaning of liberal-democratic tolerance, which does not entail condoning ideas that we oppose or being indifferent to standpoints that we disagree with, but treating those who defend them as legitimate opponents."[24] Mouffe's intention in her political

21. Mouffe, Return of the Political, p. 2.
22. Mouffe, Democratic Paradox, pp. 21, 99.
23. Ibid., p. 104.
24. Ibid., p. 102.

theory is not to leave behind liberal ideals but to create a "radical and plural democracy" that enables a fuller realization of those ideals. Indeed, she believes that democracy itself is jeopardized when the irreducibility of antagonism goes unrecognized. She sees herself trying to rescue liberal democracy from the proponents of political liberalism, as well as advocates of identity politics and unfettered pluralism, whose inadequate assumptions and goals threaten to undermine it.[25]

How so? In part, the insufficiency of most contemporary political thinking stems, according to Mouffe, from its failure to recognize the paradoxical nature of modern democracy. This paradox stems from the convergence of two distinct traditions, liberalism and democracy, that each stand for different ideas and ideals. Though today we might be tempted to assume that the two always go together, Mouffe reminds us that democracy is a form of rule that has existed and can be exercised within various symbolic frameworks (so, for example, Athenian democracy existed well before the development of liberalism). The symbolic framework in which it is exercised today is heavily influenced by the liberal discourse of human rights, individual liberty, and the rule of law. The democratic tradition, on the other hand, stands for political equality and the sovereignty of the people. Where the former could be said to be concerned with *human* rights, with reference to people generally or universally, the latter is concerned with *political* rights, associated with people within a given *demos*. The consensus that currently exists between these traditions was not attained without conflict and compromise, while even today the logic of each stands in a constitutive tension with the other that needs to be constantly negotiated.

A brief look at how equality might be understood within liberalism and democracy, respectively, may help to further illustrate how Mouffe conceives of these traditions and what the tension between them entails. A liberal invocation of equality usually involves an understanding that every person is equal to every other person and that human rights should be indiscriminately and universally accorded to all. Democracy's use of equality has more to do with the equal standing of people within a given political society, what we

25. See especially ibid., pp. 99-105; *Return of the Political*, pp. 7-8.

generally refer to as the sovereignty of the people. In short, Mouffe believes that democracy, by definition, requires that a distinction be made between those who belong to the *demos* and those who do not. Its concern with the rule of the people necessarily involves a limit to who is included in "the people," which is incompatible with the universal rhetoric of liberalism. Ideas of a global democracy or a "democracy of mankind" are unrealizable, according to Mouffe, because they draw on universal, abstract conceptions that lack the specificity needed to give them meaning ("equality can only exist through its specific meaning in specific spheres – as political equality, economic equality, and so forth"[26]). When it comes to equality within democratic conceptions, those who do not belong to the *demos* in question are in some significant sense not equal to those who do belong to it because they do not receive the same political rights. Furthermore, no guarantee exists that the decisions made through democratic procedure will not compromise what we generally consider human rights. Even though limits are set on the sovereignty of the people, usually in the name of liberty and the protection of human rights, the meaning of these rights at any given moment depends upon how the prevailing hegemony defines them.[27] There is always, therefore, a tension between the ideals of liberalism and those of democracy.

Rather than seeing this tension as the cause of the demise or inevitable failure of liberal democracy, Mouffe views it as liberal democracy's constitutive element. It provides a very important dynamic that keeps the two traditions in check, so that neither the "abstract universalism" of liberalism nor the exclusiveness of democracy completely wins the day.[28] On the flip side, failure to recognize this contradictory nature and the degree to which stabilizations found at any one time are only contingent; hegemonic resolutions of this conflict has negative, dangerous consequences. Without this recognition we assume that the way power relations are currently configured is the way they must be configured according to nature ("the way things are") and we thereby lose the

26. Mouffe, *Democratic Paradox*, p. 39.
27. Her use of hegemony draws upon her earlier work with Ernesto Laclau, *Hegemony and Socialist Strategy: Towards a Radical Democratic Politics* (London: Verso, 1985).
28. Mouffe, *Democratic Paradox*, pp. 44–45.

ability and resources to question that configuration. The acknowledgement of conflict and hegemony enables us to reenvisage the status quo, the current ordering of the tension inherent in liberal democracy, so that a fuller realization of the ideals of each remains possible.[29]

Mouffe, while recognizing that at one time such conflict and tension were acknowledged within political thought, is concerned about the degree to which contemporary "neo-liberalism" rests upon assumptions of the possibility of rational consensus and social harmony. She has in mind the paradigm of democracy that was inaugurated with Rawls' *A Theory of Justice* and which she finds represented by the two main schools of Rawls and Jürgen Habermas.[30] She finds such theories united around the belief that it is possible and necessary to reach a moral consensus in the public realm that will reconcile the ideals of liberalism and democracy.[31] But rational consensus in the public sphere cannot be attained because "every consensus exists as a temporary result of a provisional hegemony, as a stabilization of power, and ... it always entails some form of exclusion."[32] To forget this, to overlook the conflictual nature of the political that inhabits every consensus, is to open the way to overlooking and disguising the exclusions that necessarily exist under any consensus, and therefore to close the door to the multiplicity of voices that comprise contemporary pluralism.

One could wonder how Mouffe levels this claim against Rawls considering the extent to which his later work is formulated in light of his recognition of inevitable disagreement, incompatible comprehensive doctrines, and the fact of pluralism. Yet when Rawls uses "political," it is to differentiate his version of liberalism from a comprehensive doctrine not to recognize an element of conflict or antagonism within politics. His "political" has to do with, as Mouffe puts it, "a mode of reasoning which is specific to moral discourse and whose effect when applied to the field of politics is to reduce it to a rational process of negotiation among private interests under the constraints of morality. So conflicts, antagonisms, relations of

29. Ibid., pp. 2–6, 39–40, 44–45.
30. Mouffe, *Democratic Paradox*, p. 81.
31. Ibid., p. 83.
32. Ibid., p. 104.

power, forms of subordination and repression simply disappear."[33] Likewise, though he recognizes the existence of inevitable disagreement between competing comprehensive doctrines, he assumes that if these doctrines are left out of the public realm a substantive, moral, stable overlapping consensus is attainable. Through the use of devices such as the original position and the veil of ignorance and the articulation of suitable principles of justice, a sustainable consensus can be identified that will keep order at the political realm while allowing for disagreement in private.

Furthermore, Rawls' theory does not acknowledge the political element involved in establishing a definition of the "reasonable." In the name of creating an inclusive, pluralist, tolerant society, Rawls' liberalism does not allow the participation of anyone whose views are considered unreasonable. In other words, "exclusions can be denied by declaring that they are the product of the 'free exercise of practical reason' that establishes the limits of possible consensus. When a point of view is excluded it is because this is required by the exercise of reason; therefore the frontiers between what is legitimate and what is not legitimate appear as independent of power relations."[34] Instead of recognizing that the creation of a political society necessarily involves an original exclusion, Rawls writes as if a fully inclusive political society was possible if only all people would act reasonably and rationally. Likewise, instead of acknowledging that the criteria for inclusion in his society are political, involving at least a certain level and kind of power in being able to define the terms of inclusion (i.e., what is "reasonable"), instead of creating space for passions and antagonism to interact within established frameworks, he operates as if each of these elements is without relevance or influence within a well-ordered society. Mouffe's concern is that "it is not enough to eliminate the political in its dimension of antagonism and exclusion from one's theory to make it vanish from the real world. It does come back, and with a vengeance ... far from being conducive to a more reconciled society, this type of approach ends up by jeopardizing democracy."[35]

A better approach, according to Mouffe, is one that lets go of the goal of perfect social harmony and realizes the full extent and

33. Mouffe, *Return of the Political*, p. 49.
34. Mouffe, *Democratic Paradox*, p. 31.
35. Ibid.

implications of pluralism. Obviously some level of consensus is necessary for any political society to function, and Mouffe acknowledges this. At the same time, she is asking that unachievable ideals of consensus and harmony be abandoned. By asking us to abandon a picture of democratic society as "a society that would have realized the dream of a perfect harmony in social relations," Mouffe believes she is opening the way for the realization of radical and plural democracy.[36] Pluralism, in Mouffe's estimation, is the central question around which modern democracy revolves. It is what distinguishes today's democracy from that of ancient times. By pluralism she does not mean merely the fact of pluralism that was so influential for Rawls' development of political liberalism. Instead, she takes pluralism as an axiological principle that is constitutive of modern democracy and should be celebrated and increased. In her definition, pluralism is "the end of a substantive idea of the good life."[37] It has everything to do with "the dissolution of the markers of certainty," a quote from Claude Lefort that appears frequently in her writings.[38] The effects of pluralism, of the recognition that values are plural in their very nature, can be seen on the symbolic level, transforming the ordering of our social relations. When it comes to democracy, pluralism means that "we should acknowledge and valorize the diversity of ways in which the 'democratic game' can be played, instead of trying to reduce this diversity to a uniform model of citizenship. This would mean fostering a plurality of forms of being a democratic citizen and creating the institutions that would make it possible to follow the democratic rules in a plurality of ways."[39]

Mouffe does not want to see pluralism addressed merely as an empirical fact that requires us to find procedures to deal with differences, with the end result being that those differences in their particularity are deemed irrelevant (as in Rawls' theory). Nor, it is important to point out, does she seek an unfettered pluralism that celebrates all differences without limits. The latter, in her estimation, too easily hides the way in which certain differences are a result of subordination and need to be challenged rather than

36. Ibid., p. 22.
37. Ibid., p. 18.
38. For example, see ibid.
39. Ibid., p. 73.

accepted by a radical democracy. The former, on the other hand, fails to recognize that the "homogeneity and unanimity" it advocates necessarily involve exclusion and furthermore does not give difference any positive value.[40] Mouffe's radical democracy, on the contrary, "demands that we acknowledge difference – the particular, the multiple, the heterogeneous"; in short, she is working towards "a new kind of articulation between the universal and the particular."[41] This articulation involves a rejection not of modernity in its entirety, but of certain assumptions of modernity related to what Mouffe calls "the Enlightenment project of self-foundation."[42] It is not necessary to seek to find foundations for our democratic project through reason and rationality. On the contrary, appeals to rationality erase diversity and create false, dangerous dreams of the attainment of a fully inclusive consensual political society. Furthermore, "when we realize that, far from being the necessary result of a moral evolution of mankind, liberal democracy is an ensemble of contingent practices, we can understand that it is a conquest that needs to be protected as well as deepened."[43]

Similarly, we need to operate with an understanding of citizenship that recognizes the contingency of identity. Rather than operating with the understanding of the human subject upon which political liberalism relies, namely a rational or utilitarian right-bearing individual who stands independent of the society of which he or she is a part, Mouffe calls us to understand subjects as decentered, multiple, and contradictory. Our identity is never fully established but always open and ambiguous, based on our participation in a plurality of communities, social relations, and discourses. A modern democratic project is not characterized by pluralism only in relation to a multiplicity of approaches to the good life, but also in relation to the multiplicity of each subject. As Mouffe writes,

> we are in fact always multiple and contradictory subjects, inhabitants of a diversity of communities (as many, really, as the social relations in which we participate and the subject positions they define), constructed by a variety of discourses, and precariously and

40. Ibid., pp. 19–20, 134–135.
41. Mouffe, *Return of the Political*, p. 13.
42. Ibid., p. 12.
43. Ibid., p. 145.

temporarily sutured at the intersection of those subject positions. Hence the importance of the postmodern critique for developing a political philosophy aimed at making possible a new form of individuality that would be truly plural and democratic.[44]

With this understanding of what it means to be a subject, one needs to radically rethink what it means to be a democratic citizen. Again, plurality is the key: "this would mean fostering a plurality of forms of being a democratic citizen and creating the institutions that would make it possible to follow the democratic rules in a plurality of ways."[45] In Mouffe's use, citizenship becomes not just a legal status or one identity among many but a form of identification with the *res publica* and its ethico-political values of liberty and equality. It is a means for cultivating a common political identity, while recognizing that those involved in this political society have different purposes and various interpretations of the good. In other words, the principles of liberty and equality can provide a "grammar" of political conduct around which citizens are united even as they disagree about how those principles are to be interpreted.[46]

The reader versed in post-structuralist, post-Nietzschean, or so-called postmodern writings will have recognized many familiar ideas in Mouffe's political thought. Mouffe follows the political theorists we investigated in the last chapter in calling into question the larger epistemological presuppositions of the Enlightenment while seeking to retain what she calls the modern democratic project. At the same time, she seeks to radicalize democracy as we know it, bringing recognition of the ineradicable nature of conflict, the constitutive role of power, and the contingency of social relations and identity to the fore for the sake of liberal democracy itself. In her estimation, nothing less is at stake. One can see in her anti-essentialism the influence of Michel Foucault, Jacques Derrida, and Ludwig Wittgenstein, though only the latter two receive explicit engagement in her work. When it comes to Derrida, she uses his idea of the "constitutive outside" in her account of the formation of collective political identities; every social objectivity is constituted in relation to what it is not, in relation to an otherness that is outside, not in mere opposition to the inside but as the condition of

---

44. Ibid., pp. 20–21; see also pp. 12, 77; *Democratic Paradox*, p. 95.
45. Mouffe, *Democratic Paradox*, p. 73.
46. Mouffe, *Return of the Political*, pp. 65–73; *Democratic Paradox*, pp. 95–98.

the emergence of the inside, thereby "showing the radical undecidability of the tension of its constitution."[47] The constant presence of this undecidability leads to the conclusion that "politicization never ceases. . . . Every consensus appears as a stabilization of something essentially unstable and chaotic."[48]

When it comes to Wittgenstein, Mouffe uses him to explore a new way of approaching political questions that breaks with the "universalizing and homogenizing mode that has informed most of liberal theory since Hobbes."[49] Drawing upon Wittgensteinian insights, she is led to emphasize the contextual nature of liberal democracy and the way in which liberal democratic practices, institutions, and values constitute one possible "language game" or "grammar" by which political life can be ordered. This is of crucial importance to Mouffe's attempts to reenvisage democracy because, in her estimation, it enables us to leave behind the pretence that democratic values can be strengthened and proliferated by offering liberal democracy as the rational, universal, context-transcendent answer to the question of social coexistence. For democratic values to truly be instilled, we need to recognize that identification with democratic values happens through a complex process of practices, discourse, and language-games.[50] In applying the insights of Wittgenstein and Derrida, Mouffe hopes to find "a new way of thinking about democracy that departs fundamentally from the dominant-rationalist approach. A democratic thinking that incorporates their insights can be more receptive to the multiplicity of voices that a pluralist society encompasses and to the need to allow them forms of expression instead of striving towards harmony and consensus."[51]

We see here, as we saw in Corlett's writing, firmly held assumptions about seemingly inevitable dichotomies, namely, plurality *or* harmony. Much depends upon how each of these terms is defined, a matter to which we will return in our discussion of Connolly's work, but we can nevertheless raise questions as to why these are necessarily and always incompatible. We may recall that, in Mouffe's estimation, pluralism is the defining and distinguishing

47. Mouffe, *Democratic Paradox*, p. 12.
48. Ibid., p. 136. See pp. 12–13, 21–22, 135–137.
49. Ibid., p. 61.
50. Ibid., p. 70.
51. Ibid., p. 77.

characteristic of modern democracy, and once we realize its full implications, we will relinquish false, dangerous dreams of harmony and consensus. Yet some would contend, as Nancy Rosenblum does, that pluralism is and historically has always been the heart of liberalism.[52] Again different definitions of the terms in use must be addressed, but the least that can be said is that, throughout its history, liberal thought has primarily been concerned with finding a level of harmony within conditions of pluralism; for Mouffe to operate as if they are inevitably opposed is clearly a "radical" shift in political thinking that may need more explanation. It also may need to be reckoned with more fully by Mouffe herself, as it is not clear that she carries the implication of this polarization all the way through. If instability is so pervasive that every consensus is "a stabilisation of something essentially unstable and chaotic," if we take seriously the sentiment of one of her epigraphs, "Alas, poor race of mortals, unhappy ones, from what conflicts and what groans you were born," can we then realistically hope to find or attain any level of stability or order within political society?[53] With such ontological presuppositions can we think we will find even the minimal level of consensus necessary for liberal democracy to function? Clearly Mouffe thinks we can, but it may well be, as Mary G. Dietz suggests, that Mouffe can only hold this hope because her desire for reconciliation dilutes and ultimately overcomes her own account of radical agonistic democracy.[54] Fish concurs, writing that "taming politics is finally what Mouffe has in mind, despite her pronouncements to the contrary."[55]

Mouffe and Honig, according to Fish, fall prey to the same lure, namely the lure of thinking that becoming aware of an inescapable condition enables one to escape, even in some small measure, that condition.[56] Mouffe is concerned to bring to view the forces of conflict and antagonism at play in our identities, institutions, and practices, but we can wonder, along with Fish, if mere recognition

52. Nancy L. Rosenblum, "Pluralism and Self-Defense," in *Liberalism and the Moral Life*, ed. Nancy L. Rosenblum (Cambridge, MA: Harvard University Press, 1989), p. 220.
53. Mouffe, *Democratic Paradox*, p. 136; *Return of the Political*, p. viii.
54. Mary G. Dietz, "Merely Combating the Phrases of This World: Recent Democratic Theory," *Political Theory* 26, no. 1 (February 1998), pp. 112–133.
55. Fish, *Trouble with Principle*, p. 236.
56. Ibid.

of these forces equips us to account for them within our thinking and practices, particularly if they are as unruly as Mouffe suggests. Or could it be that to think that we can recognize the political assumes that we can distance ourselves from our present situation enough to see conflict for what it is? And yet, if we are as entangled in conflict and contingency as Mouffe claims, no such view would be possible. The assumption at work within Mouffe's writing that she herself occupies some sort of neutral position from which she is able to recognize conflict and develop a political theory to accommodate it may actually serve to align her more closely with the positions of neutrality she is refuting.

This raises the question of how much Mouffe actually "radicalizes" political liberalism. Clearly qualitative differences exist between her assumptions and those of the theorists and political activists to whom she is responding. Indeed, she raises very important points that have been neglected within recent political theory. The subtle ways in which power works within and on our social relations, above and beyond the more obvious influences of, for example, the sovereign state, is surely something of which we need to be constantly aware. Recognizing a level of contingency and hegemony within current configurations of institutions and identity does enable us to question the status quo in the hope of further realizing the ideals to which we adhere. Without this, we may well be prone to let particular injustices and exclusions unquestioningly stand. Mouffe's awareness of the tension between liberalism and democracy also serves as a welcome reminder for those who assume the two have always gone together. At the same time, despite her desire to emphasize democracy, based in the belief that we have lost sight of the democratic component of liberal democracy, her concerns do not seem far removed from those generally attributed to liberalism. Judith Shklar writes that the one overriding aim of liberalism is "to secure the political conditions that are necessary for the exercise of personal freedom."[57] She writes further, in her now famous description of the "liberalism of fear," that liberalism wants to prevent fear "which is created by arbitrary, unexpected, unnecessary, and unlicensed acts of force and by habitual and pervasive acts of cruelty and torture performed by military, paramilitary, and

---

57. Shklar, "The Liberalism of Fear," p. 21.

police agents in any regime."[58] Mouffe's understanding of antagonism and power may involve an expanded interpretation of what
limits personal freedom and what contributes to arbitrary acts of
force, but at root the concerns that motivate her to draw attention
to conflict are the same concerns here identified at the heart of
liberalism. For those who find some of the presuppositions of liberalism problematic, Mouffe's theory will not provide much hope
for furthering our engagement with difference and diversity. Francis
Fukuyama, for example, doubts that her solution "will do anything
but promote liberalism's inherent atomizing tendency."[59] Charles
T. Mathewes, writing of agonistic theory more generally, likewise
wonders "whether it really fulfills its claim to escape the logic of
received liberal political theory; it seems merely to represent the
recognition of intractable difficulties with the received liberalism."[60]

William Connolly shares the concern that Mouffe may come too
close to replicating the positions she is trying to counter, even as he
recognizes considerable overlap in their attempts to rethink our
understanding of liberal democracy and expand our pluralist imagination.[61] He worries that her critique of "essentialism" is made
without recognition of the faith and contestability involved in her
own position. He further wonders how far Mouffe's theory takes us
toward recognizing the positive possibilities opened to us by the
insights she puts forward.[62] Connolly's theory seeks to go further
than she does by pursuing a positive ethos that builds upon the
recognition of antagonism, conflict, and contingency at work within
our social and political relations. It is to his theory that we now turn.

William Connolly and the expansion of our
pluralist imagination

Concern with pluralism, contingency, identity and difference,
and paradox mark William Connolly's political theory, which,
similar to Mouffe's attempt to radicalize liberal democracy, seeks to

58. Ibid., p. 29.
59. Francis Fukuyama, "*The Return of the Political* (book review)," *Foreign Affairs*
73, no. 5 (September/October 1994), p. 144.
60. Mathewes, "Faith, Hope, and Agony," p. 133.
61. Connolly, *Ethos*, p. 222.
62. See also Romand Coles, *Rethinking Generosity: Critical Theory and the Politics of
Caritas* (Ithaca, NY: Cornell University Press, 1997), pp. 190–196.

push "the spirit of liberalism" into realms beyond those usually considered by liberals.[63] Like Mouffe, he is concerned about the lack of emphasis on democracy in recent political theory, viewing it as a crucial practice that needs to be recognized and cultivated alongside liberalism.[64] In his earlier work, he articulates a vision of agonistic democracy in which relations of antagonism would be converted into those of agonistic respect in the hope of cultivating a society marked by "critical pluralism."[65] In later writings, he seeks "the pluralization of pluralism" and a culture of "multidimensional pluralism" in which we are continuously seeking the expansion of the social pluralism that has been achieved thus far through the acceptance of new identities emerging out of old conceptions of difference. This involves the development of "an ethos of critical responsiveness" and a reworking of the pluralist imagination.[66] Throughout his work, Connolly is concerned to develop an ethos adequate for the embrace of difference in a pluralist culture, with paradox playing a leading role. He is likewise interested in fostering more explicit engagement with the ontological, or "ontopolitical," fundaments involved in political theory.

Beyond tolerance to an ethos of critical responsiveness

Connolly's understanding of the paradoxical relationship between identity and difference pervades his political thought. In a nutshell, the problem of "identity\difference relations" is that "difference requires identity and identity requires difference."[67] Identity is crucial to human beings, providing answers to the questions of who we are and how we are recognized, both individually and collectively, and providing the basis from which we act and interact with others. Identity is always collective and relational, and each individual is comprised of a mixture of identifications, often experienced as a tension between those intentionally sought and those bestowed through different constituencies with which

63. Connolly, Ethos, p. 29.
64. Connolly, Ethos, p. 77; William E. Connolly, Identity\Difference: Democratic Negotiations of Political Paradox (Ithaca, NY: Cornell University Press, 1991), p. 211.
65. William E. Connolly, The Augustinian Imperative: A Reflection on the Politics of Morality (Newbury Park, CA: Sage, 1993).
66. Connolly, Ethos, pp. xiv–xix.
67. Connolly, Identity\Difference, p. ix.

one interacts. This discussion of identity, then, while often referring to "self-identity," views individual and collective identifications as inextricably linked. As Connolly writes, "to be white, female, homosexual, Canadian, atheist, and a taxpayer is to participate in a diverse set of collective identifications and to be situated in relation to a series of alter identifications."[68] In addition to being formed by a mixture of identifications, identity is also formed in relation to and contrast with socially recognized differences. The existence of an identity depends upon that which it is not, so that "these differences are essential to its being."[69]

While difference is essential to the formation of identity, it is all too easy for difference to be translated into otherness or evil, while established identities come to seem as if they reflect the immutable, true order of reality. Connolly believes that we have the tendency to "normalize" identities, to see them as reflections of an intrinsic order based in "the commands of a god or the dictates of nature or the requirements of reason or a free consensus";[70] this proclivity is fostered by the role established identities play in meeting the desire for self-certainty and mobilizing collective action. To think, however, that one has a "true identity" is, in Connolly's estimation, "to be false to difference."[71] Instead of treating difference as a complementary or contending identity with which one should be engaged and to which one should give respect, belief in the truth of one's own identity leads one to treat difference as otherness. The latter results in scapegoating and oppression, while the former recognizes that life, though impossible without identity, exceeds capture by any single one.[72] Connolly uses the issue of gender to illustrate this point, drawing attention to the ways in which belief that a certain dualistic understanding of gender reflects a natural or divine order produces a number of "abnormalities." These "abnormalities" (" 'homosexuals,' 'hermaphrodites', 'bisexuals,' 'the sexually impotent,' and 'perverts' ") are labeled, marginalized, institutionalized, or subject to surgery or therapy because they are seen to be contradictory to the 'true' nature of gender and sexuality.[73]

68. Connolly, *Ethos*, p. xvi.
69. Connolly, *Identity\Difference*, p. 64.
70. Ibid., p. 65.
71. Ibid., p. 67.
72. Ibid., pp. 64–65.
73. Connolly, *Ethos*, pp. 90–91.

Instead of "normalizing" one conception of gender, I could recognize the degree to which my conception of myself as female and what being "female" means has been received through a particular configuration of identity\difference relations, is actually constituted in relation to, and dependent upon, what it is not (i.e., difference), and therefore can be reconstituted in different ways. This recognition would make me less likely to ostracize those who are different as others or as abnormalities.

In highlighting the paradoxical nature of identity\difference, Connolly is trying to foster respect for difference by drawing attention to the ways in which our identities are more contingent than we realize. He seeks to expose the degree of power and politics involved in identity by reminding us that identity, rather than being a reflection of that which is true or natural, is formed in relation and opposition to difference. As he writes, "*if* there is no natural or intrinsic identity, power is always inscribed in the relation an exclusive identity bears to the differences it constitutes."[74] Identity, then, always involves a political negotiation between itself and difference; indeed, "politics, in some sense of that protean word, pervades social life."[75] Because of the relational and collective nature of identity, the identity\difference relation necessarily involves social and public forms through which identity is acquired at the same time as some difference is excluded: "To establish an identity is to create social and conceptual space for it to be in ways that impinge on the spaces available to other possibilities."[76] Because the paradox of identity\difference cuts across all realms, it is crucial to have a political theory that adequately recognizes and engages with its ambiguities, including providing a means for public expression and questioning of current configurations of identity and difference. Acknowledgement of this paradox is at the heart of Connolly's reworking of liberal and democratic theory.[77]

Indeed, democracy itself embodies the political paradox of identity\difference, providing a means by which difference can legitimately become recognized identity at the same time as it can be a medium through which established identities become politically

74. Connolly, *Identity\Difference*, p. 66; author's emphasis.
75. Ibid., p. ix.
76. Ibid., p. 160.
77. Ibid., pp. x, 92–94.

dogmatized. Connolly's version of democracy disrupts and pro-blematizes dogmatic identities, giving

> a certain priority to life over identity, treating identity not as the deepest truth of the self or the community, but as a specific formation drawn from energies of life (diference) never exhausted by any particular organization. ... Diference (pronounced *difference*) points to the noises, energies, and remainders that circulate through every cultural configuration and are not captured by their self-identification.[78]

The idea that the protean abundance of life exceeds capture in a set of identities forms the basis for Connolly's post-Nietzschean ethic, which he develops and articulates as an ethos of agonistic respect and critical responsiveness. He views agonistic respect and critical responsiveness as two of the cardinal civic virtues needed for the sustenance of a culture of multidimensional pluralism, and he hopes that an ethos marked by these two virtues can be infused into and sustained by the many different faiths that exist and are emerging today.[79] *Agonistic respect* applies to constituencies in a political society who are already established. These constituencies, instead of treating each other as differences to be oppressed, sca-pegoated, labeled, or denied, can come to respect each other, and the excessive diversity of life, through recognition of the inter-dependence involved in the establishment of their identities and the constitutive role of difference.[80] They "absorb the agony of having elements of [their] own faith called into question by others, and [they] fold agonistic contestation of others into the respect that they convey toward them."[81] *Critical responsiveness* pertains to the ethical attitude of an entrenched constituency towards oppressed, undervalued, or unrecognized constituencies (i.e., constituencies currently under the threshold of legitimate recognition).[82] A con-stituency operating with this ethos would be open to new con-stituencies and social movements and would work towards creating space for new identities to emerge out of existing identity\difference

78. Connolly, *Ethos*, pp. 98–99.
79. William E. Connolly, *Pluralism* (Durham, NC: Duke University Press, 2005), pp. 122, 6.
80. Connolly, *Identity\Difference*, pp. 166–167.
81. Connolly, *Pluralism*, p. 123.
82. For Connolly's distinction between the ethos of agonistic respect and the ethos of critical responsiveness, see *Ethos*, pp. 234–235 and *Pluralism*, pp. 123–127.

relations. It would, further, be willing to renegotiate its own identity in light of the changes that occur as new identities are constructed and recognized.[83]

Connolly considers the ethos of critical responsiveness "the most fragile and indispensable element in a pluralizing democracy."[84] If the goal of a democracy in a pluralist culture is the pluralization of pluralism, whereby new identities are continually fashioned and recognized out of the identities, and difference, of which the current pluralism is comprised, then critical responsiveness is the ethic that makes such pluralization possible. Connolly identifies three crucial elements to this ethic, namely that it is anticipatory, critical, and self-revisionary. By being open and responding to a constituency even before that constituency has acquired its own identity (i.e., by recognizing a new constituency even before it has reached the threshold of recognition and helping it arrive at that threshold), it is *anticipatory*. This does not, however, require uncritical openness to any movement or constituency that would arise. On the contrary, it must be *critical* towards any new constituency that would make its identity a universal requirement and concomitantly seek to punish those who deviate from it. Finally, and "most crucially," it must be *self-revisionary*, recognizing that current identities may need to be modified to create space for and in light of the changes in identity\difference wrought by new constituencies.[85]

It is this last characteristic that most distinguishes Connolly's suggestion from liberal tolerance. "Tolerance," Connolly writes, "is an underdeveloped form of critical responsiveness grounded in misrecognition."[86] It neither sufficiently recognizes the degree to which identity is constructed in relation to difference nor adequately acknowledges the politics involved in the establishment of new identities out of old differences. Tolerance does not go far enough in questioning the hegemony of a given identity, resting upon the assumption that identity is self-sufficient instead of

---

83. Connolly, *Ethos*, pp. 180–181.
84. Ibid., p. 180.
85. Ibid., p. 184.
86. Ibid., p. xvii. In relation to agonistic respect, he writes that "tolerance and agonistic respect are kissing cousins, but they are not equivalent" ("Confessing Identity\Belonging to Difference," in *Identity\Difference: Democratic Negotiations of Political Paradox*, Expanded Edition [Minneapolis, MN: University of Minnesota Press, 2002], p. xxvii).

recognizing that identity itself is constituted by and needs to be modified in light of the differences it encounters. Tolerance may acknowledge difference, but a constituency that *tolerates* another constituency merely allows it to exist, often as nothing but an enclave within a culture in which one predominant identity has hegemony. The pluralizing democracy that Connolly pictures would be more like "a culture of *selective collaboration* and *agonistic respect* in relations between a variety of *intersecting and interdependent constituencies*, none of which sets the unquestioned matrix within which the others are placed."[87] Because of the interdependent and political nature of identity, tolerance as a "passive letting the other be" is insufficient.[88] Furthermore, liberal tolerance does not generally engage with the breadth of diversity with which Connolly is concerned, namely "multidimensional pluralism that covers multiple zones of diversity – in gender practice, sensual affiliation, conjugal form, ethnic identification, source of morality, language, and religious/metaphysical orientation."[89] Connolly's pluralizing democracy, then, moves beyond tolerance to an ethos of agonistic respect and critical responsiveness. When differences within this democracy meet, they "evolve toward a public ethos of agonistic respect rather than devolving entirely into the public tolerance of private differences."[90]

Democratic culture thrives, in Connolly's estimation, when the politics of pluralization is in constitutive tension with the politics pertaining to the existing plurality. Likewise, "the perfection of democratic politics" would be visible in a democratic citizen, who participated simultaneously in the representational politics of the state, and in social movements that question the arrangements of the state and other social institutions as they stand. In this understanding, democracy is not only a form of rule and governance pertaining to the existing order, which allows the existing order to become normalized, but is also an ethos, a social process, and a distinctive culture marked by the disruption of established identities and conventions. Through an ethos of agonistic respect and

87. Ibid., p. 92; author's emphasis.
88. Connolly, *Augustinian Imperative*, p. 156.
89. William E. Connolly, *Neuropolitics: Thinking, Culture, Speed* (Minneapolis, MN: University of Minnesota Press, 2002), pp. 2–3.
90. Connolly, *Pluralism*, p. 125.

critical responsiveness, existing configurations are continually questioned and pluralized, preventing the establishment of a sense of completeness and closure within political society that would do violence to difference. In other words, where this ethos is not instilled, where closure is sought, where identities and institutions remain unquestioned, where "true identity" and "harmonious community" are postulated, difference is denied and oppressed.[91] Connolly believes that this ethos can be infused into a number of different philosophies, creeds, and doctrines, and indeed that it is the ethos rather than the content of a particular faith that is the critical issue today. He urges a variety of theistic and nontheistic creeds to take on "presumptively generous sensibilities" so that antagonistic relations between faiths might be turned into relations of agonistic respect.[92]

Connolly is setting a society informed by his democratic ethos in contrast to "a normalizing society," a society that "politicizes difference by converting it into neediness or otherness; it then demoralizes and depoliticizes those constituted as abnormal and those who would call this conversion process itself into question."[93] The result, indeed the "consummate irony" is that such a society "fosters the world of antagonism, violence, and fragmentation to which it purports to be the corrective."[94] Who exactly does Connolly see as the opposition with whom he is contending for the sake of difference? Whose theories, ideas, and presuppositions result in normalizing societies of otherness and antagonism? At the broadest level, he seeks to "disturb" any person, movement, or theory that strives for a unified nation, integrated community, and/or normal individual, that believes in "true identity," "harmonious community," and/or state unity. This means that, at times, Connolly is concerned with political theorists who proffer different views within this overall matrix, while at other times he is addressing actual political constituencies who, in his estimation, foster antagonism rather than agonistic respect. He addresses these political theorists and "fundamentalists" separately, as will we shortly, but he believes that they are all characterized by "arboreal pluralism,"

91. Connolly, *Ethos*, pp. 97–104, 153.
92. Connolly, *Pluralism*, pp. 48, 6.
93. Connolly, *Ethos* p. 91.
94. Ibid., p. 90.

as opposed to the "rhizomatic pluralism" which he would like to see in place. For arboreal pluralists, diversity is understood as limbs branching out from a common trunk. That trunk can be portrayed variously as Christianity, Kantian morality, secular reason, or the history of a unified nation, but in each case the tree from which diversity grows is fed from one ("exclusionary") taproot. In contrast, Connolly would like to see a pluralism more akin to the rhizome, a stem that grows just under the ground consisting of multiple shoots and filaments rather than one trunk or root. He draws this image from Gilles Deleuze and Félix Guattari, and he, like them, is "tired of trees."[95] His rhizomatic pluralism, depicted as "a variety of human constituencies, each touched in what it is by the dense, multifarious networks, human and nonhuman, in which it partici-pates," would be marked by an ethos of generosity and forbearance.[96] The interconnectedness of constituencies who understand themselves rhizomatically fosters a sense of the contingency and interdependency of each identity, which should lead to agonistic respect and critical responsiveness. Antagonism, social fragmentation, and tyranny emerge when constituencies try to become deep and exclusionary roots, following an arboreal rather than a rhizomatic model.[97]

This understanding is what leads Connolly to stretch the defini-tion of fundamentalism, from what he identifies as its usual con-notations of the assertion of one absolute ground of authority upon which one's identity, allegiances, and political stances are unques-tionably based, "to include the refusal to acknowledge the con-testability of your own fundaments or to resist violences in the exclusionary logics of identity in which you are implicated."[98] Connolly recognizes that every identity, theory, and faith rests upon some fundamental principles or beliefs, but he wants to go further in acknowledging that strains of fundamentalism exist in each of us. Indeed, his concern is to show that those who regularly apply the label of fundamentalism only to "the other" may themselves be prone to fundamentalism, when it is understood as a set of political strategies that protects one's own fundaments by labeling those who disagree with or disturb one's fundaments as enemies, deviants,

95. See ibid., pp. 94, 103.
96. Ibid., p. 94.
97. Ibid.
98. Ibid., p. xxviii.

immoral, unnatural, or unreasonable. He wants "liberals, secularists, modernists, rationalists, scientists, [and] moderates" to see the ways in which they engage in political practices of self-aggrandizement through appeals to "a vocabulary of God, nature, reason, nation, or normality elevated above the possibility of critical reflection."[99] In this sense, his work is addressed as a corrective to those across the political spectrum (his focus here is the United States) from the Southern Baptists, who are trying to counteract what they see as the problematic infiltration of modernity into American culture and politics to the "white males" and other conservatives trying to recover a unified, reinvigorated nation in the face of relativism and multiculturalism, to liberals who argue for a secular state while failing to recognize the contestable fundaments and conceptions of the good invoked in the name of that supposedly neutral state.[100] Indeed, the search for a way beyond these "conservative and liberal fundamentalisms" motivates Connolly's *Why I am Not a Secularist*.[101] Rather than accepting secularism and Christianity as the only ways to frame our public life, he tries to bring to light the degree to which both options flow from faith commitments. Secularists do not avoid faith anymore than the explicitly religious, because "faith, on my reading, is ubiquitous, even as it is punctuated by that which exceeds its doctrinal form."[102] Furthermore, the faith held by a person impacts his or her public doctrine, as well as how he or she lives life in relation to that doctrine. For this reason, Connolly thinks it untenable to distinguish between religious faith and secular reason, between private belief and public reason, and between religious beliefs and faith practices. His vision of political life "reinstates the link between practice and belief that had been artificially severed by secularism; and it also overturns the impossible counsel to bracket your faith when you participate in politics."[103]

When different constituencies bring their faiths with them as they interact in the public realm, and when they have folded into those faiths an ethos of agonistic respect and critical responsiveness, then the political society envisioned by Connolly can emerge: one in

99. Ibid., pp. 105, 106.
100. For more on Connolly's discussion of fundamentalism, see ibid., pp. 105–133.
101. See also Connolly, *Neuropolitics*, pp. 115, 130.
102. Connolly, *Pluralism*, p. 27.
103. Ibid., p. 64.

which "the myth of a centered majority that tolerates or represses a set of discrete minorities ranged around it" has been transfigured into "a visible culture of interdependent minorities of multiple types negotiating a generous ethos of governance between them."[104] Here Connolly's argument is directed towards movements he sees on the public level that restrict and vilify difference by seeking to elevate their own view into the authoritative center of a political democracy. He wants to move out of that matrix through an expansion of our pluralist imagination that would enable constituencies to live together with different beliefs without seeking to impose those beliefs onto others or establish them as the essential core of our political culture. The result would be "a *pluralism* in which multiple possibilities of connection open up across several lines of difference because more of the parties involved appreciate the profound contestability of the faiths they honor the most, and a *democracy* in which limits are set to the probable intensity of conflict between contending parties because more partisans acknowledge their own ambiguous implication in many of the differences they engage."[105] His suggestions for a pluralized democracy are directed not only to those involved in public, political movements, however, but also to political theorists who are themselves trapped in a matrix that limits pluralization and difference.

Connolly sees most of political theory as operating within the same matrix, what he calls "the ontopolitical matrix of Anglo-American discourse in the late-modern time."[106] One axis of this matrix consists, unsurprisingly in light of the liberal–communitarian debate, of the individual and the collectivity, with different theorists placing more emphasis on one or the other. The other axis includes the categories of mastery and attunement. Mastery refers to the belief that we can master nature and make the (indifferent) world subject to human control, while attunement involves the belief that the world has a higher direction in being to which a community should become attuned. Different political theorists clearly occupy different positions within this matrix, depending upon their views of whether freedom is attained more through mastering nature or finding harmony with nature's direction and

104. Ibid., p. 62.
105. Connolly, *Not a Secularist*, p. 155; author's emphasis.
106. Connolly, *Ethos*, p. 16.

whether this mastery or harmonization is more of an individual or collective project. These differences form the basis for much of the disagreement between theorists, some of which we saw in the previous chapter. Connolly wants to move outside of this matrix altogether, by questioning the limits it establishes and thereby contributing to the expansion of our political and pluralist imagination. He views all theorists within this matrix as sharing "a demand to provide new compensations for the modern 'loss' of expressivist/enchanted understandings of the world. Most insist, therefore, that the world must be predisposed to us in the last instance, either by containing a higher direction with which we can enter into closer communion or by being a pliable medium ultimately susceptible to human mastery. Or both."[107] In response to this Connolly asks "from whence does one get the right to issue these 'musts'? Who or what says the world owes us this much, so that it must either be predisposed to the human project of mastery or to human attunement to its putative harmonies?"[108]

In Connolly's estimation the assumptions behind these views need to be "subjected to critical exploration from a genealogical perspective."[109] Such a genealogical investigation would reveal the extent to which most political theorists continue to operate in the legacy of Augustine, carrying out in different ways the "Augustinian Imperative" that insists upon the existence of an intrinsic moral order that can be authoritatively represented.[110] Whether this morality is portrayed as obedience to a transcendental command, grounded, for example, in a Kantian categorical imperative or a Rawlsian veil of ignorance, or as attunement to the intrinsic design of the world, it rests upon problematic assumptions of intrinsic moral order. In the former use, "order" is used as a verb (to order) and a command serves as the basis of morality; in the latter, "order" operates as a noun, referring to a harmonious design of being. Connolly uses "morality" to refer to moral orders that are based in one or both of these understandings, which he distinguishes from an "ethic" as a conception that "strives to inform human conduct

---

107. Ibid., p. 19.
108. Ibid., p. 20.
109. Ibid., p. 21.
110. Connolly's *Augustinian Imperative* is dedicated to this genealogical investigation.

without drawing on either as so described."[111] When disruptions to a moral order appear, instead of being taken as signs that life and identity exceed ordering, they are labeled and marginalized for their immorality. At root, any theory that believes the world is for us either in some teleological way or through our ability to master it is, according to Connolly, narcissistic, egoistic, and unethical. It is narcissistic to think the world was formed for humans or that the world is, need be, or can be subject to human efforts to tame it. It is egoistic to think that one's own identity is the only source or shape of moral life. It is, furthermore, unethical to allow a particular conception of morality, understood as a fixed code of authority or justice, to be invoked as the basis of discipline and discrimination, as the means to transcendentalize one moral identity over against differences that are then subject to violence and oppression. The ethos of critical responsiveness that Connolly puts forward is very intentionally couched in ethical rather than moral language, meaning that he wants to provide a counterpoint to a morality of command or contract with an ethic of cultivation. He is challenging "the traditional, contending moralities of command and communion with a generous ethical sensibility grounded in appreciation of the fugitive abundance of being."[112] While he shares this concern for an ethic of cultivation with certain teleological views that emphasize virtue over morality, his ethic differs from theirs in seeking not common consensus or harmony but the enhancement of our sense of interdependence and the enactment of a more generous pluralism marked by a protean care for difference.[113]

One crucial distinction between Connolly and the political theorists and activists who remain within the matrix he identifies is their relationship to contingency. In Connolly's opinion, "there is a gravitational pull within this matrix to domesticate the experience of contingency in life, either by treating contingency as a type of event susceptible to control because it is not logically necessary or by treating the contingent as an unfortunate falling away from the intrinsic ideal. But the experience of contingency persistently

111. Connolly, *Augustinian Imperative*, p. 35.
112. Connolly, *Ethos*, p. xxiii.
113. Ibid., pp. xviii, xxiii, 27–28, 127; *Augustinian Imperative*, pp. 11–13, 139–140; *Identity\Difference*, p. 29–31.

exceeds such theorizations of it."[114] Connolly's Nietzschean sensibility of the abundance of life flowing through and beyond our attempts to capture it leads him to view contingency as fundamental rather than accidental. Those who interpret their experiences of contingency as signs of fragmentation and the loss of common identity end up looking for ways to establish a more harmonious, collective unity; this ironically results in more fragmentation, as accepted ideals of identity are further entrenched and normalized while all of those labeled as difference are subject to increasing ostracization. Connolly believes that increased acceptance of the inevitability of contingency would open rather than close the circle of accepted identities and enable an embrace of difference that more adequately expresses reverence for life. This applies not only to the realm of "micropolitics," in which "by working patiently on specific contingencies in oneself, one may become more appreciative of the crucial role of contingency in identity and desire" and thereby be open to "new possibilities of ethical responsiveness to difference," but also to the politics of the nation-state.[115]

Dominant nation-states have, according to Connolly, tried to master and domesticate contingency in their internal and external environments, but their unsuccessful attempts have resulted in the emergence of global problems and possibilities, such as global warming, economic interdependence, and terrorism, that exceed the capacities of any one state.[116] Needed now are cross-national, nonstatist movements that question the identities and loyalties of states, prompting them to reconfigure themselves in the direction of ever-increasing pluralization. After pointing out that "territory" derives etymologically from "terrera," meaning to frighten, terrorize, and exclude, Connolly argues that territorial states both liberate and imprison. They liberate because they provide democratic organization and electoral accountability, but they imprison because they confine democratic energies that exceed the nation-state, and prioritize national identities and goals that are themselves contingent. The democratic ethos that Connolly seeks to foster

114. Connolly, *Ethos*, p. 22.
115. Ibid., p. 69; see also *Identity\Difference*, pp. 172–173. For more on micropolitics, see Connolly, *Neuropolitics*, pp. 108–112.
116. Connolly, *Ethos*, p. 22.

embodies, as we saw above, much more than a form of rule or governance: "its role as a mode of governance is balanced and countered by its logic as a cultural medium of the periodic dena-turalization of settled identities and conventions."[117] This dena-turalization applies to nation-states as much as any other identity. The pluralization for which Connolly strives reaches far beyond more pluralism within a given culture or nation; the democratic ethos he articulates is not confined to state walls. Territorial states will continue to exist, but their exclusive claims to loyalty, as well as their identities and priorities, must be questioned in the face of global contingency and global issues.[118] The distinctive time of late modernity, "marked by the globalization of markets, communica-tions, monetary exchanges, transportation, disease transmission, strategic planning, acid rain, greenhouse effects, resource deple-tion, terrorist activity, drug trade, nuclear threats to civilization, and tourism – just to list a familiar miscellany," must, in Connolly's estimation, be matched by "the pluralization of democratic ener-gies, alliances, and spaces of action through and above the terri-torial democratic state."[119]

Connolly's thought is, as this discussion of contingency and glo-balization suggests, deeply informed by contemporary cultural con-ditions. His desire to expand our pluralist imagination stems from the conclusion that our current political imagination "remains too stingy, cramped, and defensive for the world we now inhabit."[120] His concern to combat fundamentalisms of all varieties stems from the belief that they arise in response to the same cultural conditions that bring forward the possibility of increasing pluralization. Fun-damentalization and pluralization are two possible, contending responses to the acceleration of speed, communication, and inter-action that mark late modern life, to the increasing acknowl-edgement of contingency in the face of the "problematisation of final markers."[121] In light of these shifts in our cultural conditions,

---

117. Ibid., p. 155.
118. On why Connolly prefers "territorial politics " or "territorial state " to "nation-state," see William E. Connolly, "Cross-State Citizen Networks: A Response to Dallmayr," *Millennium: Journal of International Studies* 30, no. 2 (2001), p. 350.
119. Connolly, *Ethos*, pp. 159, 160; see also pp. xxii–xxiii, 21–23, 135–161.
120. Ibid., p. xii.
121. This is Connolly's reworking of Claude Lefort's "dissolution of the markers of certainty," the phrase used so often by Mouffe. See ibid., p. 227, fn. 29.

no " 'return' to the politics of liberal neutrality, or the privatization of public conflicts, or a restrictive pluralism rooted in a simple consensus" is possible.[122] Instead, Connolly suggests that "during a time when distance is compressed by the acceleration of speed in many zones of life, the way to move is toward a generous ethos of engagement between a plurality of faiths in private and public life."[123] According to Connolly, then, the options available to us in the face of difference are either a fundamentalist rage against difference in the name of identity or an ethos of critical responsiveness that continually redefines both identity and difference and engenders an increasingly generous pluralism.

Connolly does recognize that some limits to the ethos of pluralization must exist. Certain conditions, such as extreme economic inequality, the deterioration of public education, and incompetent care for children, must not be allowed. And certain movements must not be tolerated, specifically those that are exclusionary and unitarian, to ensure that they do not endanger pluralism.[124] In general, fundamentalist constituencies who are not trying to force others into their unitarian framework can be tolerated, but they are not to be fully included in the ethos of agonistic respect and critical responsiveness that Connolly has proposed as the more fully developed and informed counterpart to tolerance. These fundamentalist constituencies, who refuse to acknowledge the contestability of their own fundaments, must be carefully watched: no exclusionary push to condemn difference through the fundamentalization of an identity can be allowed. Because established identities always have the tendency to naturalize and fundamentalize what they are, this must be constantly guarded against, lest cultural war displace critical responsiveness. This is a difficult task, because the response to fundamentalists must be done in a way that does not continue the process of fundamentalization. As Connolly writes:

> The issue can become a paradox under unfavorable conditions: if you do not set limits to the culture of pluralization, pluralism itself might become undermined; but if you respond to its fervent

122. Ibid., p. 100.
123. William E. Connolly, "Preface to the New Edition: The Pluralization of Religiosity," *The Augustinian Imperative* (Lanham, MD: Rowman & Littlefield, 2002), p. xx.
124. See Connolly, *Pluralism*, pp. 42–43.

opponents as they would respond to you, pluralism might be defeated by the means through which it is saved. This combination registers the fragility of pluralism.[125]

The ontological turn

Connolly's recognition of the fragility of our current pluralistic society and his desire to find a way to deepen the respect and inclusivity of the diversity that exist are worthy of great respect. Unlike Rawls, who attempts to forge a tolerant, pluralist society by finding an overlapping consensus upon which all constituencies can agree without acknowledging the contestable presuppositions underlying his theory, Connolly openly admits that his ideas may not be acceptable to all. Indeed, he goes further than that: "There is considerable irony and foolishness in a call to agonistic reciprocity, since it invites the fundamentalist to incorporate an element we endorse into its own identity. The invitation may be refused. ... But the call is made in the context of acknowledging the contestability of our fundaments."[126] So what are the fundaments that inform Connolly's political theory? And why is it so important to him to address them?

To begin with the latter question, Connolly can be considered part of the group of political theorists identified earlier who think an explicit turn to ontology is in order within political theory. Connolly himself now uses the term ontopolitical, having used "ontology" in his earlier work; both word choices represent an attempt to avoid the implication of "logos" that a fundamental logic, principle, or design of being exists in or underlies the world. In contrast, then, to ontology, defined by Connolly as the study of the fundamental logic of reality apart from appearances, "ontopolitical interpretation" enables us to recognize that every political interpretation rests upon a set of fundamental beliefs about human being and the world even if those beliefs are not concomitant with assumptions of a logic or design behind the world. Connolly is concerned with the extent to which recent political theory has ignored its ontopolitical dimensions, resting upon a presumption of "the primacy of epistemology." This emphasis on epistemology usually involves one of two

125. Connolly, *Ethos*, p. 235.
126. Connolly, *Augustinian Imperative*, p. 156.

mistaken beliefs – either that one has access to criteria of knowledge without needing to invoke ontological beliefs or that one's epistemology resolves ontological questions through its use of neutral procedures. In their concern with the ways in which knowledge is known and represented, such theories do not explicitly engage with ontological questions, but they are at every moment resting unquestionably upon a social ontology that involves belief in the human being as a unified subject capable of knowledge of objects that are themselves subject to representation through use of language as a medium of representation. These are some of the very beliefs that Connolly wants to call into question. More than that, it is their uncritical acceptance that contributes to the continuation of fundamentalization over pluralization.

The "antifoundationalist" and "postmetaphysical" liberalisms presented by Rawls and Rorty are exactly, though not exclusively, what Connolly has in mind during his discussion of these matters. Rawls believes he can build his theory upon an overlapping consensus that already exists within society while Rorty, similarly, develops his thought on the basis of extant liberal values within our political culture, with both believing that they can do so without needing to defend, address, or question the fundamental assumptions upon which liberal values or their own theories rely. In Connolly's estimation, their assumption that they can keep their ontopolitical interpretations from being objects of critical investigation stems from a confidence that the most pressing conflicts and problems facing us today can be addressed without calling into question the presumptions of modernity itself.[127] But, Connolly asks, what if the modern, liberal culture that Rawls and Rorty accept in their invocation of an overlapping consensus or acceptance of liberal values also includes dangerous or exclusive elements that need to be questioned? "What ... if the points of ontopolitical convergence in late-modern nation-states turn out to be exactly the domain in need of reassessment today?"[128]

Though the theories of Rawls and Rorty may seem "ontologically minimal" compared to earlier Christian or teleological traditions with very explicit beliefs about human being and nature, they are,

127. Connolly, *Ethos*, pp. 3–4.
128. Ibid., p. 4.

in Connolly's estimation, carrying on the Augustinian Imperative that is a part of the assumptions and conceptions inscribed in western culture. As we saw above, Connolly believes that all theorists who can be located within the matrix of attunement or mastery continue on in this tradition. In the case of theorists of neutral or pragmatic liberalism, they "shift faith from God to the world, trusting that the world is *plastic* enough to respond to the drive for mastery without reacting back with a vengeance born from its indifference to their ends and the diversity of forces and energies flowing through it, and then they pretend that the withdrawal of faith from God eliminates faith altogether."[129] This may seem more obvious when it comes to Rawls; as we have already seen, his presuppositions regarding the individual, the veil of ignorance, reason, and the separation of public and private all embody contestable beliefs and result in the exclusion of many constituencies from his political society. While Rorty's embrace of contingency might lead one to assume that he and Connolly would articulate similar visions of liberalism, Connolly believes that Rorty's assumptions of the world's pliability keep him within the mastery perspective, while his support of irony in the private sphere without a concomitant recognition of its place in reconfiguring the public realm leaves him straddling rather than overcoming the individual-collectivity aspect of the matrix.[130] In Connolly's estimation, both Rawls and Rorty need to recognize that issues related to contingency, identity, and the good cannot be relegated to the private sphere while supposedly neutral notions of justice and the right form a consensus in the public sphere. As we have seen, identity has both individual and collective manifestations, and the connections between them "must be engaged overtly and politically if they are not to spawn a collective politics that unconsciously represses difference in the name of neutrality."[131] In other words, "secular liberalism calls upon you to leave your fundamental religious/existential faith in the private realm and then to confess faith in the sufficiency of reason, procedure, or deliberation in the public realm." In Connolly's version of pluralism, on the other hand, "you bring relevant chunks of your

129. Connolly, *Identity\Difference*, p. 72; see pp. 71–73.
130. Ibid., p. 227.
131. Ibid., p. 160.

faith into the public realm – as we all do inevitably anyway – while carefully cultivating comparative modesty about it."[132]

Connolly sees himself operating in the company of a diverse group of thinkers, including, among others, Nietzsche, Arendt, Foucault, Taylor, Deleuze, and Derrida, who "suspect that self-denying ordinances vindicated in various ways by 'nonfoundationalists' such as Rawls, Rorty, Habermas, Benhabib, Walzer, and Blumenberg express a refusal to engage questions most important to the late-modern time."[133] In contrast to this "nonfoundationalist" approach, the thinkers of the former group believe that every interpretation or theory rests upon fundamental presuppositions of being that should be acknowledged and critically engaged. Connolly himself draws most explicitly on the thought of Nietzsche and Foucault to craft his (self-entitled) post-Nietzschean political theory. He recognizes that both of these thinkers are subject to a variety of interpretations, which prompts him to call his use of Nietzsche "*my* Nietzsche" in places and to suggest "Fou-connoism" for his version of Foucault's thought. He likewise points out the need to critically engage with the work of both thinkers, using them to fill each other out, distancing himself from certain aspects of their thought, and pursuing various parts of their projects further until he arrives at a sustainable political theory that he is willing to endorse.[134] These are not the only two thinkers upon whom he draws; we have already seen his use of Deleuze's rhizome imagery to develop his rhizomatic pluralism, and his idea of diference certainly draws upon the work of Derrida. The democratic ethos that Connolly puts forward results, then, from reliance upon and expansion of the thoughts and strategies of a number of thinkers operating, to varying degrees, in the legacy of Nietzsche. From Foucault, for example, he draws the use of genealogy to expose how current cultural notions of identity have been constructed and become naturalized, how our identities do not reflect some harmonious design or match an intrinsic moral order, and how we can therefore hold our identities more contingently as we become increasingly open to differences. From Derrida, he takes

132. Connolly, "Preface to the New Edition," p. xxiii.
133. Connolly, *Ethos*, p. 4.
134. See ibid., pp. 30, 102–104, 208; *Identity\Difference*, pp. 184–187; "Beyond Good and Evil: The Ethical Sensibility of Michel Foucault," in *The Later Foucault: Politics and Philosophy*, ed. Jeremy Moss (London: Sage, 1998), pp. 108–128.

deconstruction as a way to show us the ambiguities involved in our understanding of rationality and decisionmaking in order to open us to aspects of difference that might currently exist outside prescribed notions of rationality and identity. While he views these "strategies of detachment" as indispensable to his political project, he does not think they enable us to go far enough towards the development of a "positive ontopolitical interpretation," so he adds to them "a strategy of attachment that stands in a precarious relation of implication and dissonance with them."[135] A crucial part of this strategy is the explicit acknowledgement of the ontopolitical dimensions of our theory and interpretations. This involves not only recognizing that such dimensions exist but also acknowledging that our implicit projection of them into our theory and interpretations exceeds our capacity to explicitly formulate them, while whatever explicit formulations we do make exceed our ability to demonstrate their truth.[136]

What, then, are the ontopolitical dimensions of Connolly's theory, as far as he is able to articulate them? Because Connolly believes in being explicit about the presuppositions operating within his theory, we have, in essence, been discussing them since the beginning of our investigation of his thought. Nevertheless, it is worthwhile drawing more definite attention to the main fundaments upon which his political theory rests. One of these fundaments is his belief in the abundance and rich diversity of "life," with life understood as a "protean set of energies" that exceeds every attempt to capture it within a given identity or organize it within a particular political structure.[137] This understanding of life, drawn from Nietzsche, serves as "an indispensable, non-fixable marker, challenging every attempt to treat a concept, settlement or principle as complete, without surplus or resistance."[138] Life understood this way is concomitant with nontheistic gratitude for the abundance of being, which Connolly refers to as his highest existential faith and which serves as the source of his pluralizing ethic.[139] Closely connected to this ontopolitical assumption about life is the belief that "nothing is fundamental" (this is drawn from Foucault). This should be interpreted

135. Connolly, *Ethos*, p. 36.
136. Ibid.
137. Ibid., p. 28.
138. Connolly, "Beyond Good and Evil," p. 113.
139. Connolly, "Preface to the New Edition," p. xix; *Ethos*, p. 31; *Neuropolitics*, p. 197.

in two ways. The first reading emphasizes the "fundamental" aspect: no fundamental law, purpose, contract, design, deity, moral order, or plasticity marks the world. The second focuses on the "nothing" component, with nothingness understood as a fullness, as "life," as differences and protean energies that circulate through and exceed the "perpetual gaps" in social constructions of identity and institutions.[140] "Nothing is fundamental" is equivalent to "diference is fundamental." In either articulation, the implication he draws is that no identity is complete or uncontestable, and any attempt to establish an identity as such will result in unnecessary exclusion or violence to difference. He then acknowledges that this view is an article of faith, profoundly contestable.

Even this acknowledgement of the contestability of his ontopolitical projections is supposed to further the goal of all constituencies operating in light of the contingency of their identities and beliefs: the hope is that in revealing the contestability of his fundaments others will notice the contestability of their own fundaments and begin to see the violence involved in attempting to impose those fundaments upon everyone. He believes that incorporating "a deep plurality of religious/metaphysical perspectives" into public discourse is a crucial component in the quest to develop a positive ethos of engagement out of the pluralism in contemporary life, but these perspectives need to recognize "the shakiness of the ground upon which they themselves stand" for such an ethos to emerge.[141] In short, the consensus for which one can work within a pluralizing ethos is limited to "an ironic consensus," one "mobilized above all around reciprocal appreciation of the contestability of contending presumptions about the fundamental character of being."[142] Politics, in this understanding, is a way to engage the ambiguities concomitant with this level of contestability and contingency, serving both to foster common purposes and to expose and disturb the "musical harmonies" into which these common purposes tend to be transposed. Connolly says of this alternative liberalism that "it is not the best liberalism that can be dreamt, only the highest regulative ideal to pursue if we are

140. Connolly, *Ethos*, p. 39; "Beyond Good and Evil," p. 119.
141. William E. Connolly, *Why I am Not a Secularist* (Minneapolis, MN: University of Minnesota Press, 1999), p. 185; *Ethos*, p. 104.
142. Connolly, *Ethos*, p. 104.

incomplete without social forms in a world not predesigned to mesh smoothly with any particular formulation of social and collective identity."[143]

It is clear from this last quote, as it has been throughout this discussion of Connolly's thought, that at every point his version of liberal democracy is affected by his ontology. The honesty with which he recognizes that his theory invokes "big articles of faith" that are "about as big as the ones they contest" is a refreshing change from those who operate as if their variants of liberalism would be acceptable to any one who is reasonable, rational, or sane without acknowledging that controversial, potentially unacceptable presuppositions inform their thinking.[144] It, indeed, opens the door to explicit engagement and conversation at the ontological level within political theory, which in some senses allows certain constituencies that are excluded from the liberal societies of Rawls and Rorty to be more fully a part of his envisaged society. We cannot help but appreciate his concern for a society that is ever-increasing its acceptance of difference. This is clearly the motivation behind his ethos of agonistic respect, by which he hopes that established constituencies can come to honor each other rather than carrying on the cultural wars that currently mark political discourse and interaction. It is likewise behind his ethos of critical responsiveness, which would serve to enable currently unrecognized constituencies to reach the threshold of recognition and respect. We only have to think of the ways in which slaves and women had to fight for this recognition, recognition that we now take for granted, to realize that it is important to be open to, and further to help open the way to, those who may even now be unfairly oppressed and marginalized. We can see this same motivation for an increased openness to difference operating in his desire to move beyond the liberal–communitarian debate through a recognition that the relationship between and establishment of our individual and collective identities is much more nuanced than either side of the debate generally acknowledges. In addition to recognizing that identity is more complex than current political theory acknowledges, Connolly is also to be admired for attempting to account for the

---

143. Connolly, *Identity\Difference*, p. 94.
144. Connolly, *Augustinian Imperative*, p. 126.

increased sense of contingency and globalization that mark our current cultural *milieu*.

Yet in every area where we can respect the direction of Connolly's thinking, we can also raise significant questions as to how far his concern for difference is actually realized within the political theory he is presenting. We can further wonder if the suggestions he raises, and the alternatives he rules out, represent the only way forward for those concerned to increase the respect for and acknowledgement of diversity. In other words, are his ontopolitical interpretations and his ethos of agonistic respect and critical responsiveness the only or the best ways to deal with an increasing sense of contingency and an elevated sensitivity towards difference? To take his understanding of contingency as an example, he writes that

> by contrast to the necessary and universal, it means that which is changeable and particular; by contrast to the certain and constant, it means that which is uncertain and variable; by contrast to the self-subsistent and causal, it means that which is dependent and effect; by contrast to the expected and regular, it means that which is unexpected and irregular; and by contrast to the safe and reassuring, it means that which is dangerous, unruly, and obdurate in its danger[145].

On this rendering, given the contrasts he presents, to try to come to terms with contingency means to accept the particular at the expense of the universal and to grant, seemingly unproblematically, that uncertain, unexpected, unruly danger frames our experience of reality. But must the contrasts be set so strongly? We raised a similar question with regard to the other agonistic political theorists we have considered, pointing out the extent to which their thought depends upon assumptions of certain inevitable polarizations. Connolly, too, seems to assume that unity and difference, solidarity and diversity, and the universal and the particular must stand as irreconcilable opposites. Joseph M. Schwartz, after noting these dichotomizations within Connolly's writing, wonders if they must be transcended politically for social justice to be achieved.[146] Such transcendence is precisely what Connolly rules out, presenting his thought as if we must choose either harmony or difference. In

145. Connolly, *Identity\Difference*, p. 28.
146. Joseph M. Schwartz, "*Ethos of Pluralization* (book review)," *Journal of Politics* 59, no. 2 (May 1997), p. 618.

addition to questioning if this option is one with which we must or should be willing to rest content, we also need to question what Connolly understands by harmony.

Connolly's liberalism leaves us without hope for harmony or unity, without a picture of anything beyond the attainment of an ironic consensus. Such a consensus is "ironic" because it is based in recognition of the contestability of the contending presumptions we each bring with us. Connolly's understanding of consensus is drawn from Foucault's oft-cited remark: "The farthest I would go is to say that perhaps one must not be for consensuality, but one must be against nonconsensuality."[147] Connolly is nervous about the damage that can be caused and the difference that can be oppressed when we are overly concerned with seeking consensus, even while he recognizes that no political society can exist if "non-consensuality" wins the day. The ironic consensus or harmony he envisions would consist of an increased sense of interdependency between different constituencies and a more generous pluralism based in a protean care for difference. How different is this from the visions of harmony and consensus he is trying to counter? Benjamin Barber speaks of the harmony sought by liberal democracy as a musical harmony, characterized by multiple, distinct voices coming together, "creating not the ennui of unison but a pleasing plurality."[148] This is harmony used in its technical, musical sense in which a common voice emerges from a mixture of different voices rather than from an imposed unity or monism. Connolly, however, is not content with even this description of harmony, drawing a picture of political society in which the recognition of ambiguity and contingency constantly disturbs the "musical harmonies" into which common purposes tend to be transposed.[149]

At the same time, Connolly himself recognizes that the pursuit of harmony has been a goal and a need for centuries. The medieval time period, according to the story Connolly weaves, was one in which "signs of harmony were everywhere in the world." The

147. Michel Foucault, "Politics and Ethics: An Interview," in *The Foucault Reader*, ed. Paul Rabinow (New York: Pantheon, 1984), p. 379. Cited in Connolly, *Ethos*, p. 102.
148. Benjamin R. Barber, "Liberal Democracy and the Costs of Consent," in *Liberalism and the Moral Life*, ed. Nancy L. Rosenblum (Cambridge, MA: Harvard University Press, 1989), p. 65.
149. Connolly, *Identity\Difference*, p. 94.

increased tempo of life in early modernity, along with the greater sense of interiority of the "Christian/Kantian self," called these external signs of harmony into question, causing a new guarantor of harmony to come forth, namely "common sense." In late modernity, however, "everything now moves faster and there is not enough time to install the same common sense into everyone inhabiting the same space. Now contending drives to *fundamentalize* 'common sense' or to *pluralize* it escalate into a series of cultural wars."[150] The solution he proposes, in light of the conditions of late modernity that, in his estimation, make an appeal to anything universal problematic, is to relinquish harmony in favor of unhindered pluralization and particularity. Given the importance of harmony within the story he tells, we must surely raise questions about the feasibility of such a solution. If harmony was a crucial aspect of medieval life and the importance of its preservation was precisely what called forth the Kantian common sense that has been sustaining us since early modernity, is it not naïve to think that we can now suddenly live without harmony? Rather than assuming that harmony necessarily involves "fundamentalization" in the name of the universal or that because we are facing new experiences as part of our particular cultural moment, we must abandon an idea that has been an integral part of political societies for centuries, might we not use our political and pluralist imaginations to rethink the relationship between the universal and the particular in ways that allow for harmony to be retained as a goal? In other words, does the need for harmony disappear just because its realization seems more and more unattainable in light of certain cultural conditions and ontological presuppositions about the nature of antagonism and conflict? Or should we perhaps be concerned to find more adequate and creative ways to think about harmony in light of our heightened awareness of and concern for difference?

This is just one of the ways in which we can wonder how helpful Connolly's agonistic political theory is in solving the problems raised by difference, problems likewise left unresolved by the versions of political liberalism we considered in the last chapter. In short, how far does Connolly take us towards resolving certain problem areas we noted in reference to political liberalism? Despite

150. Connolly, *Not a Secularist*, p. 174.

his attempts to move beyond liberalism of a Rawlsian variety, he may continue to operate in its legacy and be plagued by its short-comings. This seems to be the case when it comes to liberal indi-viduality, which may be surprising given that we have already commended Connolly for providing a more nuanced picture of identity that seeks to move beyond the main terms of the liberal–communitarianism debate. While true, Connolly also recognizes that his political theory follows liberalism in terms of "its appre-ciation of the claims of individuality."[151] He speaks of the need for a "political theory of individuality" that questions "state, corpor-ate, and associational institutions of normalization" rather than assuming that individuality can flourish within the paradigms that currently exist. Every established definition and potential site of normalization needs to be questioned, in the public realm as well as those realms usually associated with individuals, and attention needs to be given to relations of power and difference that keep certain identities from being recognized.[152] Again, we can appreci-ate his concern to draw attention to these often unrecognized influences upon our conceptions of identity, a concern which is clearly also undergirded by his belief that identity is collective as well as individual and that humans are incomplete without social form. Yet at root his concern is motivated by a certain ethos of individuality.[153] For is not his motivation behind drawing attention to the elements of conflict, power, politics, and ambiguity in the establishment of identity\difference the desire to see every *individual* respected and recognized? Do we not need to hold our own beliefs and identities contingently precisely so those beliefs and identities do not get in the way of any new *individuals* crossing the threshold of recognition? And does this not mean that once again, despite Con-nolly's attempts to create a more nuanced picture of the relation-ship between them, individual identity is prioritized over collective identity? Does he not assume that no collective identity can or should be so integral to a person's identity that it cannot be held loosely and contingently? How much respect is actually accorded to

---

151. Connolly, *Identity\Difference*, p. 94.
152. See ibid., pp. 73–94 for an elaboration of these themes.
153. I draw this term from Barry Allen, "Foucault and Modern Political Philosophy," in *The Later Foucault: Politics and Philosophy*, ed. Jeremy Moss (London: Sage, 1998), pp. 164–198.

a collective identity that is not allowed to be held with anything but a contingent sense, that is not understood to be constitutive of identity in and of itself but only in relation to difference? While he may not buy into the "unencumbered self" which political liberalism is accused of presupposing, he nevertheless seems to operate in the legacy of liberals who prioritize individual over collective goals. We may well be able to transfer to Connolly Barry Allen's description of Foucault's thought, namely that his work

> is an effort to specify the most significant forces now aligned against the modern ethos of individuality, and to reaffirm, if in an unexpected way, the traditional message of modern political individualism: that political government is properly subordinate to ethical ends, to the ethos of individuality, to what makes *individual* life worth living, rather than to collective ends imposed on individuals for whatever reason, in the name of whatever stirring ideal (social justice, democracy, progress, and so on).[154]

Connolly, then, openly rejects the "normal individual" upon which much contemporary liberal theory unquestioningly bases itself, but this rejection is ultimately for the sake of giving more respect and more recognition to a greater number of individuals, which seems like a mere continuation of liberalism's prioritization of the individual.[155]

Connolly's belief in the need to hold identities, including the various individual, collective, and relational components of which they are comprised, with a certain lightness reveals another place in which his theory seems not all that different from a particular strategy of the liberalism he is trying to overcome. Can we really hold our commitments and aims as loosely as Connolly and other agonistic theorists seem to think we can or, as Mathewes suggests, is the "lightness" that agonistic theorists commend predicated on a self-contradictory and false human psychology?[156] Do not some commitments by their very nature and definition require a level of involvement that is not so easily discarded? And is Connolly, therefore, assuming that we can and should change the nature of such commitments so that they become compatible with his ethos?

154. Ibid., p. 190.
155. Cf. Barry Harvey, "*Why I am Not a Secularist* (book review)," *Journal of Church and State* 43 (Winter 2001), p. 141.
156. Mathewes, "Faith, Hope, and Agony," pp. 134–135.

We saw in the previous chapter that Rawls, despite his concern for accommodating the inevitable pluralism of ("reasonable") comprehensive doctrines, admits that comprehensive doctrines should be revised in order that liberal principles of justice are prioritized. Connolly, in the name of his ethos of critical responsiveness rather than liberal principles of justice, asks for considerable alterations to be made to the views of identity and morality of many constituencies within our liberal democratic culture. Indeed, as we discussed above, the third and most crucial aspect of his ethos is that of self-revision, meaning that current identities need to be ready to modify themselves in light of new constituencies that arise and the changes they bring to identity\difference. To some degree openness and adaptability are necessary to any attempt to accommodate and welcome difference, but the extent of the adaptability is what is in question here. The difference between Connolly and Rawls on this point might be that Connolly recognizes that this is controversial, and that asking identities to change in the way he suggests goes deeper than liberal tolerance. There will presumably be, however, a number of constituencies who would find themselves unable to agree with or adapt to the changes that Connolly commends. For example, Connolly would like to see an expansion of the kinds of diversity considered legitimate, to include not just different faith traditions and cultural practices but diverse "gender practices, marriage arrangements, linguistic use, sensual affiliations, and household organizations."[157] Furthermore, he hopes that as these kinds of diversity become more accepted in societal institutions, such as schools, corporations, and the military, in which members of faith communities participate, these members will put pressure on their faith communities to change: "numerous constituencies now acquire more leverage to press their faith communities from within to honor that variety."[158] Similarly to Rawls, Connolly hopes that outside values will influence and alter the constituencies of our political society. Many faith communities have deep theological, philosophical, and doctrinal reasons for their current practices, and would be scarcely recognizable were they to alter themselves along some of the lines Connolly is suggesting.

157. Connolly, *Pluralism*, p. 61.
158. Ibid.

That being said, we should recognize that the political society envisioned by Connolly is more inclusive than those described by Rawls and Rorty, for those who do not adopt the ethos he recommends and thereby remain "fundamentalists" are not excluded but rather tolerated. As we discussed earlier, in Connolly's theory tolerance is one step short of the ethos of agonistic respect and critical responsiveness; it remains content with passively letting other identities remain as they are rather than questioning the identity\difference relation involved in the establishment of constituencies and allowing one's own identity to be shaped and changed in light of that power relation. To treat certain fundamentalisms with tolerance allows Connolly to avoid excluding "moralities of god, home, and country"; such an exclusion would, as he acknowledges, "depluralize this model of pluralism."[159] At the same time, it keeps him from having to fully include, respect, and recognize certain problematic constituencies. Indeed, to limit his attitude towards such identities to one of tolerance rather than extending to them his ethos of critical responsiveness means that the self-revisionary aspect of his ethos has its limits. He does not seem not open to learning from and adapting his own views in light of any identity that has universal intent. Is he open to the possibility of moral order or harmonious design, or even to learning from constituencies who hold such beliefs, while not accepting their fundaments *tout court*? At the end of the day, as he openly acknowledges, even his tolerance has its limits, not being extended to "identities that must define what deviates from them as intrinsically evil (or one of its modern surrogates) in order to establish their own self-certainty" or those who "compel the universalization of what they are."[160] For the pluralism that Connolly supports "prizes cultural diversity along several dimensions and is ready to join others in militant action, when necessary, to support pluralism against counterdrives to unitarianism."[161]

What is it that provides the basis for Connolly's belief that toleration must not extend to certain constituencies? His desire to stop fundamentalization and universalization seems to stem from a deep belief that every person, and the identity and difference that help constitute each person, is worthy of respect, and that this respect

159. Connolly, *Ethos*, p. 202.
160. Connolly, *Identity\Difference*, p. 15; *Ethos*, p. 203.
161. Connolly, *Pluralism*, p. 41.

should not be mitigated by certain constituencies who ostracize, label, or oppress those who are different from themselves. In short, Connolly's concern that difference be recognized and respected at all times and in all ways could be seen as an updated version of the belief in the equal moral worth and inherent dignity of all persons that many liberal thinkers draw from Kant. Could it be that Connolly is motivated by a commitment to certain Enlightenment ideals, and that the radical nature of his project consists not in inculcating new values but in attempting to find a different way to attain those values now that some parts of the so-called Enlightenment project appear untenable?[162] Connolly himself acknowledges this, at least in certain areas; writing of the relationship between religion and politics, he believes that "exclusionary variants of Judaism, Christianity, Islam, and atheism could all profit from going through the Enlightenment."[163] Perhaps here Connolly helps us understand Alasdair MacIntyre's claim that aspects of post-Enlightenment thought "are ... the negative counterpart of the Enlightenment, its inverted mirror image."[164]

If Connolly's concern for difference is in some way an inverted mirror image of the Enlightenment-based concern for human equality, then it may not be surprising that Connolly tends to focus on diversity while traditional liberal thinkers focus on unity. That is to say, whereas the concern for equality within liberal thought leads to an emphasis on how humans can be equally unified regardless of belief or faith, when inverted to result in the concern for difference within Connolly's thought, it leads to a rejection of the concept of unity. One can see why it is important to emphasize that our particularity is significant, and plays a constitutive role in who we are as persons and as citizens, especially in light of liberalism's emphasis on the universal over the particular. At the same time, one can also see ways in which an unchecked emphasis on difference might lead to its own set of problems. How does one adjudicate between differences that are welcome and those that are detrimental or harmful? Is the only allowable criterion whether a constituency is harmful to the

162. See also Diane Rubenstein, "The Four Discourses and the Four Volumes," *Journal of Politics* 56, no. 4 (November 1996), p. 1130 and Schwartz, "*Ethos of Pluralization* (book review)," p. 618.
163. Connolly, *Pluralism*, p. 52.
164. MacIntyre, *Whose Justice? Which Rationality?* p. 353.

identity and difference of other constituencies? Will an unmitigated celebration of difference provide societies polarized by their differences with adequate resources and reasons for their constituencies to look beyond their own particularities to find reconciliation with those who are different? Or, despite its best intentions, does it lend itself to a narcissistic emphasis on one's own self and one's own particularity?

This leads us to a consideration of whether Connolly's noble vision provides enough to sustain commitment to the values and ethos he endorses. We are not the first to raise this question. Even Stephen White, who is largely sympathetic to Connolly's project, wonders if Connolly's "central ontological figure of abundance, by itself, inadequately prefigures the ethical qualities Connolly assigns to critical responsiveness."[165] White questions whether Connolly's ontology is too underdetermined to provide the criteria by which we can adjudicate between that which respects and that which harms human equality and dignity. White concludes that "Connolly is taking us in a normative direction toward which his ontology has not given enough orientation."[166] John R. Wallach similarly wonders if Connolly has left us with enough resources to combat the injustices to which he seeks to draw attention, noting that such resources are drawn from the unities, constituencies, ethics, and ideas that Connolly either drains of their substantive content or regards as necessary but unwelcome in political life.[167] Perhaps in response to this concern about the adequacy of the basis provided for his ethical vision, in his more recent work Connolly tries to offer his ethos as one that can be adopted and sustained by a wide variety of faiths. In this way it does not need to be linked to or motivated by his ontological commitments but can be infused into a number of creeds, doctrines, and philosophies, and supported by beliefs internal to those faiths.[168] This is, of course, reminiscent of John Rawls' efforts to offer his theory of justice as one that can be supported by a wide variety of comprehensive doctrines, although its roots clearly lie in his own comprehensive doctrine. While one would hope that certain

165. White, *Sustaining Affirmation*, p. 127.
166. Ibid., p. 128.
167. John R. Wallach, "*The Ethos of Pluralization* (book review)," *Political Theory* 25, no. 6 (December 1997), p. 891.
168. See Connolly, *Pluralism*, pp. 6, 65, 66.

aspects of the humility, generosity, and receptivity of Connolly's ethos would resonate with other creeds, doctrines, and faith communities, it remains to be seen just how they would foster support for Connolly's ethos using their own language and doctrines.

Let us turn our attention more directly to Connolly's ethos, since it lies at the heart of his political theory. Do we find in his writings a sense of the positive definition he gives to the term "ethical" or the motivation he would provide for adhering to his ethic? He speaks of it as a "sensibility," and he asks, "what makes such a sensibility *ethical?*"[169] When it comes to actually answering that question, however, he generally reverts to describing what it is not, so we know that it is *not* based in a moral order (used in either the verb or the noun sense) and it is *not* reducible to a moral code. In one instance he goes on to describe his "anti-teleological ethic" as one that cultivates "possibilities of being imperfectly installed in established institutional practices," drawing its sustenance from "(a) a contingent identity affirming (b) the rich abundance of 'life' exceeding every particular organization of it."[170] This sounds like it has a positive component, but even here "life" is described primarily in terms of its function in challenging every alternative that tries to bring closure. He writes that "an ethical sensibility is to be cultivated *because* there is no compulsory basis for ethics," but is that really an adequate motivation?[171] Even if we would agree with Connolly in wanting to question the ethicality or morality of those who base their ethic or moral code solely in a moral command, even if we would concur that we hope for an ethic that would hold even if no divine or moral command made it compulsory, we are still left wondering if nontheistic reverence for the "effervescent energies flowing through and over identity, the universal, and the real" is enough to be the source of Connolly's ethic.[172] Can an ethic that does not provide any substantive content to the distinctions between good and bad, or just and unjust, hold sway? How do we actually move, as Slavoj Zizek asks, from an " 'ontological' assertion of multitude to ethics (of diversity, tolerance)?"[173] Or is Connolly's

169. Connolly, *Augustinian Imperative*, p. 140; author's emphasis.
170. Ibid., pp. 141, 142.
171. Connolly, *Ethos*, p. 233; author's emphasis.
172. Ibid., p. 188.
173. Zizek, *Ticklish Subject*, p. 172.

ethos an example of the recent predominance of ethics in contemporary society identified by Alain Badiou, in which ethics has come to designate an incapacity "to name and strive for a Good," so that the reign of ethics "is one symptom of a universe ruled by a distinctive combination of resignation in the face of necessity together with a purely negative, if not destructive will?"[174]

The theological turn

Badiou further maintains that "every effort to turn ethics into the principle of thought and action is essentially religious."[175] Connolly is clearly engaging with many "religious" themes throughout his work: his language is imbued with theological terms, and his turn to ontology opens the door for his proposal to be viewed as a faith alongside other faiths. In his political society, we would each place our projections, positions, and fundaments on the "ontological register, where alternatives contend with each other while, hopefully, acknowledging the fundamental and reciprocal contestability of these contending articles of faith."[176] Yet more than just recognizing his own fundaments as articles of faith, he engages very explicitly with traditional religions, particularly Christianity, throughout his work. As Tracy B. Strong points out, a major component of Connolly's project is the argument that contemporary political theory cannot ignore Christianity.[177] While his *Why I am Not a Secularist* (whose title is an intentional play on Bertrand Russell's *Why I am Not a Christian*) opens with an autobiographical account of his experience of being a childhood atheist surrounded by Southern Baptists, his earlier *Identity\Difference* begins with a discussion of the problem of evil. He identifies two problems of evil, the first referring to "human efforts to save the benevolence of an omnipotent god by exempting that god from responsibility for evil."[178] This manifests itself on the political level as we continue the task of protecting our own identities by labeling those who threaten that identity as evil. This is, indeed, the second problem of

174. Badiou, *Ethics*, p. 30.
175. Ibid., p. 23.
176. Connolly, *Ethos*, p. 188.
177. Tracy B. Strong, "*Identity\Difference* (book review)," *Ethics* 102, no. 4 (July 1992), p. 864.
178. Connolly, *Identity\Difference*, p. ix.

evil, "the evil that flows from the attempt to establish security of identity for any individual or group by defining the other that exposes sore spots in one's identity as evil or irrational."[179] An exploration of whether it is possible to retain the functions served by identity without perpetuating this second problem of evil through dealing with difference as otherness as evil is, as Rengger notes, "*the* defining question of the book."[180]

Connolly's main opponent in this discussion is Augustine, who "tried to save his god from any trace of responsibility for evil while protecting that god's omnipotence and its capacity to promise the possibility of eternal life."[181] Indeed, one chapter of *Identity\ Difference* is "A Letter to Augustine," which serves, as Strong notes, as the emotional centre of the book.[182] His next book is dedicated to an exploration of the Augustinian Imperative, which serves as the book's title. While Connolly admits that the book is not about Augustine as much as the imperative of which he was an exemplary articulator and with which much of contemporary political culture continues to operate, he explores Augustinian texts and ideas to find "Augustinian tactics of moralization" that problematically pervade our thinking today. His goal is to "approach Augustine from a critical distance, from a (post-) Nietzschean perspective that seeks to reassess and modify effects of the Augustinian legacy on the present."[183] As we saw earlier, he traces two models of morality to Augustine, one which pictures morality as obedience to a transcendental command and one which thinks of morality as attunement to a harmonious design of being. Neither one, not even their secular variants and offspring ("secularism," Connolly tells us, "constitutes the afterlife of Augustinianism"[184]), allows for the full

179. Ibid., p. 8.
180. N. J. Rengger, "*Identity\Difference* (book review)," *Millennium: Journal of International Studies* 20, no. 3 (Winter 1991), p. 532; see also Connolly, *Identity\Difference*, p. 8.
181. Connolly, *Identity\Difference*, p. 4. For an account of Connolly's intellectual development in light of his relationship with Augustine's writings, see K. Roberts Skerrett, "The Indispensable Rival: William Connolly's Engagement with Augustine of Hippo," *Journal of the American Academy of Religion* 72, no. 2 (June 2004), pp. 487–506.
182. Strong, "*Identity\Difference* (book review)," p. 864. See also Anne Norton, "*Identity\Difference* (book review)," *Journal of Politics* 54, no. 3 (August 1992), pp. 919–920.
183. Connolly, *Augustinian Imperative*, p. xviii.
184. Connolly, *Identity\Difference*, p. 145.

appreciation and recognition of the abundance of being and diversity of life, which leads him to counter morality with his ethical cultivation.

Connolly does admit, from time to time, that Augustine shared a certain sense of the abundance and mystery of life.[185] He even admits that, "much more than most versions of secularism, Christianity honors a role for mystery, paradox, and existential struggle in life."[186] Yet at the same time as he commends Augustine's appreciation for mystery and plurality and the contribution his insights may have made towards future reflections on these matters, he accuses Augustine of deploying mystery as a dogmatic instrument of power to protect his own doctrine, denounce competing doctrines, and draw stringent lines around the diversity that could be considered tolerable.[187] In his most recent work, he draws parallels between the doctrines held by Augustine and those put forth by the radical Muslim cleric, Sayyid Qutb, whose ideas are said to have influenced Osama bin Laden, writing that he finds them "too close for comfort."[188] Augustine has been one of the most influential figures in political theory, and perhaps in Western society more broadly, so it is in some senses not surprising that he would receive such explicit attention in Connolly's work. At the same time, we may want to raise questions about the accuracy of Connolly's use and interpretation of Augustine. Rengger writes of Connolly's interpretation of Augustine as "a reading that occasionally strains my credulity."[189] Strong wonders if Augustine's thought, particularly on original sin, could not be interpreted in such a way that his critiques come very close to Connolly's own.[190] If Augustine is indeed such a central figure in the history of political thought, if even his "opponents" feel the need to engage him in conversation as they seek to develop a more adequate contemporary political theory in light of our sense of contingency and concern for difference, if he addresses issues of mystery and plurality that continue to be of relevance, might it be worthwhile to look back to Augustine more directly – to see what aspects of Augustine's thought might

185. See, for example, ibid., p. 156.
186. Connolly, *Augustinian Imperative*, pp. 156–157.
187. Ibid., pp. 112–113, 77.
188. Connolly, *Pluralism*, p. 17.
189. Rengger, "*Identity\Difference* (book review)," p. 534.
190. Strong, "*Identity\Difference* (book review)," p. 865.

have been misunderstood as it has been appropriated and interpreted through the years, and to see how his thought and his
ontology might help us find more adequate ways to engage with
difference and diversity?

Connolly is certainly not alone in his attempts to draw Augustine into contemporary conversations about political society.
John Milbank, for example, has developed a "postmodern critical
Augustinianism"[191] and cites Augustine as one interested in "dena-
turalising" and "deconstructing" the political order of his day so
that he could show the dynamics and contingency involved in its
construction.[192] Milbank's "Augustinian" theology also leads him to
question the "secular" and to counter the predominance of morality
based in law or command with an "ethic of gift."[193] Though these
concerns are similar to those of Connolly, Milbank believes that a
tenable ethic needs to be grounded in an abundance and plenitude
that go much deeper than that which can be drawn from Nietzsche.
At the ontological level, he sees in Augustine the prioritization
of peace over conflict, so that the tragic, conflictual condition in
which we live is a contingent result of the fall and peace rather than
conflict is our ontological reality.[194] For the agonistic recognition of
conflict is not, according to Jean Bethke Elshtain, shocking news to
those who study history and have an awareness of human sin and
evil. It is "a wakeup call only for those who were first lulled to sleep
by consensus theory or some such."[195] The difference between
agonistic and Christian thinkers is not, as Elshtain notes, recognition

191. A label he uses for his own project in John Milbank, "Postmodern Critical
Augustinianism: A Short *Summa* in Forty-two Responses to Unasked
Questions," in *The Postmodern God*, ed. Graham Ward (Oxford: Blackwell, 1997),
pp. 265–278.
192. John Milbank, "An Essay Against Secular Order," *Journal of Religious
Ethics* 15 (Fall 1987), pp. 208–210. See also Milbank, *Theology and Social Theory*,
pp. 380–438.
193. On the secular, see Milbank, "Against Secular Order," pp. 199–224;
Theology and Social Theory; "Problematizing the Secular: The Post-Postmodern
Agenda," in *Shadow of Spirit: Postmodernism and Religion*, ed. Philippa Berry
and Andrew Wernick (London: Routledge, 1992), pp. 30–44. On why "morality"
is not equivalent to Christianity and cannot be Christian, see John Milbank,
The Word Made Strange: Theology, Language, Culture (Oxford: Blackwell, 1997),
pp. 219–232.
194. John Milbank, "The Midwinter Sacrifice: A Sequel to 'Can Morality be
Christian?' " *Studies in Christian Ethics* 10, no. 2 (1997); *Theology and Social Theory*,
p. 390.
195. Jean Bethke Elshtain, "Response to Panel Papers," *Annual of the Society of
Christian Ethics* 21 (2001), p. 154.

of conflict, but the assertion that this conflict and violence comprise our ontological reality, for "Hobbes and Jesus of Nazareth cannot both be right."[196]

A brief conclusion

It may well be that the ontology of Augustine offers us a way to move beyond the seemingly hopeless ontology of violence put forward by Connolly and the other agonistic theorists we have considered. These agonistic political theorists have contributed much to the conversation about how we might live together in a pluralist political society. They have helpfully demonstrated ways in which political liberalism is not as tolerant as it hopes to be nor as free from ontological assumptions as it claims to be. They have given us a picture of a society in which differences can be recognized and particularity can be acknowledged, in the political realm alongside other realms, even as they have reminded us that the task of creating "inclusive" political societies may not have the neat and tidy solution for which we are hoping. And they have inspired us to think about humility and generosity as the guiding virtues of our interactions with one another. By so thoroughly ontologizing and naturalizing conflict, however, agonistic theorists may be guilty of the charge leveled against them by Mathewes, namely, that of "refusing all imaginative possibilities for some sort of ideal absolute harmony." Such a refusal "stands in manifest tension with the agonists' own insistence that patterns of human interaction are radically contingent, always open to contestation and re-imagination."[197] For, as Milbank wonders "how does one establish, without a renewed form of foundationalism, that the *agon* is inescapable, or that epistemological uncertainty is endless conflict rather than the tensional but 'peaceful' participation of the finite in the infinite?"[198]

Our agonistic political theorists believe that harmony in the midst of our plurality is no longer a plausible ideal because of the conflict and chaos that mark our ontological reality. In their thinking a move beyond liberal tolerance in the name of difference is concomitant with the relinquishment of hope of unity amidst diversity.

196. Elshtain, "Response," p. 154.
197. Mathewes, "Faith, Hope, and Agony," p. 137.
198. Milbank, "Against Secular Order," p. 212.

This post-Nietzschean political thought attempts to overcome certain binary oppositions which they find in modern theory, moving
beyond strict delineations between Self and Other, identity and
difference, inside and outside, in the name of and for the sake of
plurality and multiplicity. Yet in the place of these "modern" bin-
aries they establish their own oppositions, unnecessarily establishing strict dichotomies between harmony and difference, unity and
diversity, the universal and the particular. Furthermore, some of the
very changes and movements that they applaud and encourage, such
as the multiplicity of identity and the increased sense of contingency
experienced under conditions of pluralism, do not seem liberating
to significant parts of the world's population. As Zizek and Michael
Hardt and Antonio Negri note, outside of elite intellectual circles,
increased hybridity, mobility, and contingency are often experienced
traumatically and associated with increased suffering.[199]

We are left wondering what hope we have in this world of difference and plurality in which we find ourselves today. Does agonistic political thought, despite its insufficiencies, represent the
best prospect for engaging with diversity? Or is it possible that an
alternative ontology could help us develop different pictures of
what is possible when it comes to questions of difference? Could it
be that a Trinitarian ontology would enable us to imagine communities of harmony that respect the universal *and* the particular?
We would do well to walk through the ontological door opened by
agonistic political theorists and walk towards Christianity's ontology of peace as a possible way to expand our political and pluralist
imagination.

199. Zizek, *Ticklish Subject*, pp. 220–221; Hardt and Negri, *Empire*, pp. 154–155.

4
_____

Augustine and the theological turn

Introduction

We have now considered the contributions of two important voices to the conversation about how we might live together in a pluralist and diverse society, one represented by political liberalism and the other by agonistic political thought. We have learned from these voices and appreciated the theories they put forward, and yet as we tried to picture the solutions they offer we wondered if they were able to welcome diversity and bring together difference as sufficiently as they hope to. We sensed the need for another contribution to the conversation, another voice to help us think further about the relationship between unity and diversity in a pluralistic age. This other voice is an old voice, one that has been a part of such conversations in the past but in recent times has not been as much of a contributor. It is the voice of Christian theology. In this chapter, we supplement the ontological turn of recent political theory with a theological turn, as we listen to Augustine of Hippo's voice as representative of one Christian understanding of the nature of human being and reality. We will try to hearken back to what Augustine was saying in his own time and discern how that might augment our political imagination today.

The writings, letters, and sermons of Augustine reveal a picture of the nature of reality and human being that is vastly different from the pictures that emerge out of political liberalism or post-Nietzschean political thought. Whereas the post-Nietzscheans see chaos and conflict predominating, Augustine believes peace and harmony to be the most fundamental realities. Whereas political liberals seek

a political realm in which conflict is overcome through consensus, Augustine is aware of the ineradicable presence of lust for domination and power in our earthly *polis*. Indeed, Augustine was neither naïve about the pervasiveness of power games within society nor unaware of the complexities concomitant with situations of plurality and diversity. And yet his theological thinking about humanity, community, and political life reveals ideas and pictures that have long been absent from mainstream political theory. That being said, we are not the first, as we saw in the last chapter, to turn to this writer, thinker, and bishop from the fourth century in an effort to address the question of difference as it faces us in the twenty-first century.

A turn to Augustine within certain pockets of political theory, philosophy, and theology may perhaps best be understood as a response to the deep questioning of modernity, and many of its presuppositions and institutions, that marks our contemporary *milieu*. This questioning has wrought changes in political theory, as we have seen, and seems to have opened the door for considerations of new and different resources that might help our political imagination in the face of pluralism. Agonistic political thought is one such resource, while Augustine, as a political thinker who predates modernity, is another. As Joshua Mitchell remarks, in an attempt to explain why changing circumstances have enabled recent political thought to reconsider the work of Augustine, "under such circumstances as these, Augustine ceases to be a figure who quietly administers the sedative of faith to the Western world – the effects of which take a millennium to wear off. Another possibility emerges."[1] Peter Brown likewise believes that because "the whole emphasis on what is fruitful in political theory has shifted," Augustine now seems like a thinker who stands very close to the preoccupations of our age.[2] At the same time, certain changes in our intellectual climate have revealed the degree to which the concerns of political philosophy are integrally related to ontological beliefs about the nature of reality and human being, so that, as Charles T. Mathewes

1. Joshua Mitchell, "The Uses of Augustine, After 1989," *Political Theory* 27, no. 5 (October 1999), p. 696.
2. P. R. L. Brown, "Political Society," in *Augustine: A Collection of Critical Essays*, ed. R. A. Markus (New York: Doubleday, 1972), p. 312. See also Eugene TeSelle, *Augustine the Theologian* (London: Burns & Oates, 1970), p. 119.

writes, "what initially seems a contingent political question is revealed to be a deep and inescapable metaphysical issue."[3] This means that questions related to pluralism and difference need to be addressed, as Mathewes points out, not only because they mark our current sociopolitical reality but for properly theological reasons. To look at the question of pluralism in theological terms, we may need to look beyond and behind modern theology to recover earlier sources, of which the Augustinian tradition stands as a rich and fruitful spring.[4]

Although Augustine's situation was significantly different from ours today, so that it is important to treat his work in light of his historical circumstances rather than merely appropriating it for our purposes, we need not assume that he lived in a time of simplicity and likemindedness while we are the first to face complexity and plurality. As Charles Norris Cochrane writes, "Augustine was born into a world the perplexities of which have probably never been exceeded by any period, before or since, in human history."[5] Nor need we assume that agonistic theorists operating in Nietzsche's legacy are the first to expose the underlying power games at play in society and politics. Augustine believes that the *libido dominandi* is at the very heart of the city of this world, "a city which aims at dominion, which holds nations in enslavement, but is itself dominated by that very lust of domination."[6] Augustine furthermore recognizes that a certain degree of contingency marks the world as we know it, particularly when it comes to such forms of security as power. For Augustine, the lust for domination and the contingency of worldly power provide all the more reason to acknowledge the insufficiency of the "earthly city," the city and political society of this *saeculum*,[7] in contrast to the Heavenly City, the City of God, the city that is on pilgrimage in this age and therefore coexists with the

3. Charles T. Mathewes, "Pluralism, Otherness, and the Augustinian Tradition," *Modern Theology* 14, no. 1 (January 1998), p. 86.
4. Mathewes, "Pluralism," p. 84.
5. Charles Norris Cochrane, *Christianity and Classical Culture: A Study of Thought and Action from Augustus to Augustine* (Oxford: Clarendon Press, 1940), p. 380.
6. St. Augustine, *Concerning the City of God Against the Pagans* (hereafter *City of God*) I, preface, trans. Henry Bettenson (Harmondsworth, England: Penguin Books, 1972).
7. We follow Peter Brown's definition of the *saeculum* as "the sum total of human existence as we experience it in the present, as we know it has been since the fall of Adam, and as we know it will continue until the Last Judgement" ("Political Society," p. 321).

earthly city, while having a fundamentally distinct origin, basis, love, and telos.

Peace, everlasting and perfect, is the Supreme Good of the City of God, which its citizens look forward to on the basis of faith and hope. Love for God rather than lust for domination defines this city. Its citizens come from all nations and speak all languages, adorning different dress and adhering to different manners of life, unrestrained by conformity of customs, laws, and institutions, free to have "their innumerable variety of desires and thoughts and everything else which makes human beings different from one another."[8] Its peace is vastly different from that of the earthly city, so different that Augustine believes it is the only peace worthy of the name.[9] It is a peace that is inextricably connected to harmony, "for this peace is the perfectly ordered and completely harmonious fellowship in the enjoyment of God, and of each other in God."[10] Unlike the post-Nietzschean political theorists of the last chapter, then, who, in the name of difference and in recognition of the prevalence of conflict and power, give up all hope for harmony, Augustine speaks of a world that has harmony amidst diversity at its very center. It is through a close look at the writings of Augustine that the distinctness of the ontology with which he operates becomes visible, in stark contrast to that offered either by political liberalism or agonistic political thought. Once his ontology is before us, we can then turn to see how it might benefit and expand our current political imagination.

Before we begin this task, it may be helpful to clarify what the ambitions of this chapter are, and what they are not. The overarching goal is an immersion into the ontology that underlies Augustine's thought, as it can be drawn out from an investigation of a distinct number of his works.[11] This will obviously involve

---

8. *Enchiridion* XXVII, 103.
9. *City of God* XIX, 17.
10. Ibid.
11. Because of the magnitude of Augustine's corpus, for the purposes of this investigation it was only possible to engage in depth with those writings that seemed most relevant to the discussion at hand. These include *On Music*, trans. Robert Catesby Taliaferro, in The Fathers of the Church, vol. 4 (New York: The Fathers of the Church, Inc., 1947); *On Christian Doctrine*, trans. D. W. Robertson, Jr. (Indianapolis, IN: Bobbs-Merrill, 1958); *Confessions*, trans. Henry Chadwick (Oxford: Oxford University Press, 1991); *The Trinity*, trans. Edmund Hill, O.P., ed. John E. Rotelle, O.S.A. (Brooklyn, NY: New City Press, 1991); *Enchiridion* and *City of God*. For relevant letters and sermons I have relied upon *Augustine: Political Writings*, ed. E. M. Atkins and R. J. Dodaro (Cambridge: Cambridge University Press, 2001).

a certain amount of selectivity, both in the works that are considered and in the parts of those works that are directly addressed. The aim, however, is to step back from isolated works so that a picture emerges of the ontology that undergirds his thought, informing it both implicitly and explicitly. This is not, then, an investigation focused on articulating the relationship between the two cities, as many works of Augustinian political theory are, nor is it an attempt to come to terms with his understanding of the self, as is much modern interaction with Augustine. Though discussions of these important realms of Augustine's thought will certainly be a part of our endeavor, they are only that – one part of Augustine's larger ontology. As we step into that ontology, the hope is that some new possibilities will begin to emerge for helping us picture life together. We are not trying to transfer Augustine wholesale into our political moment, but we are trying to see which parts of his ontology might augment our current political and theological imagination.

We begin this chapter with a broad articulation of the framework which Augustine assumes and develops as the nature of the world and human being in certain of his writings, and then move into a more detailed discussion of the specific components of which his ontology is comprised. Within the broader picture of order and harmony that he paints, we will need to deal closely with his understanding of God's creation of nature, humanity, and order; the disorder and disharmony that result from sin; the role of Jesus Christ and the Trinity more generally in creating and redeeming the world, making possible and providing eschatological hope for renewed peace and unity amidst diversity; and how God's redemption plays out in terms of the Heavenly City and the Church. With these in mind, we will then be able to turn to how Augustine conceives of the relationship between the Heavenly City and the earthly city, and what hopes citizens of the Heavenly City can have for the earthly city while they are on pilgrimage in its midst.

Harmony and diversity

An overview

Peace, harmony, and order are fundamental to Augustine's picture of the world, implicitly underlying his thought if not

explicitly articulated in a given piece or text. They are at the heart of his understanding of the creation of nature and humanity, the fall and the manifestation of sin in the world, the redemption of creation that comes through Jesus Christ, and the eschatological hope that marks the Heavenly City. One of Augustine's earliest works is, in fact, entitled *De ordine (On Order)*,[12] and his belief in the underlying order of God's created world continues throughout his lifetime, certain changes in his thinking on the matter notwithstanding.[13]

In his earliest works, this belief in God-created order is articulated in terms of music and number, which, according to Augustine, reveal the beauty and unity of God's world.[14] For number begins from the unity of one and has beauty in its equality and likeness, just as nature, though comprised of a variety of different forms and sizes, comes from one beginning and has beauty in its equality and similitude. The diversity of nature stems from the riches of God's goodness and is "joined together in charity as one and one gift from one."[15] Throughout his works, Augustine maintains that creation has one beginning, namely the fullness of God's goodness, out of which God created, giving form and particularity to that which was formless, endowing the vast diversity of creation with measure, form, and order, giving each part of creation its place within God's order.[16] Creation, then, is manifold *and* interconnected within a divine order. Humanity, too, is part of this picture of diversity and harmony, for, according to Augustine, God chose to begin all humanity from one single individual so that the human race would "be bound together by a kind of tie of kinship to form a harmonious unity, linked together by the 'bond of peace'."[17]

The divine order that Augustine identifies with God's creation is fundamentally relational, involving a harmony of relation between

12. St. Augustine, "De ordine," in *Contra academicos. De beata vita. De ordine*, ed. William M. Green and Klaus D. Daur (Turnholti: Typographi Brepols, 1970).
13. See, for example, St. Augustine, "Of True Religion," xli, 76 and "Retractions," I, xiii, 8, in *Augustine: Earlier Writings*, trans. John H. S. Burleigh (London: SCM, 1953).
14. See esp. *On Music* VI.
15. *On Music* VI, 56. See also W. F. Jackson Knight, *St. Augustine's De Musica: A Synopsis* (London: The Orthological Institute, 1949), pp. 122–125.
16. *Confessions* XII, iii (3), XIII, ii (2); *Enchiridion* III, 9; "The Nature of the Good," in *Augustine: Earlier Writings*, translated by John H. S. Burleigh (London: SCM, 1953), iii.
17. *City of God* XIV, 1.

and within God, angels, humanity, animals, and nature.[18] This
harmony is rooted in Augustine's belief that God's order involves a
hierarchy of goods in which each good has its proper place.[19] The
highest goods in this hierarchy are immortal goods related to eternal peace and the everlasting enjoyment of God and others in God.
When things are properly ordered, humans delight in and refer all
else to these immortal goods, "where the highest unchangeable
undisturbed and eternal equality resides," so that "terrestrial subjects are subject to celestial, and their time circuits join together in
harmonious succession for a poem of the universe."[20] This reveals
another sense in which the divine order is relational: within God's
divine order all things were created to be related and referred to
God. As Brown writes, "the word *referre*, 'to refer', or 'relate', is
central to Augustine's discussion of human activity; and for
Augustine, of course, this human activity of whatever kind, can only
reach fulfillment when it can take its place in a harmonious whole,
where everything is in relation to God."[21] All goods, then, are to be
referred to the greater, unchanging good of God. Even love of self
and love of neighbor are ultimately undertaken for the sake of God;
a person, in "loving his neighbour as himself ... refers the love of
both to that love of God which suffers no stream to be led away from
it by which it might be diminished."[22]

And yet humanity turned away from the greatest goods to lower
ones, choosing self-love over love of God, and thereby disrupting the
harmonious unity of creation and allowing "disordered chaos" and
the prevalence of disunity over unity to hold sway in this world.[23]
As Augustine writes in *The Trinity*, "by wickedness and ungodliness
with a crashing discord we had bounced away, and flowed and faded
away from the one supreme true God into the many, divided by the
many, clinging to the many."[24] From the initial act of creation came

---

18. N.B. This is in contrast to William Connolly's interpretation of Augustine's
order as fundamentally *moral*. The relational nature of the divine order, as
Augustine describes it, certainly has an accompanying ethics, but at heart it is
concerned primarily with relationality rather than morality.
19. See Cochrane, *Christianity and Classical Culture*, pp. 486–487 and Gerard
O'Daly, *Augustine's City of God: A Reader's Guide* (Oxford: Clarendon, 1999),
pp. 140–141.
20. *On Music* VI, 29.
21. Brown, "Political Society," p. 318.
22. *On Christian Doctrine* I, 21.
23. *Confessions* XIII, xxxiv (49).
24. *The Trinity* IV, 11.

the many from the One, united in order and harmony, but from the fall of humanity came the disruption of order and the division of the many into ever-increasing disharmony, into the many without the unity of the One. Whence the need for the redemption and reconciliation that came through Jesus Christ, the "one" of the following passage:

> And so it was fitting that at the beck and bidding of a compassionate God the many should themselves acclaim together the one who was to come, and that acclaimed by the many together the one should come, and that the many should testify together that the one had come, and that we being disburdened of the many should come to the one; and that being dead in soul through many sins and destined to die in the flesh because of sin, we should love the one who died in the flesh for us without sin, and that believing in him raised from the dead, and rising ourselves with him in spirit through faith, we should be made one in the one just one; and that we should not despair of ourselves rising in the flesh when we observed that we the many members had been preceded by the one head, in whom we have been purified by faith and will then be made completely whole by sight, and that thus fully reconciled to God by him the mediator, we may be able to cling to the one, enjoy the one, and remain for ever one.[25]

This passage resonates with the neoplatonic language of the one and the many of Plotinus to make the point that through the one Jesus Christ, the one who as God and man was able to be the mediator between God and humanity, those who are many can again become one.[26] This unity is not merely one of nature or kinship, but one of charity: those who are one in Christ are bound in the fellowship of love.[27] This love is love of God and neighbor, and a soul that "loves Him above itself, that is, God and fellow souls as itself," is a soul that is in order.[28]

---

25. Ibid.
26. The degree to which Augustine is influenced by Platonic and Neoplatonic thought is a matter of no small discussion and debate. For Augustine's thoughts on Platonists, both how they influenced him and how their thought falls short, see *Confessions* VII, ix (13), x (16), xx (26), xxi (27); *City of God* VIII, 4–22; X; XXII, 25–29; "Of True Religion" i–iv, 11. For a helpful review of differing evaluations of Augustine's relationship with Platonism, see Robert Crouse, "*Paucis Mutatis Verbis*: St. Augustine's Platonism," in *Augustine and His Critics*, ed. Robert Dodaro and George Lawless (London: Routledge, 2000), pp. 37–50.
27. *The Trinity* IV, 12.
28. *On Music* VI, 46.

This love is what binds the Heavenly City together:

> the children of grace, the citizens of the free city, the sharers in
> eternal peace, who form a community where there is no love of a
> will that is personal and, as we may say, private, but a love that
> rejoices in a good that is at once shared by all and unchanging – a
> love that makes "one heart" out of many, a love that is the whole-
> hearted and harmonious obedience of mutual affection.[29]

Furthermore, once the Heavenly City reaches its fulfillment in
"eternal bliss," an even deeper state of harmony will be reached.
Harmonies of the body that were heretofore hidden will be revealed
and harmonies of archangels, angels, and humans that in this age
exceed the powers of our imagination and description will be made
known.[30] No lust for domination will be evident between humans in
this divine order, nor will humans have dominion over each other.
Such things arise only when human sin replaces genuine dutiful
concern and compassion with the pride that "hates a fellowship of
equality under God, and seeks to impose its own dominion on fellow men, in place of God's rule."[31] Indeed, just such a disruption of
the divine order, caused by a "perverted imitation of God," resulted
in the need for government that involves power, compulsion, and
coercion.[32] This government is a providential provision that can
help towards the attainment of limited peace between people in the
earthly city, but because of humanity's disruption of the divine
order through its preference for the lower goods of power and self-
love, the only true hope for equality and harmony lies in the City
whose founder is Jesus Christ.

It is when humans turn from the highest, unchangeable goods
and prioritize lower goods that the harmony God intended for the
world is disrupted. The harmony of the universe is, according to
Augustine, inextricably connected to harmony within humans, for
when humans choose to prioritize lower goods over higher ones,

---

29. *City of God* XV, 3.
30. *City of God* XXII, 30.
31. *City of God* XIX, 12; XIX, 14.
32. This view clearly goes with interpretations of Augustine in which politics is
seen as a God-ordained result of the fall but not God's original intention for
creation. For an account of recent scholarship covering the range of possible
positions on this issue (i.e., that Augustine views politics as natural, as "bad,"
or as somewhere in between), see Peter J. Burnell, "The Status of Politics in
St. Augustine's *City of God*," *History of Political Thought* 13, no. 1 (Spring 1992),
pp. 13–29.

they disrupt God's intended order for their internal and their external lives, meaning the harmony within themselves and the harmony between themselves and the rest of God's creation. As Rowan Williams notes, "the *pax* of the individual soul and the *pax* of the universe are parts of a single continuum, so that attempts at peace on the lower levels without regard to the higher are doomed to disaster."[33] We see this in the following passage, in which Augustine moves from the peace of the body to the peace of the soul, to the peace of man and God to peace between men, and ultimately to the peace of the Heavenly City in which the whole universe resides in perfectly harmonious fellowship in the enjoyment of God and mutual fellowship in God, in the tranquility of order:

> The peace of the body, we conclude, is a tempering of the compo-
> nent parts in duly ordered proportion; the peace of the irrational
> soul is a duly ordered repose of the appetites; the peace of the
> rational soul is the duly ordered agreement of cognition and action.
> The peace of body and soul is the duly ordered life and health of a
> living creature; peace between mortal man and God is an ordered
> obedience, in faith, in subjection to an everlasting law; peace
> between men is an ordered agreement of mind with mind; the
> peace of a home is the ordered agreement among those who live
> together about giving and obeying orders; the peace of the Heavenly
> City is a perfectly ordered and perfectly harmonious fellowship in
> the enjoyment of God, and a mutual fellowship in God; the peace of
> the whole universe is the tranquillity of order – and order is the
> arrangement of things equal and unequal in a pattern which assigns
> to each its proper position.[34]

The details: loves, peace, hope, and ends

This broad framework of harmony and order has given us a glimpse of many of the key ideas and concepts to which we now turn in more detail as we seek to enter more fully into Augustine's ontology. This is a vast endeavor, and we do not presume to be able to place all of his many ideas and concerns into one overarching schema even as we hope to address some of the most important and relevant aspects of his thought. We must also bear in mind that although

33. Rowan Williams, "Politics and the Soul: A Reading of the *City of God*,"
Milltown Studies no. 19/20 (1987), p. 63.
34. *City of God* XIX, 13.

Augustine is invoked time and again within the world of political thought, not a single one of his books, as Peter Brown points out, is devoted to political theory as such.[35] At times, then, our discussion may seem to be drawing us far away from the question of how to engage with difference and diversity within political society that dominates the previous chapters of this project, but the connections should become increasingly evident as the discussion progresses.

Let us return to the beginning, namely Augustine's understanding of creation. Creation comes from the fullness of God's being and goodness, so that God is the source of all existence and being is a gift from God flowing from the abundance of God's own being.[36] At the heart of Augustine's picture of creation is God as "Almighty Artist," a "wonderful and indescribable craftsman" who fashioned and made all created things out of His own goodness.[37] This is God understood as the Trinity of Father, Son, and Holy Spirit, and the creation fashioned by this Triune God is full of wonder and beauty:

> For a Christian it is enough to believe that the cause of created things, whether in heaven or on earth, visible or invisible, is nothing other than the goodness of the creator who is the one true God, and that there is nothing that is not either himself or from him, and that he is Trinity, that is, Father, the Son begotten from the Father and the Holy Spirit who proceeds from the same Father, and is one and the same Spirit of Father and Son. By this Trinity, supremely, equally, and unchangeably good, all things have been created ... and at the same time all things are very good, since in all these things consists the wonderful beauty of the universe.[38]

Indeed, Augustine has seemingly endless appreciation for the wonders of creation, from humans who could move their ears and produce sounds from their behind at will "without any stink" to the ability of peacocks to resist putrefaction, from wood that floats instead of sinks to mountains that belch out fire.[39] His sense of wonder and appreciation for the diversity of creation is especially evident in the following passage:

> How could any description do justice to all these blessings?
> The manifold diversity of beauty in sky and earth and sea; the

35. Brown, "Political Society," p. 311.
36. *Confessions* XIII, i (I)-iv (5); *City of God* V, 11.
37. *City of God* XXII, 11; *Enchiridion* XXIII, 89.
38. *Enchiridion* III, 9, 10.
39. See *City of God* XIV, 24; XXI, 4; XXI, 5; XXII, 11; XXII, 24.

abundance of light, and its miraculous loveliness, in sun and moon and stars; the dark shades of woods, the colour and fragrance of flowers; the multitudinous varieties of birds, with their songs and their bright plumage; the countless different species of living creatures of all shapes and sizes, among whom it is the smallest in bulk that moves our greatest wonder – for we are more astonished at the activities of the tiny ants and bees than at the immense bulk of whales. Then there is the mighty spectacle of the sea itself, putting on its changing colours like different garments, now green, with all the many varied shades, now purple, now blue ... Think, too, of all the resources for the preservation of health, or for its restoration, the welcome alternation of day and night, the soothing coolness of the breezes, all the material for clothing provided by plants and animals. Who could give a complete list of all these natural blessings?[40]

Yet in God's original design for creation some of these blessings would have been less necessary than others, for man would have enjoyed perfect health in body and complete tranquility in soul as long as "he lived in the enjoyment of God, and derived his own goodness from God's goodness."[41] Neither desire nor fear, neither scarcity nor sadness, neither disease nor fatigue was present in the paradise that was marked instead by ease and plenty, by joy flowing from God to humans and a "blaze of love" going from humans towards God, by mutual respect and love between man and woman, and by "a harmony and a liveliness of mind and body."[42]

And so the world would have remained full of goodness and harmony had no one sinned. Indeed, then the distinction between the earthly city and the Heavenly City would never have arisen, for the only city would have been "the vast and all-embracing republic of the whole creation" governed by God its creator and Jesus Christ its king.[43] Augustine is, in some ways, most well known for his conception of "original sin," namely the belief that sin came into the world through the one man Adam and was thereby passed to all humanity so that even infants are sinful and stand in need of baptism and rebirth.[44] This sin violated the harmony and hierarchy that

40. *City of God* XXII, 24.
41. *City of God* XIV, 26.
42. Ibid.
43. *The Trinity* III, 9.
44. For the first occurrence of "original sin" within his writing, see *Confessions* V, ix (16). See also *Confessions* I, vii (11); *Enchiridion* XIII, 45, 46; *City of God* I, 9.

were part of God's order for the universe. As such, sin can be understood as a disruption of the relational harmony that God intended for God's creation, between God and humanity, between and within humans themselves, and between humanity and creation. How does Augustine describe sin?

> What happens is that the soul, loving its own power, slides away from the whole which is common to all into the part which is its own private property. By following God's directions and being perfectly governed by his laws it could enjoy the whole universe of creation; but by the apostasy of pride which is called the beginning of sin it strives to grab something more than the whole and to govern it by its own laws; and because there is nothing more than the whole it is thrust back into anxiety over a part, and so by being greedy for more it gets less.[45]

Sin, then, is turning away from God and the common good towards oneself and one's private concerns and property. It is neglecting the way God created the world and the greater whole and harmony of the universe. It is, in short, falsehood. "Every sin is a falsehood," Augustine writes, and "falsehood consists in not living in the way for which he was created." Indeed, man "forsakes God by sinning, and he sins by living by his own standard."[46]

This, in fact, is the defining mark of the difference between the city of man and the City of God, and that to which the cities owe their existence: the former lives by the standard of humanity, or the standard of the flesh, while the latter lives by God's standard, or the

---

45. *The Trinity* XII, 14. See also "The Literal Meaning of Genesis" XI, 19, in *On Genesis*, trans. Edmund Hill, O.P., ed. John E. Rotelle, O.S.A. (Hyde Park, NY: New City Press, 2002); *On Music* VI, 53.

46. *City of God* XIV, 4. This understanding of sin is clearly linked to Augustine's larger view of evil. Augustine's rejection of Manichaean dualism in favor of the view that "evil has no existence except as a privation of good" was based on the belief that evil is the decrease of good in a creature and is thereby dependent on the existence of the good (*Confessions* III, vii [12]; see also VII, xiii [19] and *The Nature of the Good* iv). This leads Augustine to a "surprising conclusion," namely that every being is good, so calling something evil means only that it is a contaminated good, not evil in and of itself (*Enchiridion* IV, 13). Augustine is willing to leave some questions unanswered when it comes to evil and its origin, but he is not willing to compromise the belief that all that is created by God is good. We should note, contra William Connolly's interpretation, that he is more concerned with showing that all beings and all goodness depend on God for their existence than with developing an account of evil in which God has no responsibility; if the latter were his driving concern, the Manichaean notion of a separate force of evil would surely have seemed more compelling.

standard of the Spirit.[47] This is primarily a matter of love for, as Augustine writes,

> the two cities were created by two kinds of love: the earthly city was created by self-love reaching the point of contempt for God, the Heavenly City by the love of God carried as far as contempt of self. ... In the former, the lust for domination lords it over its princes as over the nations it subjugates; in the other both those put in authority and those subject to them serve one another in love, the rulers by their counsel, the subjects by obedience. The one city loves its own strength shown in its powerful leaders; the other says to its God, "I will love you, my Lord, my strength."[48]

So the earthly city is marked by love for itself, and its citizens likewise are concerned primarily with love for themselves, whereas the Heavenly City and its citizens live for the good of God, others, and creation more generally.

For Augustine, the question of love is integrally connected to the question of order, for when humans live by God's standard and love God accordingly, then they will be living in harmony with God's order and design for the universe. As he says in one sermon, "I simply want your loves to be properly ordered. Put heavenly things before earthly, immortal things before mortal, everlasting things before transitory ones. And put the Lord before everything, and not just by praising him, but also by loving him."[49] It is worth noting that for Augustine love of God, neighbor, and self are all inextricably connected, so that when God enjoins His people to love God and neighbor, He is also enjoining them to love themselves. For to truly love themselves, humans must also love God, and through this love of God they will be themselves renewed and enabled to love others: " ... when the mind loves God, and consequently as has been said remembers and understands him, it can rightly be commanded to love its neighbor as itself. For now it loves itself with a straight, not a twisted love, now that it loves God; for sharing in him results not merely in its being that image, but in its being made new and fresh and happy after being old and worn and miserable."[50] Furthermore, if all people were to follow these two precepts of

47. *City of God* XIV, 4.
48. Ibid, 28.
49. Sermon 335c, 13, in *Augustine: Political Writings* (p. 59).
50. *The Trinity* XIV, 18.

loving God and loving neighbor, the result would be peaceful, ordered harmony:

> Now God, our master, teaches two chief precepts, love of God and love of neighbour; and in them finds three objects for his love: God, himself, and his neighbour; and a man who loves God is not wrong in loving himself. It follows, therefore, that he will be concerned also that his neighbour should love God, since he is told to love his neighbour as himself; and the same is true of his concern for his wife, his children, for the members of his household, and for all other men, so far as is possible. And, for the same end, he will wish his neighbour to be concerned for him, if he happens to need that concern. For this reason he will be at peace, as far as lies in him, with all men, in that peace among men, that ordered harmony.[51]

Such harmony, the kind that "makes 'one heart' out of many," is possible only when a community is based on an unchanging good that all can share, rather than on a love which is private and dependent on the changing nature of human wills.[52] For in Augustine's thinking, as John Burnaby notes, "the *Summum Bonum* is by its very nature the *bonum commune*, a good which can be possessed only by being shared. ... "[53] It is because of the shared nature of the highest good, combined with the social nature of humanity, that calls to love God, others, and oneself are not in opposition to each other.

That Augustine believes that humans are inherently social should come as no surprise, in light of the discussion thus far. In this, Augustine sees himself in agreement with the ancient philosophers who "hold the view that the life of the wise man should be social; and in this we support them much more heartily."[54] Augustine acknowledges that "God created man as one individual," and yet, he continues, "that did not mean that he was to remain alone, bereft of human society."[55] Indeed, God began with the creation of one individual and had the rest of humankind come from that one individual so that all of humanity would be knit together by a sense of kinship and bound together in the midst of their differences: "God started the human race from one man to show to mankind

51. *City of God* XIX, 14.
52. *City of God* XV, 3.
53. John Burnaby, *Amor Dei: A Study of the Religion of St. Augustine* (London: Hodder & Stoughton, 1938), p. 127.
54. *City of God* XIX, 5.
55. *City of God* XII, 22.

how pleasing to him is unity in plurality."[56] And yet this human race, as we now see it, is "at once social by nature and quarrelsome by perversion."[57] In the face of the disharmony that results from fallen human nature, Augustine turns again to the fact that God began the human race from one man, counseling his readers to remember that they come from one parent, "who was created by God as one individual with this intention: that from that one individual a multitude might be propagated, and that this fact should teach mankind to preserve a harmonious unity in plurality."[58]

The difficulty, of course, with preserving this harmonious unity in plurality is that humans are now marked by sin, understood, as we saw above, as turning away from God and the common good towards oneself and one's private concerns and property. The result is disorder and disharmony both between and within individuals, for the fall did not only involve a turn away from the common good, but it also interrupted the order and harmony found within persons. To offer a complete account of Augustine's understanding of the human self is a task that lies beyond the parameters of this project, and yet it is important to identify certain key aspects of his understanding of the person and the impact of sin on the self. Each person, according to Augustine, is comprised of "body and soul together," with the body being that which God made out of dust and the soul being that which was implanted in the body by the breath of God.[59] Body and soul can also be thought of as the "outer man" and the "inner man," terms that Augustine draws from 2 Corinthians 4:16.[60] Augustine uses this terminology in *The Trinity* to offer a complex human psychology in which both the inner and outer man are further delineated in terms of their various functions and aspects, all of which have been disordered by sin. For, in Augustine's view, before the fall, and again in the City of God, the body would have been properly ordered in subjection to the mind and soul. Yet with the first sin of Adam "the soul, in fact, rejoiced in its own freedom to act perversely and disdained to be God's servant;

56. Ibid., 23.
57. Ibid., 28. See also XIX, 5.
58. *City of God* XII, 28.
59. *City of God* XIII, 24.
60. Ibid. See also *The Trinity* XII, 12; *City of God* XXII, 24. A contemporary rendition of 2 Cor. 4:16, NRSV: "So we do not lose heart. Even though our outer nature is wasting away, our inner nature is being renewed day by day."

and so it was deprived of the obedient service which its body had at first rendered."[61] In other words, for Augustine, as we saw above, the peace of the individual is dependent upon the proper ordering of its various components; sin disrupts this peace by disrupting this ordering, so that the individual's inner components, desires, and loves are disordered just as his or her relationships with God, others, and creation are disrupted.[62]

Because of this disruption, then, humanity and its loves and desires are in need of reordering. This is precisely what, according to Mathewes, "the whole of De trinitate is meant to teach": its goal is "to educate the agent's desires towards right love of God, and to teach the agent that their desires, however crooked, have always already had God as their final end all along."[63] And this reveals that which undergirds all of Augustine's anthropological musings, or what Mathewes calls "the ultimate theological point of Augustine's analysis of selfhood," namely "that the self finds itself, in fact it is a self, only insofar as it is engaged by an other, a divine other."[64] Rowan Williams reaches similar conclusions in relation to the search for selfhood and The Trinity, arguing that Augustine's probings into self-knowledge reveal that "self-knowledge is precisely the knowledge of the self as incomplete, as seeking."[65] This is because "we are not able to know or love ourselves 'accurately' unless we know and love ourselves as known and loved by God."[66] Augustine's understanding of the self does not, according to Williams and Mathewes, result in the establishment of the solitary human ego or "Cartesian solipsism," as it is often accused;[67] instead, it establishes

61. City of God XIII, 13.
62. City of God XIX, 13.
63. Mathewes, "Pluralism," p. 99.
64. Ibid.
65. Rowan Williams, "'Know Thyself': What Kind of an Injunction?" in Philosophy, Religion and the Spiritual Life, ed. Michael McGhee (Cambridge: Cambridge University Press, 1992), pp. 221–222.
66. Rowan Williams, "Sapienta and the Trinity: Reflections on the De trinitate," in Collectanea Augustiniana: Mélanges T. J. Van Bavel, vol. 1, ed. B. Bruning, M. Lamberigts, and J. Van Houtem (Leuven: Augustinian Historical Institute, 1990), pp. 319–320.
67. For other arguments along these lines, see Michael Hanby, "Desire: Augustine Beyond Western Subjectivity," in Radical Orthodoxy: A New Theology, eds. John Milbank, Catherine Pickstock, and Graham Ward (London: Routledge, 1999), pp. 109–126 and Augustine and Modernity (London: Routledge, 2003); Lewis Ayres, "The Fundamental Grammar of Augustine's Trinitarian Theology," in Augustine and His Critics, eds. Robert Dodaro and George Lawless (London: Routledge, 2000), pp. 51–76.

the self firmly in relation to God and in need of the otherness of God for its own self-knowledge and self-love. Further, the self cannot be known "without a grasp of the inseparability of its good from the good of all."[68] Thus, according to Mathewes, "on Augustine's picture, otherness no longer appears as necessarily heteronomous." Instead, "Augustine offers a picture of selfhood inextricably intertwined with otherness and community," for "otherness and selfhood intermingle at every level of the self's reality."[69]

Of course, The Trinity is not only about the self's quest for self-knowledge but also about the Trinity, without which there would be no self for which to search, nor any hope for the reeducating of that fallen self's desires. For it is only through the grace and aid of the Triune God that an individual can come to recognize the "otherness" that is at its core and the communal, social nature of its existence. In this sense, what is needed is not merely reeducation but renewal, reformation, and, indeed, reconciliation, all of which are given by the gift and work of God.[70] Even love for God is a gift from God, a gift made possible only through the Holy Spirit. Augustine's frequently offers "the Gift of God" as the name for the Holy Spirit, for the Holy Spirit is given to humanity to pour out the love of God, to make known the charity of God the Father and God the Son.[71] It is God's gift of the Spirit that "makes us abide in God and him in us," that "fires man to the love of God and neighbour when he has been given to him."[72] The Father, the Son, and the Spirit can all be called charity and together comprise one charity, and yet Augustine identifies the Spirit closely with love because of the distinctive work of the Spirit in actualizing the salvific love of Christ in the life of those called to be part of God's family.[73] The mediating life and work of Jesus Christ lie at the heart of the love that the Spirit pours into humanity, because without Christ no renewal of humanity and no reconciliation between humanity and God are possible.

68. Williams, "Know Thyself," p. 222.
69. Mathewes, "Pluralism," pp. 99–100; Williams, "Sapienta and the Trinity," p. 331. Within The Trinity, see esp. XIV, 15–26.
70. The Trinity XIV, 22–24.
71. The Trinity XV, 32. See also Enchiridion XII, 40 and The Trinity V, XV.
72. The Trinity XV, 31.
73. Ibid., 28–31.

According to Augustine, Jesus Christ is the means by which the lost harmony of God's created world is restored. Through his life, ministry, death, and resurrection, he took that which was disordered in humanity and ordered it back to God, thereby opening the way for humanity and the rest of creation to be reordered and restored to its original, created harmony. Jesus Christ was able to do this because he was both God and human and could thereby act as a mediator. This idea of Jesus Christ as mediator between God and humanity, drawn from 1 Timothy 2:5, is central to Augustine's christology.[74] Because sin had separated the human race from God, a mediator was needed to reconcile humans to God; to fulfill the role such a mediator needed to have something in common with both God and humanity. Jesus Christ, as both Word of God and Son of Man, became "the mediator who alone was born, lived and was killed without sin, that human pride might be rebuked and healed by the humility of God and that man might be shown how far he had wandered from God when he was called back by God incarnate. ... "[75] The mediating work of Christ enables a restoration of that which was intended for humanity in creation, namely participation in the Triune God.[76] As Augustine writes,

> we were absolutely incapable of such participation and quite unfit for it, so unclean were we through sin, so we had to be cleansed. Furthermore, the only thing to cleanse the wicked and the proud is the blood of the just man and the humility of God. ... So God became a just man to intercede with God for sinful man. The sinner did not match the just, but man did match man. So he applied to us the similarity of his humanity to take away the dissimilarity of our iniquity, and becoming a partaker of our mortality he made us partakers of his divinity.[77]

The key to Augustine's conception of the Incarnation is, as Gerald Bonner puts it, "the Word of God descending to man, so that man might in turn ascend to God."[78] This understanding of the work of

---

74. 1 Tim. 2:5, NRSV: "For there is one God; there is also one mediator between God and humankind, Christ Jesus, himself human." Augustine generally quotes a shorter portion of the verse, translated "the one mediator between God and men, the man Jesus Christ" (see, for example, *City of God* XVIII, 47).
75. *Enchiridion* XXVIII, 108; see also *Confessions* X, xlii (67).
76. *City of God* IX, 15.
77. *The Trinity* IV, 4.
78. Gerald Bonner, "Christ, God and Man in the Thought of St. Augustine," *Angelicum* 61 (1984), p. 280. See *City of God* XXI, 15.

Christ as Mediator involves not only the remission of sins but also the fulfillment of humanity's created destiny, what Augustine refers to as participation or deification.[79] He draws this concept from Platonic thought while "radically Christianizing" it, as did the Greek Fathers, so that it comes to mean not just that humanity exists by participating in God but that such participation is only possible because of the Incarnation and mediation of Jesus Christ as the God-man. To put it differently, the salvation of humanity by Christ enables humans to partake of the divine life through Christ, because the humanity of Christ serves as the vehicle through which sinful humanity is reunited with and reordered to the divine. Through this participation in God, brought about by the indwelling of the Holy Spirit, humans become transformed into children of God, adopted as sons, part of the family of their Triune God.[80] Or, to use different language, they become citizens of the Heavenly City, living as pilgrims in their earthly cities while their lives and loves are ordered around God as their *summum bonum*, their unchanging and communal Good.

These citizens of the Heavenly City are no longer merely individuals, turned in on themselves and their lower, private goods, but are together united around the common good of God in the Body of Christ, the Church of Christ, by the Holy Spirit. But this does not mean that a return to harmony and order is always evident in the institutional Church as it exists in the here and now, for the City of God is not equivalent to the Church in the *saeculum*. Although in places Augustine writes of the City of God as the Church,[81] his writings, particularly those against the Donatists, leave no doubt that he harbored no illusions about the perfectibility of the Church or those who attend Church on earth. He differentiates between the Church as it exists now, in which both the faithful and the unfaithful, the redeemed and the unredeemed, are its members, and the Church "as it will be," when it will consist only of citizens of the Heavenly City.[82] Augustine's vision of the Church and the

---

79. Bonner notes that Augustine uses the term "deification" sparingly, but deification nevertheless has a strong conceptual presence in his thought. See Gerald Bonner, "Augustine's Concept of Deification," *Journal of Theological Studies* 37 (1986), p. 369.

80. See Augustine, Letter 153, 13, in *Augustine: Political Writings* (p. 78).

81. See, for example, *City of God* VIII, 24; XIII, 16; XX, 11.9.

82. *City of God* XX, 9. See also Carol Harrison, *Augustine: Christian Truth and Fractured Humanity* (Oxford: Oxford University Press, 2000), p. 220; Herbert A. Deane, "Augustine and the State: The Return of Order Upon Disorder," in

Heavenly City is ultimately eschatological, as he anticipates the day when the citizens of the Heavenly City who are now pilgrims on earth are joined together with the angels who have always remained with God in heaven; they "will together form one company in eternity, which is one already by the bond of charity, established to worship the one God."[83] And yet this does not diminish the importance of the visible Church, for the Heavenly City is already present within the Church; as Nicholas Healy writes, "Augustine clearly affirms the ontological relation between the City of God and the church."[84] In Augustine's view, Christ is inseparable from His body, which is the Church.[85] This is why, as Patricia Wilson-Kastner notes, "For Augustine the Church is the extension of the Christ in space and time. He is the head and we are his members, and through being joined in communion with him we are admitted to communion with God."[86] Further, one must share in the sacramental life of the Church, for the Holy Spirit and Christ, the great high priest, work through the sacraments.[87] For these reasons, not to mention the communal nature of both humanity and its *summum bonum*, Augustine can conceive of no "individual" life of faith, separated from the Church and its sacraments. As Bonner writes, "for Augustine deification is an ecclesial process, in that it takes place within the communion of the Church, to which the Christian is admitted by baptism. For this reason, it can be called a sacramental process, in that the Christian grows in grace by being nourished by the eucharist, which he receives as part of the worship of the Church."[88]

The Church, then, despite its recognizable imperfections, is the place in which humans, through participation in God by the gift of the Holy Spirit, are reconciled to God and each other. Through this participation, they begin to have their loves and desires reordered

The City of God: A Collection of Critical Essays, ed. Dorothy F. Donnelly (New York: Peter Lang, 1995), p. 58.
83. *Enchiridion* XV, 56; *City of God* X, 7.
84. Nicholas M. Healy, *Church, World and the Christian Life: Practical-Prophetic Ecclesiology* (Cambridge: Cambridge University Press, 2000), p. 55.
85. *Enchiridion* XV, 56; XVII, 65. See also Bonner, "Christ, God, and Man," p. 288; Bonner, "Deification," pp. 375, 383; Patricia Wilson-Kastner, "Grace as Participation in the Divine Life in the Theology of Augustine of Hippo," *Augustinian Studies* 7 (1976), pp. 147–148, 151.
86. Wilson-Kastner, "Grace as Participation," p. 148.
87. On the latter, see *City of God* X, 20.
88. Bonner, "Deification," p. 383.

so that they can again partake of and contribute to the harmonious unity that God intended for His creation. This radical reordering of relationships and loves takes them out of the earthly city and into the City of God, in the sense that their primary identity is now given by their participation in God and His Kingdom. Once they receive the saving love of Christ through the Spirit and become partakers of the divine life, they are citizens of the Holy City of God, abiding as pilgrims in this present life as they seek to live by the love, virtues, and standards of the City which has their primary allegiance.[89] With this change in allegiance, their perception of the earthly city is radically altered. As they go through the present age on pilgrimage, they do not cling to it or its blessings as do those who only know citizenship in the earthly city.[90] Instead, they recognize that a certain degree of contingency marks the goods and customs of the temporal life, including some of the goods that seem most important.[91] They are given a new lens through which to view the disorder, disunity, and lust for power that mark the earthly city, at the same time as they begin to see the differences between the aims and ends of the two cities more distinctly. How does being a citizen of the Heavenly City impact one's view of the earthly city, according to Augustine? How does it affect one's efforts to love, serve, and live in the earthly city? It is to these questions that we now turn.

The two cities: different ends, different goods

The two cities, as we saw above, were created by two kinds of love, so that the Heavenly City is marked by love of God and the earthly city by love of self. This distinction between two loves goes back to Augustine's earliest articulation of the two cities in *The Literal Meaning of Genesis*. This distinction carries with it a host of other differences, as the following passage makes clear:

> These two loves – of which one is holy, the other unclean, one social, the other private, one taking thought for the common good because of the companionship in the upper regions, the other putting even what is common at its own personal disposal because of its lordly arrogance; one of them God's subject, the other his

89. *City of God* XIV, 9.
90. *City of God* I, 29.
91. See *City of God* XIX, 17; *On Christian Doctrine* III, 19–22.

rival, one of them calm, the other turbulent, one peaceable, the other rebellious; one of them setting more store by the truth than by the praises of those who stray from it, the other greedy for praise by whatever means, one friendly, the other jealous, one of them wanting for its neighbor what it wants for itself, the other wanting to subject its neighbor to itself; one of them exercising authority over its neighbor for its neighbor's good, the other for its own – these two loves were first manifested in the angels, one in the good, the other in the bad, and then distinguished the two cities, one of the just, the other of the wicked, founded in the human race under the wonderful and inexpressible providence of God as he administers and directs everything he has created. These two cities are mixed up together in the world while time runs it course, until they are sorted out by the last judgment.[92]

What is it that causes such differences between the two cities, that directs their loves to such different ends? Perhaps it can best be viewed through the lens of humility, for according to Augustine humility leads to dependence on God while humility's opposite, exaltation, leads to domination.[93] As Brown writes, Augustine characterizes "the most basic relationship in the divine order as one of dependence, and so the most basic symptom of the dislocation of this order, as one of domination – of the need to secure the dependence of others."[94] This domination, this *libido dominandi*, marks the earthly city. Indeed, Augustine is so concerned about the predominance of this lust for domination that, as he confesses at the beginning of *City of God*, he "cannot refrain from speaking about the city of this world, a city which aims at dominion, which holds nations in enslavement, but is itself dominated by that very lust of domination."[95]

The Heavenly City is not unaware of or unconcerned with power, but it fails to give power the preeminence it receives in the earthly city and it (ideally, of course) refuses to use the means of domination to achieve power within this world. The City of God gives prominence to justice over power, and to humility over pride, for power is only bad when it becomes an end in itself rather than being referred to the greater good of justice.[96] The challenge is

---

92. *The Literal Meaning of Genesis* XI, 20.
93. *City of God* XIV, 13.
94. Brown, "Political Society," p. 320.
95. *City of God* I, Preface.
96. So Augustine can write of the "power of humility" in *City of God* I, Preface.

convincing the proud that humility is the way to true power, meaning power that is subsumed under the greater good of justice rather than pursued for its own sake. The mistake of the devil, according to Augustine, was precisely the desire to play the power game rather than the justice game, while the means to overcome his authority comes through and in imitation of Jesus Christ who prioritized justice over power:

> The essential flaw of the devil's perversion made him a lover of power and a deserter and assailant of justice, which means that men imitate him all the more thoroughly the more they neglect or even detest justice and studiously devote themselves to power, rejoicing at the possession of it or inflamed with the desire for it. So it pleased God to deliver man from the devil's authority by beating him at the justice game, not the power game, so that men too might imitate Christ by seeking to beat the devil at the justice game, not the power game. Not that power is to be shunned as something bad, but that the right order might be preserved which puts justice first.[97]

What happens when power is placed over justice? The fall of Rome, for one thing, for the lust for power found in the Roman people "first established its victory in a few powerful individuals, and then crushed the rest of an exhausted country beneath the yoke of slavery."[98] The love of domination, which Augustine describes as the greed for praise and glory, became the primary concern of the Romans, when it was love of justice that would have served them better.[99] Augustine counsels people not to pursue lives of honor or power, nor to pursue high position, unless it is done under the compulsion of love or for the sake of promoting the well-being of the people.[100] For the truth is that all power belongs to God ("what, after all, could be more powerful than the all-powerful, or what creature's power could be compared with the creator's?"[101]), but in God a radical inversion of the human understanding of power takes place. Jesus Christ incarnate, instead of demonstrating the power of dominion that comes from pride, exhibits the power of charity that results from humility. This is evident in the "marvellous

97. *The Trinity* XIII, 17.
98. *City of God* I, 30.
99. *City of God* V, 13, 14.
100. *City of God* XIX, 19.
101. *The Trinity* XIII, 17.

gentleness" of Jesus as he interacts with the woman caught in adultery (this passage from John, it is worth noting, is one Augustine often uses to examine the nature of judicial authority):

> He brought the truth, then, as a teacher, gentleness as a liberator, justice as a judge. That's why the prophet foretold that he would reign in the Holy Spirit. When he spoke, his truth won recognition; when he wasn't roused against his enemies, his gentleness won praise. His enemies, then, were tormented by spite and hatred because of these two, his truth and his gentleness, and they put a stumbling-block in the path of the third, his justice.[102]

For Augustine, truth, gentleness, and justice belong together, as they are embodied together in Jesus Christ, and they take priority over and transform common understandings of power.[103]

This is all part of Augustine's understanding of order, in which higher goods are to be preferred to lower goods and all things enjoyed for the sake of God. The original divine order was one of perfect justice; when goods are used for the wrong ends or prioritized incorrectly (e.g., if power is placed over justice), then not only

---

102. "Commentary on the gospel of John, 33" 419/421, 4, in *Augustine: Political Writings* (p. 103).

103. This may be the best place to address how, in light of this emphasis in his thought, Augustine later came to endorse the use of coercion to bring Donatists back into the Catholic Church. We must first remember, as Peter Brown helpfully reminds us, that Augustine lived in an age of intolerance, in which "religious intolerance was part and parcel of the peculiar nature of the exercise of power in late antiquity" ("The Limits of Intolerance," in *Authority and the Sacred: Aspects of the Christianisation of the Roman World* [Cambridge: Cambridge University Press, 1995], p. 53; pp. 27–54). To endorse coercion at all, however, represents a significant shift in Augustine's thinking; his earlier writings are concerned not with forced conversion but with persuasion (see, for example, "Of True Religion" xvi, 31 and *On Christian Doctrine*, esp. IV). Augustine himself writes that his "opinion originally was that no one should be forced to the unity of Christ, but that we should act with words, fight with arguments, and conquer by reason," and yet his thinking was changed by the examples of Donatists who seemed to be thankful to have been coercively returned to the Catholic church ("they give thanks that they have been reformed and freed from this disastrous madness. Those who used to hate now love."). See Letter 93, in *Letters 1–99*, trans. Roland Teske, S. J., ed. John E. Rotelle, O.S.A. (Hyde Park, NY: New City Press, 2001) (p. 387) and Letter 185, in *Augustine: Political Writings* (p. 176). It may help, too, to remember that Augustine's views on coercion developed in response to particular situations rather than taking shape as a fixed theory, and that he would never have anticipated the degree to which his writings would be appealed to to justify religious persecution in later times (see introduction to *Augustine: Political Writings*, p. xxiii). For these reasons, Eric Gregory's assessment that religious coercion is not a conceptual requirement of Augustine's political thought seems a valid one (Eric Sean Gregory, "Love and Citizenship: Augustine and the Ethics of Liberalism" [Ph.D. dissertation, Yale University, 2002], p. 9).

is the divine order disrupted but justice is not upheld.[104] For this reason, it is only in relation to God that true justice can be realized, for only through Jesus Christ can a people's disordered loves and priorities be reordered, can power and domination be subsumed under justice and love. The only association, therefore, in which justice will be found is one in which people are united in love for God and love for neighbor:

> It follows that justice is found where God, the one supreme God, rules an obedient City according to His grace, forbidding sacrifice to any being save himself alone; and where in consequence the soul rules the body in all men who belong to this City and obey God, and the reason faithfully rules the vices in a lawful system of subordination; so that just as the individual righteous man lives on the basis of faith which is active in love, so the association, or people, of righteous men lives on the same basis of faith, active in love, the love with which a man loves God as God ought to be loved, and loves his neighbour as himself.[105]

In short, the only city that is capable of true justice is that which has Jesus Christ as its founder and ruler, namely the City of God.[106] To put it another way, as Robert Dodaro writes, "Augustine maintains that justice cannot be known except in Christ, and that, as founder (*conditor*) and ruler (*rector*), Christ forms the just society in himself. United with Christ, members of his body constitute the whole, just Christ (*Christus totus iustus*), which is the city of God, the true commonwealth, and the locus for the revelation of justice."[107]

This understanding of justice leads Augustine to deny that the Roman commonwealth of which Cicero wrote actually existed, according to Cicero's definition of a commonwealth as "the weal of the people" in which the people are an "association of men united by a common sense of right." For without true justice there can be no true right, no common sense of right around which people can unite. "The irresistible conclusion" Augustine reaches is that "where there is no justice there is no commonwealth."[108] While

104. *City of God* XIX, 13.
105. Ibid. 23.
106. *City of God* II, 21.
107. Robert Dodaro, *Christ and the Just Society in the Thought of Augustine* (Cambridge: Cambridge University Press, 2004), p. 72.
108. *City of God* XIX, 21.

Cicero would agree that a society requires justice, Augustine finds his conception of justice wanting, asking "what kind of justice is it that takes a man away from the true God ... ?"[109] For, as we have just seen, a man's loves need to be reordered in relation to God for justice to be realized. If the justice of a people depends upon the justice of the individuals who comprise that people, and if individuals cannot be just unless they participate in God, how can a society that turns people away from God ever be truly just? The upshot for Augustine is that "if a soul does not serve God it cannot with any kind of justice command the body, nor can a man's reason control the vicious elements in the soul. And if there is no justice in such a man, there can be no sort of doubt that there is no justice in a gathering which consists of such men."[110]

Based on this view of justice, it is of no surprise that Augustine does not restrict his critique of a lack of justice to Rome, but expands it to include Athens, Babylon, and any city that does not have God as its ruler and the common basis of its faith and love, meaning any city that is not the City of God. Augustine does provide an alternative definition of a people, one that depends not on a common weal or sense of right but on "a common agreement about the objects of its love."[111] In this way a people can be a people even if it is devoid of justice, identified by examining the objects of its loves. One love that is sure to be found within every city is a love of peace, for desire for peace is a part of human nature, and even in war peace and victory are the ultimate goals.[112] Indeed, Augustine believes that "peace is so great a good that even in relation to the affairs of earth and of our mortal state no word ever falls more gratefully upon the ear, nothing is desired with greater longing, in fact, nothing better can be found."[113] Earthly cities seek peace, and even attain it at times, and such peace is to be enjoyed as a good and as a gift from God.[114] Earthly peace can indeed be considered the single aim of the many diverse customs, laws, and institutions of various nations. And yet if this peace is sought after for its own sake or for the sake of lower rather than higher goods, "if the higher

109. Ibid.
110. Ibid.
111. Ibid., 24.
112. Ibid., 11.
113. *City of God* XIV, 11.
114. *City of God* XV, 4.

goods are neglected, which belong to the City on high, where victory will be serene in the enjoyment of eternal and perfect peace ... , the inevitable consequence is fresh misery."[115]

The problems that arise in the pursuit of peace come when people prefer a prideful peace of injustice to the just peace of God. Under the just peace of God all would have equality under God's rule, but under the unjust peace of pride some humans seek to impose their will and dominion on others.[116] In light of these conditions, the earthly city can only aim at an earthly peace; the harmony to which it is limited is that of a compromise between human wills about things pertaining to the mortal life. The peace of the Heavenly City, by contrast, "is the perfectly ordered and harmonious fellowship in the enjoyment of God, and of each other in God."[117] It is a peace of immortality, given once humans arrive at that state where life no longer ends in death but lasts for the eternal enjoyment of God and one's neighbor in God.[118] Augustine believes that "the Supreme Good of the City of God is everlasting and perfect peace," writing "we could say of peace, as we have said of eternal life, that it is the final fulfilment of all our goods."[119] All of this leads Augustine to conclude that the peace of the earthly city does not compare to the peace of the Heavenly City, "which is so truly peaceful that it should be regarded as the only peace deserving the name."[120]

This peace of the Heavenly City, despite its eschatological nature, is relevant for pilgrims in the earthly city. At the least, this is because Augustine believes peace to be a necessary prerequisite for the creation of humans, who "could have no existence without some kind of peace as the condition of their being."[121] Furthermore, citizens of the Heavenly City look forward in hope to their promised peace, even as they enjoy and use the peace of the earthly city while they are on pilgrimage in this world. Hope for the fulfillment of the heavenly peace provides strength to pilgrims in the face of the lack of peace found in the temporal world; without hope of the

115. Ibid.
116. *City of God* XIX, 12.
117. Ibid., 17.
118. Ibid., 17, 13.
119. Ibid., 20, 11.
120. Ibid., 17.
121. Ibid., 13.

realization of a greater good in the age to come, present reality turns into misery and despair.[122] As Augustine writes,

> We see, then, that the Supreme Good of the City of God is ever-lasting and perfect peace, which is not the peace through which men pass in their mortality, in their journey from birth to death, but that peace in which they remain in their immortal state, experiencing no adversity at all. In view of this, can anyone deny that this is the supremely blessed life, or that the present life on earth, however full it may be of the greatest possible blessings of soul and body and of external circumstances, is, in comparison, most miserable? For all that, if anyone accepts the present life in such a spirit that he uses it with the end in view of that other life on which he has set his heart with all his ardour and for which he hopes with all his confidence, such a man may without absurdity be called happy even now, though rather by future hope than in present reality. Present reality without that hope is, to be sure, a false happiness, in fact, an utter misery.[123]

According to one scholar, Augustine's emphasis on living in hope is a "profound change" that may in fact signal the end of classical thought, in which the emphasis was instead on what people could do and achieve.[124] It is true that Augustine's understanding of hope and the eschatological realization of peace give him reason to be cautious about what can be achieved within the earthly city. For this eschatological emphasis within Augustine does not, as Eugene TeSelle points out, mean that the Heavenly City needs to be constructed on this earth, nor that the earthly city is to be transformed into the Heavenly City.[125] Quite the opposite, for the realization of the Heavenly City belongs to the age to come rather than to this age. Citizens of the Heavenly City, while here on earth in the *saeculum*, instead of trying to force the eschatological peace of the Heavenly City, can and should enjoy the earthly peace of the earthly city as a good from God, as a good suitable to the temporal life and one they seek to foster, even as they recognize that it is not the highest good for which they hope. The conclusion to which all of this points is that, for Augustine, the earthly city is neither the ultimate

---

122. *City of God* XV, 18, 21; Letter 155, in *Augustine: Political Writings* (p. 92).
123. *City of God* XIX, 20.
124. Brown, "Political Society," p. 323.
125. Eugene TeSelle, "Towards an Augustinian Politics," *The Journal of Religious Ethics* 16 (1988), p. 102.

community nor the primary frame of reference, and it should not be looked to for the realization of the goals of peace, justice, and love that can only be realized in the Heavenly City. This is not to deny that the earthly city has its necessary place and role, but rather to keep from placing false hopes in what can be accomplished in the *saeculum*. And this is no small thing, as Cochrane notes, because while not destroying the structures of the earthly city, it enables them to be viewed in a new light, in which the "state" is seen "no longer as the ultimate form of community, but merely as an instrument for regulating the relations of what Augustine calls the 'exterior' man."[126]

The answer to what all of this means for the relationship of citizens of the Heavenly City to the earthly city lies somewhere in between the two extremes of completely abandoning the earthly city and looking to the earthly city to achieve utopian-like harmony and peace. Augustine is clear that citizens of the Heavenly City share in the goods of the earthly city, making use of its earthly peace and helping to defend and sustain the limited harmony that is possible in the earthly city, "a kind of compromise between human wills about things relevant to mortal life."[127] The harmony and order that can be achieved in the earthly city, though they may be perversions of God's original intentions for creation, are still part of God's order for the fallen world. For "even what is perverted must of necessity be in, or derived from, or associated with ... some part of the order of things among which it has its being or of which it consists. Otherwise it would not exist at all."[128] So every disorder is predicated on a prior order, and even the most disordered persons and institutions do not fall outside of the providence of God.[129] The earthly city can, then, achieve limited goods, even if not the greatest goods for which humankind was created. And citizens of the Heavenly City can help foster those goods in the many different earthly cities in which they find themselves.

As these citizens contribute to the goods of their earthly cities, they need not try to force their different earthly cities into one

126. Cochrane, *Christianity and Classical Culture*, p. 509.
127. *City of God* XIX, 17.
128. Ibid., 12. See also Oliver O'Donovan, "Augustine's *City of God* XIX and Western Political Thought," in *The City of God: A Collection of Critical Essays*, ed. Dorothy F. Donnelly (New York: Peter Lang, 1995), p. 143.
129. See *City of God* IV, 35; V, 1. See also Deane, "Augustine and the State," p. 67.

supposedly God-prescribed political arrangement. For when Augustine offered a definition of a "people" based on its common loves rather than the realization of true justice, he opened a way for a variety of political institutions and societies with different concerns and ends to be considered a "people" or a *res publica*, even if they cannot attain the true justice for which humankind was created. That is to say, no one political arrangement or order is prescribed by the Christian faith, or, as Williams puts it, "no particular *ordo* is identical with the order of God's city, and so no state can rightly be defended as an absolute 'value' in itself."[130] A variety of political arrangements can produce earthly peace and justice, limited as those ends are, so citizens of the Heavenly City are not to seek a utopian political arrangement for this age. On the contrary, the Heavenly City transcends earthly political arrangements, even as she shares them:

> While this Heavenly City, therefore, is on pilgrimage in this world, she calls out citizens from all nations and so collects a society of aliens, speaking all languages. She takes no account of any difference in customs, laws, and institutions, by which earthly peace is achieved and preserved – not that she annuls or abolishes any of those, rather, she maintains them and follows them (for whatever divergences there are among the diverse nations, those institutions have one single aim – earthly peace), provided that no hindrance is presented thereby to the religion which teaches that the one supreme and true God is to be worshipped[131]

Citizens of the Heavenly City can and should follow the laws and institutions of their earthly cities for the sake of earthly peace, so long as they do not hinder the worship of the God who provides their true *summum bonum*.

Does Augustine really call these citizens to be involved in the earthly city given his understanding of the disordered power and domination that mark and define it? Augustine recognizes the degree to which injustice and the *libido dominandi* are inevitably part of political and civil life, he laments it, particularly when it comes to the need for judges and judgments against fellow humans, and yet he still maintains that some are called to be involved in the political

---

130. Williams, "Politics and the Soul," p. 66. See also Deane, "Augustine and the State," p. 55.
131. *City of God* XIX, 17.

and judicial life of the earthly city.[132] Indeed, they are called to be
involved as Christians, bringing their faith and their perspective to
bear on their positions. This becomes particularly clear in his correspondence, as he writes to Christian judges and proconsuls to be
as gentle and humble as possible, to soften their judgments as much
as they can without promoting injustice, to observe the humanity of
those who are being judged, and to set an example of Christian faith
and gentleness.[133] When, to use Williams' language, a member of
the City of God is called to be in a position of power in the earthly
city, Augustine believes that he or she "continues in a practice of
nurturing souls already learned in more limited settings."[134]
Augustine goes even further than this, believing that Christians
bring unique and beneficial contributions to the earthly city
because of their humility, their mercy, their desire to place justice
above power and to love the Heavenly City more than the earthly
city.[135] As Williams argues, for Augustine it is only a Christian ruler
who can truly safeguard political values because only such a ruler
can resist the temptations of the *libido dominandi* in light of the
recognition that political values and all else are ultimately safe-
guarded by God in God's providence.[136] This does not mean that
Augustine found ready examples of such restrained Christian rulers
in his time. According to Dodaro, Augustine looks for models of civic
virtue in the saints: figures such as Job, David, Peter, and Paul
"openly confess their sins while also praising God for his forgiveness
and for the strength to live in his virtue."[137] Neither does this mean
that a Christian ruler is called to make the political realm itself
Christian. Indeed, such a task would be impossible exactly because of
the injustice and *libido dominandi* that always mark the earthly city
and the individuals of which it is comprised. As Herbert A. Deane
writes, no matter how pious or well-intentioned a ruler might be,
"the state itself – the political order – can never be truly just."[138]

---

132. See Ibid., 5, 6. See also Peter J. Burnell, "The Problem of Service to Unjust
Regimes in Augustine's *City of God*," in *The City of God: A Collection of Critical
Essays*, ed. Dorothy F. Donnelly (New York: Peter Lang, 1995), pp. 37-49.
133. See, for example, his letters to Marcellinus (133 and 139), Apringius (135),
and Macedonius (152-155), in *Augustine: Political Writings* (pp. 61-99).
134. Williams, "Politics and the Soul," p. 68.
135. See *City of God* V, 24. N.B.
136. Williams, "Politics and the Soul," p. 67.
137. Dodaro, *Christ and the Just Society*, p. 183; see pp. 182-214.
138. Deane, "Augustine and the State," p. 63; see also pp. 56-58, 62-66.

To draw this discussion together, let us summarize what we have concluded thus far. Because of the fallen nature of the world and the eschatological nature of the Heavenly City, citizens of the Heavenly City, while they are on pilgrimage here on earth, do not look to the earthly city for the realization of true justice, peace, order, or harmony. Instead, they experience the firstfruits of the reordering of their loves and relationships through participation in God through Jesus Christ and Christ's Body, the Church. On their pilgrimage they are part of the earthly city and share some of its earthly goods, they accept calls to positions within the earthly city, and yet they do not view the earthly city as their primary community, nor do they view its arrangements as ultimate or final. Indeed, an awareness of the passing, contingent nature of the temporal world provides a basis for not treating its contingent arrangements as natural or inevitable, thereby providing a basis from which they can question the *status quo*.[139] The recognition that earthly peace and the institutions and laws that contribute to that peace are a good desired by heavenly citizens supplies sufficient motivation for the pilgrims of the Heavenly City to support and engage the temporal world. At the same time, their involvement with the earthly city is tempered by their citizenship in the City of God, for they refer lower temporal goods to the greater goods of their eternal God. As Augustine writes:

> it is clear that when we live according to God our mind should be intent on his invisible things and thus progressively be formed from his eternity, truth and charity, and yet that some of our rational attention, that is to say some of the same mind, has to be directed to the utilization of changeable and bodily things without which this life cannot be lived; this however not in order to be *conformed to this world* (Rom 12:2) by setting up such goods as the final goal and twisting our appetite for happiness onto them, but in order to do whatever we do in the reasonable use of temporal things with an

139. For more on how Augustine's eschatological perspective makes his political perspective "radical" and critical, see R. A. Markus, *Saeculum: History and Society in the Theology of St Augustine* (London: Cambridge University Press, 1970), pp. 168–170. Not all agree on this point, noting that Augustine's skepticism towards the possibility of any significant change in the human situation and his lack of an account of an ideal earthly city may have prevented him from imagining, for example, the possibility of a world without slavery. See TeSelle, "Towards an Augustinian Politics," pp. 92–93; Williams, "Politics and the Soul," pp. 63, 67.

eye to the acquisition of eternal things, passing by the former on
the way, setting our hearts on the latter to the end.[140]

Citizens of the Heavenly City are never to forget that to seek the
goods of the earthly city for their own sake is to seek disorder, but
to pursue the goods of the Heavenly City through participation in
God is to pursue that which enables God's diverse creation to come
together in unity, harmony, justice, equality, and love, the firstfruits
of which can be tasted even now.

This immersion into the ontology that underlies Augustine's
thought reveals a remarkably different picture of the nature of
reality and human being than those that inform contemporary
political theory. This different ontology leads to a distinct understanding of the political realm and what can and cannot be accomplished through it. It, likewise, leads to different pictures of how
the diversity of creation can be reharmonized and reunited. How
might these pictures help us as we contemplate how to engage with
difference within contemporary society? What might Augustine's
ontology have to offer to our current political imagination? The
following chapter attempts to answer these questions by putting
Augustine's thought into conversation with the political theorists of
our previous chapters and with contemporary theologians who are
concerned with similar matters.

140. *The Trinity* XII, 21.

5
───────

Towards a theology of public conversation

Introduction

Let us review where in our story we were before the "theological turn" of the last chapter, after we had listened to some of the conversation happening within political theory about ways to picture collective life marked by deep diversity. We were, in fact, in a bit of a quandary. We agreed with the agonist political theorists that the theory of political liberalism entails quite a bit more, ontologically speaking, than political liberals want to admit, and results in a theory that is neither as tolerant nor as inclusive as they desire it to be. Like the post-Nietzscheans, we desired a way to move forward that more honestly recognizes and respects the particularity of the differences in our midst. Unlike the post-Nietzscheans, however, we were unconvinced that ontologies deeply rooted in conflict and power can sustain the ethos they commend. We raised serious questions about the necessary dichotomization such theorists posit between unity and diversity, harmony and particularity, wondering if an unmitigated celebration of difference enables us to identify harmful differences or move beyond current political, cultural, and religious divisions and polarizations to a workable collective life. We hoped that our political imagination would benefit from considering an ontology that is distinctly Christian, rooted in a Trinitarian understanding of God as the source and redeemer of reality, creation, and human being. Towards this end, in an effort to supplement the ontological turn begun by post-Nietzschean political theorists with a theological turn, we immersed ourselves in the voice of Augustine of Hippo, well known to be one of the most influential political and social theorists in Western history.

In this chapter, we will draw the different voices to which we have been listening together, putting a theological ontology into conversation with the ontologies of political liberals and post-Nietzscheans. Our goal is to discern if a way exists to move beyond liberal tolerance and an agonistic celebration of difference. Such a way can be found, according to Augustine, but not in our current political society or any earthly city. If Augustine is right, this has significant implications for conversations within political theory. These implications are explored in the first part of this chapter, in which Augustine's belief that the Heavenly City is the only place in which difference can be fully recognized, respected, and embraced is linked with our need to limit our expectations for what can be accomplished in our "earthly" political structures. From there, we move into a conversation with another theologian who has attempted to posit a unique relationship between Christianity and difference, namely John Milbank. Milbank draws heavily upon Augustine, but his reappropriation of Augustine's thought looks rather different than ours, in ways that are illuminating for the present discussion and make a brief excursus into his thought worthwhile.

We then turn to look again at this question of the Heavenly City vis-à-vis the earthly city. If it is necessary to remember that certain realities of our ontological condition prevent us from being able to find unity and celebrate difference to the degree we would like to within the political realm, then what can we try to accomplish within political society? More specifically, as Christians how are we to think about the earthly city and its connection to the Church? And how can we assure those who are not part of the Church that our belief in the necessity of Jesus Christ for the reconciliation and recognition of differences does not mean that we intend to make our political societies into Christian theocracies, even as we hope for a political life which welcomes the particularity of Christianity alongside other particularities? To begin to answer these questions, we explore the nature of the relationship between the Church and the political realm by putting Augustine into conversation with Milbank and Karl Barth. We then turn to look more specifically at contemporary Western political society, for if critics are right that today's liberalism does not allow for the differences of its constituents to be recognized, this has surely impacted Christianity

as well. Part of this discussion takes place by trying to articulate what sort of relationship between Christianity and the political realm would allow Christianity to be true to its particularity as a public, social, embodied reality. This is undertaken both for the sake of the Church as it tries to make sense of its calling and place within a pluralist, liberal, "tolerant" society and for the sake of other constituencies who are trying to bring their particularity to bear in public life. The final section offers a picture of how these different particularities might come together in rich conversation within the earthly city. This will not be an attempt to attain the celebration and reconciliation of diversity that are only possible in the Heavenly City, nor to find in Christianity a political theory for the earthly city, but it will be hopeful of deep conversation of word and practice rooted in the particular identities of differences who reside alongside each other in contemporary life. Such conversation both acknowledges particularity and enables diverse constituencies to genuinely learn from each other, in ways that allow for the possibility of persuasion, change, and even conversion. This picture of conversation does not solve all of the problems we face in our attempts to find a degree of unity in the midst of our diversity, but it does move us a little closer to humbly and charitably engaging and reconciling – rather than tolerating, ignoring, or indiscriminatorily celebrating – our differences.

Augustine's ontology: beyond tolerance

When we turned to Augustine in the last chapter, we discovered a vastly different picture of the nature of reality and human being than that uncovered in the ontologies of political liberals and post-Nietzscheans. If we have been on a quest to imagine a society that is marked by more than tolerance, in which particularity comes together in community while still being retained, respected, and even encouraged, then the theological ontology found in Augustine offers a way towards the fulfillment of our quest. In an Augustinian view, such imaginings can become reality, but only in the society known as the Heavenly City, understood both ecclesiastically and eschatologically. The Kingdom of God has been inaugurated and members of the Church already participate in and witness to its firstfruits, and yet the full realization of the City marked by love,

embrace, and a peaceful coming together of difference will not occur in this *saeculum*. If we look for these goals to be fulfilled in the here and now, in the earthly city or the nation-state or the global world, we will be sorely disappointed. We may even be dangerously motivated to seek something that is beyond the reach of fallen human nature. At the least, we will remain in the place in which we find ourselves now, after two hundred or so years of the liberal democratic experiment, wondering, along with Charles Taylor, what sources can underlie and sustain our far-reaching commitments to benevolence, justice, tolerance, and, now, difference.[1] In short, political society cannot be the site of the fulfillment of utopian dreams of harmony in the midst of diversity. This side of the fall, even with the far-reaching consequences of the cross and the ever-important role of hope in sustaining the society known as the Church, we dare not look for too much in the earthly city.

It is not difficult to see just how different the picture of the world presented by Augustine is from the pictures considered in earlier chapters. Harmony, order, peace, kinship, and love are at the heart of God's design for the created, and redeemed, world. Underlying all the conflict, struggles for power, and disunity evident in this world a deeper harmony remains, a harmony visible in the Trinity, and offered to humans through participation in the Trinity. Life as it should be consists of neither primordial conflict, as for the post-Nietzscheans, nor individuals in a state of scarcity, as for political liberals. These are contingent results of the fall of humanity but they do not have to comprise humanity's primary reality. Indeed the situation is quite the contrary, for the Christian believer.

For Augustine, creation is marked by a diversity of people (from the One came the many), a diversity that results from the fullness and abundance of God's own being and is united as one in love for God and each other. All being is gift, flowing from God's goodness; humanity was meant to forever live in the enjoyment of God's goodness, in conditions marked by ease and plenty, abundance and joy, and love and harmony between God and humanity and between all creatures. In Augustine's view, God purposefully had the creation of humankind begin with just one person so that all people would

---

1. Taylor, *Sources of the Self*, p. 515.

"be bound together by a kind of tie of kinship to form a harmonious unity"[2] and "to show to mankind how pleasing to him is unity in plurality."[3] We fail to see this kinship and this unity in plurality when we have ceased to live in the harmony for which we were created, when we have turned away from God and each other to ourselves, when, in short, we see ourselves fundamentally as individuals.

This is clearly a different picture of humanity from that with which John Rawls, Richard Rorty, Chantal Mouffe, and William Connolly are operating. For Rawls and Rorty, the individual rightly and unapologetically forms the basis of their political theory and ontology. For Mouffe and Connolly, though they attempt to eschew an emphasis on the individual that comes at the expense of communal identities, concern for respect of the individual still provides a foundational motivation for their thought. The very language of the individual, standing alone, conceivable apart from social existence and a common *summum bonum*, is foreign to Augustine's understanding of the way humanity ought to be. Indeed, God's creative purpose was to have a united, harmonious people; through the grace offered by and through Jesus Christ, humans can be restored to a right relationship with both God and the family that God began in creation, becoming God's children by the Holy Spirit.

For those who accept the free gift of grace offered by Jesus Christ through the Holy Spirit, their identity becomes rooted in being a part of God's family and community. They are first and foremost children of God, citizens of the Heavenly City, abiding as pilgrims in this present life. To use the Pauline language of Scripture, they have been rescued and transferred into the kingdom of the beloved Son; they are citizens with the saints and members of the household of God; their citizenship is now in heaven.[4] They still live in the earthly city, but they no longer view themselves primarily as individual citizens of political society. They will not have the same hopes for what can be accomplished in the earthly city, that is to say in political society, that citizens of the earthly city might have. The political society or nation-state in which they happen to find themselves will not be viewed as ultimate, nor will it provide their telos, their hope, or their common good. At the same time, they will

2. *City of God* XIV, 1.
3. *City of God* XII, 23.
4. Col. 1: 13–14; Eph. 2: 19–20; Phil. 3:20, NRSV.

not have the same hopelessness as the post-Nietzscheans, for they believe that the grace of God is present in the earthly city even as they wait in faith and hope for the eschatological peacefulness of the City of God.

Citizens of the Heavenly City can and should contribute to the earthly city and its goods of peace and justice, recognizing that such goods are worthy of pursuit while at the same time acknowledging their limits. The justice and peace of the earthly city are not the same as the justice and peace that are theirs in part and will one day be theirs in full through participation in the Triune God. As we saw in the last chapter, for Augustine, true justice and true peace, true equality and true harmony, can only be realized in relation to God. The harmony, equality, peace, and justice for which we work in this age are hardly, if even, shadows of that which can be found through Jesus Christ in the Heavenly City, partially visible in the Church now, reaching true fulfillment in the age to come. All of these ideas are linked and inseparable for Augustine: the just peace of the Heavenly City "is the perfectly ordered and harmonious fellowship in the enjoyment of God, and of each other in God,"[5] in which all people are equal. In this understanding, and therefore for citizens of the Heavenly City, neither justice nor peace, neither harmony nor equality, can be attained outside of a right relationship with God that restores the disorder that marks the fallen world and earthly city and reorders the disordered loves and goods of fallen humanity. This means that any attempt to, for example, achieve complete harmony in the midst of diversity outside of the context of the Trinity is doomed to failure.

The question of diversity and harmony has been at the heart of this study: how are we, in a political society marked by pluralism, going to find ways to either tolerate each other or move beyond tolerance to a deep respect of the particularity of the difference we encounter? We have seen and questioned how political liberalism answers this question, and we have likewise seen and questioned the response of agonistic political theorists. Indeed, at the end of the third chapter, we were left still looking for answers, for there seems to be little hope of achieving what the post-Nietzscheans desire on the basis of the ontology and ethos they provide. This is what

5. *City of God* XIX, 17.

prompted our turn to Augustine, to see if the ontology that under-girds his thought might provide us with some answers, with ways to expand our pluralist political imagination that move us beyond the strict dichotomies of unity and diversity, harmony and plurality. In what sense and to what degree can we respect difference *and* be a unified political entity? We can start to answer this question by noting that we need not assume, as the post-Nietzscheans do, that unity is equivalent to homogeneity or uniformity, nor that unity and diversity are at odds with one another. As Oliver O'Donovan helpfully writes, "We should never allow ourselves to speak of a 'contrast' or 'tension' between unity and diversity. Diversity is the historical content of unity, the material in which the unity becomes concrete."[6] The world in its complexity, O'Donovan goes on to say, reflects the creator's unity. And the church, in its diversity, is unified in the word of God that acknowledges Jesus as his Son. A Christian ontology, rooted in the Triune God who both creates and redeems the manifold diversity of this earth, provides a way for unity and diversity to be reconciled without either one being lost. As Robert Jenson notes, "Humanity's End is a perfectly mutual community between differentiated persons, foundationally enacted by the Spirit as the love of the Father and the incarnate Son ... We will be as different from one another as the Father is different from the Son; just as such we will be perfectly united to one another by the Spirit."[7]

Where does this reconciliation between unity and diversity take place? On an Augustinian view, the Heavenly City is the only place where unity and diversity can truly coincide. Jean Bethke Elshtain is right to acknowledge that "to celebrate unity within the diversity of sentient humanity, and diversity within the unity, is a central feature of Augustine's work,"[8] yet she is not careful in articulating that, for Augustine, such a celebration is only possible through participation in the Christ who reconciles the One and the many. Through Christ we rediscover the kinship that exists between all of humanity, we become part of God's family, we move away from our

6. O'Donovan, *Desire of the Nations*, p. 177.
7. Robert W. Jenson, *Systematic Theology*, vol. 2, The Works of God (New York: Oxford University Press, 1999), p. 319.
8. Jean Bethke Elshtain, *Augustine and the Limits of Politics* (Notre Dame, IN: University of Notre Dame Press, 1995), pp. 43–44.

private self-absorption to concern for the other and the common good. Reconciliation to God through Christ and the Holy Spirit provides the only way for humans to move beyond toleration of difference or narcissistic celebration of difference to love for each other in the midst of difference. The more far-reaching goals desired by the post-Nietzscheans can, ironically, only be realized through Christ. Without belief that the diversity of creation is God-given, created by God through Christ, we do not have enough to sustain the belief that diversity is a good to be cherished and embraced. Without the redemption of creation by God through Christ, we have no ability to see that the diversity of creation is at the same time a beautifully, interconnected harmony. Without the promise of Christ's return, we have no hope that the Heavenly City will one day come down from heaven to earth, uniting great multitudes from all nations, tribes, peoples, and languages before Christ their King.[9]

This picture of diversity unified around common purpose and worship does not, contrary to popular belief, require homogeneity. Another look at Augustine's picture of the Heavenly City should amply reveal this:

> while ... on pilgrimage in this world, she calls out citizens from all
> nations and so collects a society of aliens, speaking all languages.
> She takes no account of any difference in customs, laws, and
> institutions, by which earthly peace is achieved and preserved – not
> that she annuls or abolishes any of those, rather, she maintains
> them and follows them (for whatever divergences there are among
> the diverse nations, those institutions have one single aim – earthly
> peace), provided that no hindrance is presented thereby to the
> religion which teaches that the one supreme and true God is to be
> worshipped.[10]

United in Christ, differences of nationality and culture cease to be divisive without thereby ceasing to exist. In other words, such differences are taken seriously in their particularity while simultaneously being recognized as contingent rather than ultimate. Furthermore, no national identity is seen as absolute, and no political system as beyond questioning. Such identities and systems can always be queried and critiqued in terms of how well they are upholding the ideals which they are intended to uphold, whether

9. See Rev. 7:9; 21:1-4, NRSV.
10. *City of God* XIX, 17.

that be peace, justice, or respect for difference. An Augustinian perspective on the earthly city can provide just the sort of questioning of the status quo that is of such importance to our post-Nietzscheans, as well as provide deep reasons to limit the role of nation-states in defining identities and subsuming local cultures. Robert Dodaro identifies just this sort of legacy in Augustine, "one capable of offering at least a partial antidote to the ideological pull of statehood, race, philosophy and religion, class and national security."[11] Dodaro locates this "antidote" in Augustine's view of the ongoing confessional nature of humanity: because we are sinful, we must accept responsibility for contributing to the breakdown of harmony in society, we must look to see the reflections of our images in the images of our enemies, and we must try to be reconciled with those images. To put it differently, there are connections between humanity, in its createdness, sinfulness, and redemption, that far surpass the connections that arise from a common nation-state or class identity. And yet the deeper kinship that comes from God and through participation in God does not erase local customs and national identities that are in some sense constitutive of persons and practices.

Stepping back for a moment, we have well seen by now that how one understands and views difference is related to one's deepest beliefs about the nature of reality and human being. This project has disclosed some very different approaches to difference, which in turn yield very different political suggestions. As Rowan Williams writes,

> The question of how we are to construe difference is in the long run a metaphysical one; that is, it is not a question that can be settled by appeal to a tangible state of affairs or set of facts, yet at the same time not a question that can be relegated to a matter of taste or private judgement, since the matter is one that ... shapes decisively the way in which political options are understood.[12]

In political liberalism, for example, the fact of pluralism is precisely that, a fact, to be acknowledged and accommodated, whereas in post-Nietzschean political theory, pluralism is a condition to be celebrated and cultivated in the name of ever-increasing respect for

11. Robert Dodaro, "Augustine's Secular City," in *Augustine and His Critics*, ed. Robert Dodaro and George Lawless (London: Routledge, 2000), p. 251.
12. Rowan D. Williams, "Between Politics and Metaphysics: Reflections in the Wake of Gillian Rose," *Modern Theology* 11, no. 1 (January 1995), p. 5.

difference. When it comes to Christianity, it is a commonplace that Christianity is opposed to difference, inasmuch as it purports to offer the one way to universal truth to which all people must adhere in order to find salvation. We, however, have tried to show that Christianity and difference do not inherently conflict with one another. As O'Donovan remarks, "it is not a Christian or a Jewish view that sin is difference ... Plural self-consciousness is not itself the fall."[13]

At the same time, Christianity does not offer an unequivocal endorsement of all kinds of difference, nor does it focus on difference to the exclusion of humanity's commonalities. As we think of Augustine's ontology, it may be helpful to identify two views of difference, one "positive" and one "negative." Some differences are part of God's very purposes for creation, part of God's overflowing abundance and generosity, to be celebrated and recognized both now and evermore (i.e., positive difference). Other levels and kinds of difference are understood to be a result of the fall of humanity, to be divisive and contrary to God's created purposes for humanity. Such differences will remain with us in the earthly city, not as a cause for celebration but as a fact of this fallen world (i.e., negative difference). This is what makes the post-Nietzscheans nervous, for they view any attempt to curtail difference as a sign of a misuse of power in the name of self-protection and self-aggrandizement. Yet we must all surely recognize that unlimited difference is neither plausible nor desirable, and that too much emphasis on our own particularity can lead to narcissism and increased divisiveness. Speaking of drives for "inclusion" that are reticent to acknowledge the need for some boundaries, Miroslav Volf notes that "without boundaries we will be able to know only what we are fighting against but not what we are fighting for. Intelligent struggle against exclusion demands categories and normative criteria that enable us to distinguish between repressive identities and practices that should be subverted and nonrepressive ones that should be affirmed."[14] As Elshtain astutely observes, "for the time being we seem to have lost the *via media* between denying differences or

13. Oliver O'Donovan, *Common Objects of Love: Moral Reflection and the Shaping of Community* (Grand Rapids, MI: William B. Eerdmans, 2002), p. 40.
14. Miroslav Volf, *Exclusion and Embrace: A Theological Exploration of Identity, Otherness, and Reconciliation* (Nashville, TN: Abingdon, 1996), p. 63.

absolutizing them definitively; between presuming a too thoroughgoing unanimity and negating the possibility of any commonality."[15] Although the efforts of the post-Nietzscheans are undertaken in the name of an ever-expanding embrace of difference, they clearly, as we saw, operate with criteria for evaluating difference and deciding which differences are to be embraced, which tolerated, and which excluded. Perhaps the uniqueness of a Christian ontology lies in the fact that the primary political society with which it is concerned is the Heavenly City, so that its exclusivity need not determine who can be involved in the earthly city.

That is to say, the claims of this section that participation in the Heavenly City offers the only way for sinful differences to be reconciled and God-given differences to be celebrated, that participation in God provides the only means by which unity and diversity can be brought together in harmony, do not lead on to a political picture in which the ontology of Christianity takes over the political realm. Christianity does uniquely offer resolution to the problems that plague our political societies, problems that have led us to try to address the dilemmas left unresolved by both modern and post-Nietzschean attempts to create pluralist societies marked by tolerance and/or deep embrace of difference. But this resolution will not be fully visible this side of the eschaton, nor, with its understanding of sin and the *libido dominandi*, does it expect that any earthly city could reflect the realities of the Heavenly City. It hopes, of course, that citizens of the earthly city will become citizens of the Heavenly City, finding through participation in the Triune God the community, the peace, the justice, and the love that many had hoped to find in the earthly city. It cares for the earthly city and its members, offering, at least ideally, service that is not marred by lust for glory and power, in joint pursuit of the goods which the Heavenly City shares with the earthly city while it is on its pilgrimage. And it influences how its citizens view and contribute to earthly justice and peace through its understanding of heavenly justice and peace. But, for reasons that will be entered into more fully below, it does not seek the realization of its picture of reconciliation, or any picture of complete restoration, in the earthly city. Indeed, its role in

---

15. She continues, "This is but one of the many reasons we, as a society, are in trouble." Elshtain, *Limits of Politics*, pp. 104–105.

reminding the earthly city to limit its ambitions and be realistic about its aspirations is a crucial one.

Before turning to explore this more fully, we shall pause briefly to engage with the work of John Milbank. We are not the first to try to engage in a theological account of difference that seeks to show, contra liberals and post-Nietzscheans, that Christianity offers the site for the true embrace of harmony and difference. Drawing on Augustine and writing of Christianity ontologically, Milbank has given considerable attention to questions of theology and difference. His work represents an attempt to take certain insights of post-Nietzscheans (e.g., concern for difference and the linguistic and contingent nature of reality), demonstrate that such insights were latent within Christianity, and thereby offer a theological account that is both "radical" and orthodox. Because of our overlapping concerns, it will be fruitful for us to spend some time engaging with his thought.

Theology and difference according to Milbank: a brief excursus

We have seen how the ontological picture offered by post-Nietzschean theorists shapes their embrace of difference. We have also questioned whether such ontologies can sustain the positive ethos towards diversity that they commend, given their despairing roots and the all-pervasive realities of conflict and power they perceive. John Milbank has raised similar questions, while further claiming that rather than breaking with liberalism and the Enlightenment, post-Nietzschean thought, or what he terms "postmodern nihilism," remains in continuity with it.[16] He presents Christianity as the only persuasive alternative to either liberal or postmodern thought, for in his estimation Christianity is unique in positing a universality that does not come at the expense of difference and in offering a way to move beyond tolerance *and* inevitable resignation to conflict. We quote him at some length:

> Christianity ... , unlike many other discourses, pursued from the
> outset a universalism which tried to subsume rather than merely
> abolish difference: Christians could remain in their many different

16. Milbank, "Postmodern Critical Augustinianism," p. 267.

cities, languages, and cultures, yet still belong to one eternal city ruled by Christ, in whom all "humanity" was fulfilled. In this way it appears as a "precursor" of enlightenment, and any claim of outright Christian opposition to enlightenment is bound to be an oversimplification. But the liberty, equality, and fraternity latent as values in Christianity do not imply mere mutual tolerance, far less any resignation to a regulated conflict. On the contrary, Christianity is peculiar, because while it is open to difference – to a series of infinitely new additions, insights, progressions toward God, it also strives to make of all of these differential additions a harmony, "in the body of Christ," and claims that if the reality of God is properly attended to, there can be such a harmony. ... Christianity, there-fore, is not just in the same position as all other discourses vis-à-vis postmodernity; it can, I want to claim, think difference, yet it per-haps uniquely tries to deny that this necessarily (rather than con-tingently, in a fallen world) entails conflict.[17]

Here some of the major themes of Milbank's thought emerge. He is concerned to persuade his readers that the picture described by post-Nietzscheans in which conflict and violence appear as primary and inescapable is not the only ontological possibility; indeed, Christianity offers a "counter-ontology" in which peace has priority over conflict, for conflict is a contingent result of the fall rather than a description of the inevitable nature of (created) reality, and only with such an ontology can difference be truly acknowledged and respected. The description put forward by post-Nietzscheans is but one *mythos*, while the description proffered by Christians is another; Milbank's rendering of this description draws heavily on his inter-pretation of Augustine. The overlap between Milbank's project and our own should be obvious by now, in that both are concerned with presenting Christianity ontologically, drawing upon Augustine and paying attention to the question of how difference is to be under-stood within his ontological picture. These attempts have yielded some similarities as well as many differences, even while this pro-ject has, admittedly, been greatly influenced by Milbank's theolo-gical approach.

When Milbank discusses post-Nietzschean, or what he more often refers to as postmodern or nihilist, thought, he is referring to the work of Nietzsche, Heidegger, Deleuze, Lyotard, Foucalt, and

17. Ibid., pp. 267–268.

Derrida.[18] While he is not, then, explicitly engaging with the post-Nietzscheans with which our investigation has been concerned, he is focusing on many of the thinkers who have greatly influenced their thought. He is particularly concerned with the sufficiency of their accounts of difference. He sees in such thinkers the desire to articulate a positive view of will-to-power in which pure difference is affirmed and nothing is negated. Yet, given their understanding of the primacy of conflict and competition for power, he wonders how difference can enter common cultural space without competing, displacing, or expelling others or other differences, without, in other words, *negating* some type of difference. On their account, difference cannot escape being "oppositional difference," for "there is a transcendental assumption of a negative relation persisting between all differences."[19] How might one get to a *positive* view of difference, in which the affirmation of difference is not concomitant with assumptions of conflict and competition? According to Milbank, it is possible only through a recovery of a scholastic or Thomistic understanding of analogy.

Milbank draws upon analogy as a way to think about created reality that does not rely on the rigid classification systems based in genera and species that emerged in modernity. Whereas the latter try to determine what is held in common, what commonalities of essence can tie objects together, analogy links different objects by noting both what objects have in common and where they are different. Again, whereas the latter, in an effort to group things together by common classification, require abstraction from the particularities of the objects at hand and rely upon the assumption that each object has an univocal meaning, analogy depends upon identifying both the similarities and the differences in objects being compared so that they are never abstracted or given one single absolute meaning. That is to say, as Milbank puts it, analogy refers to "a 'common measure' between differences which does not reduce differences to mere instances of a common essence or genus. In other words a likeness that only maintains itself through the differences, and not despite or in addition to them."[20] Milbank

---

18. Milbank, *Theology and Social Theory*, p. 278. Note that he intentionally treats their writings as "elaborations of a single nihilistic philosophy, paying relatively less attention to their divergences of opinion" (ibid).
19. Ibid., p. 289.
20. Milbank, *Theology and Social Theory*, p. 289.

would like to see "all unities, relations and disjunctures" understood analogically because he believes it would enable likenesses
between entities to be discovered *and* rediscovered along the way
while simultaneously allowing for recognition of the actual content
and difference of each entity.[21] Because of analogy's ability to
recognize the differences and particularity of each entity, Milbank
believes that analogy provides the way for difference to be positively
rather than negatively related.

Milbank's support for analogy is concomitant with a concern for
the dangers of univocity, or the belief that "things 'are' in the same
way," that Being is the same in every instance.[22] Milbank blames
Duns Scotus for the first articulation of such univocity, for by
conceiving of Being as univocal, by positing that both finite and
infinite (man and God) "are" in the same way, Duns Scotus invented
the separation between ontology and theology and subverted the
scholastic understanding of being as analogical. As Michael Hardt
and Antonio Negri tell the story, Duns Scotus' belief that "every
entity has a single essence" essentially "subverts the medieval
conception of being as an object of analogical, and thus dualistic
predication – a being with one foot in this world and one in a
transcendent realm," and thereby contributed to what they identify
as the primary event of modernity, namely "the affirmation of the
powers of *this* world, the discovery of the plane of immanence."[23]
This is precisely where Milbank identifies the problem of modernity, and it is what he continues to identify in the thought of
so-called postmodern thinkers. For according to Milbank, the ontologies of Heidegger, Derrida and Deleuze all rely upon Scotus'
transcendental, contentless univocity, even while they add "a
nihilist twist by denying the hierarchy of genera, species and indi-
viduated *res*. There are no stable genera, but only complex mixtures,
overlappings and transformation" (we're reminded here of Connolly's preference for the rhizome over the tree, which he takes
from Deleuze).[24] This results, in one sense, in an absolute diversity
of genera, but, in another sense, "the reverse side of this diversity
remains the univocity of being: only Being, declares Derrida, has

21. Ibid., pp. 304–306.
22. Ibid., p. 303.
23. Hardt and Negri, *Empire*, p. 71; see also pp. 70–82.
24. Milbank, *Theology and Social Theory*, p. 303.

a literal and not a metaphorical sense. Likewise, for Deleuze, every differential happening is also the eternal return of the same, the eternal repetition of a self-identical existence."[25] Milbank questions the assumption of these theorists that their philosophy of univocity is any more "fundamental" than a Catholic understanding of analogical difference, and he maintains that an analogical approach is equally viable.

Yet Milbank distances himself from the traditional presentation of analogy, for he wants to argue that analogy is not necessarily concomitant with identity, presence, and substance. Here he agrees with much postmodern philosophy that these categories have become problematic. Indeed, his larger theological project is one in which notions that have traditionally been associated with Christianity, and which have recently been discredited by postmodern philosophers, such as presence, substance, and the rational essence of subjects, are no longer seen as necessary to theology, while other notions that have been the subject of postmodern critique are retained as essential to a Christian ontology. These latter notions include "transcendence, participation, analogy, hierarchy, teleology (these last two in modified forms) and the absolute reality of 'the Good' in roughly the Platonic sense."[26] It is worth noting that, on Milbank's account, the subject of the postmodern critique has often been forms of Platonism and metaphysics that postmodern thinkers conflate with Christianity without recognizing the degree to which ideas originally garnered from Platonic and metaphysical sources are often radically altered by the Church Fathers; in this sense, Milbank, in jettisoning ideas that have seemed to be integral to Christian thought, does not see himself doing something radically different, but merely carrying on in the tradition of certain earlier Christian thinkers who modified or abandoned these notions.[27] In short, Milbank is able to combine his understanding of analogy with a Deleuzian conviction of the need to recognize the overlapping nature and mixtures of life:

> analogy does not imply "identity", but identity and difference at once, and this radical sense can be liberated if one jettisons the

25. Ibid.
26. Ibid., p. 296.
27. See ibid., pp. 295–296. The thinkers he has in mind are, as he lists them, Augustine, Eriugena, Gilbert Porreta, Thomas Aquinas, Nicholas of Cusa, Leibniz, Berkeley, Vico, Hamann, Kierkegaard, and Blondel.

genera/species/individuals hierarchy and recognises, with the nihilists, only mixtures, *continua*, overlaps and disjunctions, all subject in principle to limitless transformation. If the Aristotelian categories are abandoned, then the way is open to seeing analogy as all-pervasive, as governing every unity and diversity of the organized world.[28]

Milbank is asking for nothing short of a radical reworking of how we approach the world, one that opts for a dynamic "analogizing process" that discovers likenesses between entities by paying attention to their actual content, without relying on preestablished categories or a univocal process that ignores particular differences.[29] This analogizing process is part of participation in divine Being, and the divine Being to whom Milbank refers, the God of Christianity, both is and creates difference. In Milbank's estimation, difference lies so close to the heart of Christianity that one can offer a redescription of God, creation, and charity using the language of difference. So Milbank writes that God *is* difference, as such including and encompassing every difference, while also being the One who *differentiates*. Creation is understood, therefore, as God's gratuitous giving of existence and thereby of difference. This is why Milbank links charity so closely with difference, because creation, as God's original charitable act, is "the gratuitous, creative positing of difference, and the offering to others of a space of freedom, which is existence."[30] This creative charitable act does not set down a fixed hierarchy but is better understood as a serial emanation from God, in which each individual has its own unique place in the series; this, Milbank writes, "makes difference ontologically ultimate and worthy of the highest valuation."[31] God is, furthermore, continually creating, continually differentiating, so that creation is not a finished product in space but continues *ex nihilo* in time. This understanding of God is reliant on Milbank's invocation of the view of Dionysius the Areopagite, who sees God as an internally creative power. God is, mysteriously, both "infinite realized act and infinite unrealized power"; this "power-act" plays out through the Trinity in a movement from unity to difference.[32]

28. Milbank, *Theology and Social Theory*, p. 304.
29. Ibid., p. 305.
30. Ibid., p. 416.
31. Ibid.
32. Ibid., p. 423.

Milbank goes on to offer a description of the Trinity in terms of difference. The relation between Father and Son can be seen as the "first difference," a move from unity to difference "in which unity *is* through its power of generating difference, and difference *is* through its comprehension by unity."[33] The "second difference," referring to the Holy Spirit, is what allows the Trinity to be a "'musical' harmony of infinity," revealing God's "radically 'external' relationality."[34] Through the Spirit the relation becomes more than just one that is locked between the two poles of Father–Son in a way that might seem to deny difference, but instead enables a movement of difference beyond the Father–Son relation. Difference in the first instance (speculatively speaking) constitutes unity between the Father and the Son and in the second instance (speculatively speaking), in the Spirit, it is a response to unity that is actually more than unity. Or, as Milbank writes elsewhere, the first difference (i.e., the relation between the Father and the Son) is the articulation of the content of God, though that content is inseparable from Godself, and the second difference (i.e., the Holy Spirit) is the interpretation of that articulation. With the second difference comes a moment of response to the expression of God as found in the first difference, and this response "is 'excessive' in relation to the expression."[35] Thus the love between the Father and the Son is communicated through the Spirit "as a further difference that always escapes";[36] this escape is what involves and enables human participation in the Trinity. The Trinity consists in this interplay between Father, Son, and Spirit, rather than in a finished or static totality, which is what leads Milbank to write of the Trinity both as community[37] and as a "'musical' harmony of infinity."[38]

This God who is difference and who, in continuously creating, is continuously differentiating, is the God in whom the created world of time participates. In this participation, humans are themselves "radically creative and differentiating."[39] Indeed, in Milbank's

33. Ibid., pp. 423–424.
34. Ibid., p. 424. For more on his understanding of the Holy Spirit, see Milbank, "The Second Difference," chap. 7 in *The Word Made Strange*, pp. 171–193.
35. Milbank, "Postmodern Critical Augustinianism," p. 274.
36. Ibid.
37. Ibid.
38. Milbank, *Theology and Social Theory*, p. 424.
39. Ibid., p. 425.

understanding of participation, "it is vital to realize that contingent 'making' should naturally be conceived by Christianity as the site of our participation in divine understanding."[40] Participation is at the heart of Milbank's theological picture, but it is participation that goes further than most theological renditions, which focus on shared being and knowledge in the Divine, for it takes into account issues related to the making and creating of culture, language, time, and historicity that are often, according to Milbank, downplayed by those espousing the traditional notion of participation.[41] In other words, postmodern philosophy has uncovered ways in which language and culture, for example, are subject to change and contingency, dependent on different power struggles and attempts to posit "truth." Milbank has tried to respond to this, theologically, with his accounts of participation and analogy. His analogical approach is dependent upon participation in divine creativity, or differentiation ("the analogizing capacity *itself* is 'like God' "[42]). His emphasis on the dynamic nature of analogy results from his belief that the likenesses discovered through analogy are constructed, either by natural or cultural processes, and are open to refashioning and reshaping.[43] On this account, language and concepts are flexible and schematic, being based on analogies that result from a constant exchange of predicates rather than being fixed in definite categories or classifications. When humans undertake the analogical process, when they engage in "making," they are participating in the divine.[44] An excerpt from Milbank may further elucidate this point:

> I have always tried to suggest that participation can be extended also to language, history and culture: the whole realm of human *making*. Not only do being and knowledge participate in a God who is and who comprehends; also human making participates in a God who is infinite poetic utterance: the second person of the Trinity. Thus when we contingently but authentically make things and reshape ourselves through time, we are not estranged from the

---

40. Ibid. Cf. Milbank, "A Christological Poetics," chap. 5 in *The Word Made Strange*, pp. 123–144.
41. John Milbank, *Being Reconciled: Ontology and Pardon* (London: Routledge, 2003), p. ix.
42. Milbank, *Theology and Social Theory*, p. 305.
43. This is linked to the idea presented in *The Word Made Strange* that language, rather than representing ideas, *constitutes* ideas (p. 29).
44. See Milbank, *Theology and Social Theory*, pp. 304–306.

eternal, but enter further into its recesses by what for us is the only possible route.[45]

The details, nuances, and implications of Milbank's thought in these areas are neither possible to explore within the confines of this work nor fully articulated by Milbank. He continues many of the themes introduced in *Theology and Social Theory* in later writings, particularly in many of the essays included in *The Word Made Strange*. In these, the extent to which Milbank believes that language should be one of the central concerns of theological inquiry, and indeed that reality and existence are fundamentally linguistic, becomes clear. Frederick Bauerschmidt's summary of this book's argument brings this to light: "That argument, briefly put, is that postmodernism is correct in seeing reality as fundamentally linguistic, but that this is something that had already been realized, at least incipiently, in the Christian doctrine of the Triunity of God and the equiprimordiality of Word and Spirit with the Father. Therefore, the task for theology at the end of modernity is to rethink itself in light of this, its own most basic insight."[46] In some ways, then, Milbank is trying to take into account some of the very same insights that our post-Nietzschean political theorists have, and to emerge with a theology that can respond to the concerns over difference that certain so-called postmodern thinkers have raised. Indeed, the level of engagement by Milbank over these issues far exceeds that of most other theologians, but it may be debatable whether that is to Milbank's credit. Indeed, we must wonder whether he has so imbued the philosophy and language of these thinkers that he lets them position his thinking, even as he decries theology for letting itself be positioned by modernity.[47]

Milbank helpfully demonstrates that theology is not necessarily incompatible with concern for difference. More than that, he shows that the post-Nietzscheans' approach to difference has some inherent problems, for difference must always be negatively related within an ontology in which conflict and power define the very

45. Milbank, *Being Reconciled*, p. ix. This book is an attempt to further Milbank's earlier work on participation in terms of *poeisis* to include an understanding of participation in terms of *donum*, or gift.

46. Frederick Christian Bauerschmidt, "The Word Made Speculative? John Milbank's Christological Poetics," *Modern Theology* 15, no. 4 (October 1999), p. 418.

47. Cf. Wayne J. Hankey, "*Theoria versus Poesis*: Neoplatonism and Trinitarian Difference in Aquinas, John Milbank, Jean-Luc Marion, and John Zizioulas," *Modern Theology* 15, no. 4 (October 1999), p. 387.

parameters of reality and therefore of interaction between differences within that reality.[48] We are again led to the conclusion that a positive embrace of difference is not possible within such a negative ontology. We must look elsewhere for sustenance for the strong ethos towards difference that the post-Nietzscheans desire. In this, Milbank is right, and his presentation of a picture of Christianity in which difference can be seen as part of God's creative purposes provides a way to root difference positively. And yet theologians must be wary of being so imbued by the spirit of the age that they let the concerns of that age set the terms of their theological conversation. Efforts to redescribe theological doctrines that have been handed down through the ages using language that derives from recent scholarship and contemporary concerns need, if undertaken at all, to be done with considerable caution and humility.[49] Milbank's strongly presented redescriptions of traditional concepts, in which he ascribes "difference" to the very heart of the Christian doctrine of creation, indeed to the very heart of God's Trinitarian self, in which he alters and expands the notion of participation that dates back to the early Church Fathers to emphasize human construction of meaning and language, seem to indicate a lack of just such humility. These efforts furthermore raise the question of authority; as Paul D. Janz points out, to claim orthodoxy, as Milbank does, is, by definition, to pronounce a kind of binding authority.[50] What authority is Milbank claiming as he alters Christian doctrines that have been handed down through the centuries and as he asserts that a revised analogical approach towards the created world is the only way forward? Orthodoxy connotes submission and conformity to a set of doctrines and beliefs that are part of a larger tradition, yet it is precisely these doctrines and beliefs that Milbank is eager to change. In Milbank's defense, he believes that as he undertakes his project of theological modification and redescription' he is in continuity with a tradition initiated by certain great theological

48. See John Milbank, "The End of Enlightenment: Post-modern or Post-secular?" in *The Debate on Modernity*, ed. Claude Geffré and Jean Pierre Jossua (London: SCM, 1992), p. 46.

49. Kathryn Tanner's efforts to talk about difference in trinitarian terms may be an example of this type of theological humility. See Kathryn Tanner, *Jesus, Humanity and the Trinity: A Brief Systematic Theology* (Edinburgh: T&T Clark, 2001), pp. 13–14.

50. Paul D. Janz, "Radical Orthodoxy and the New Culture of Obscurantism," *Modern Theology* 20, no. 3 (July 2004), pp. 385–387, 398–400.

thinkers, as we saw above. Furthermore, he believes that this is the only hope for theology's survival ("the only chance lies in the composing of a new theoretical music. Hence my endeavour to make the Christian *logos* sound again afresh, even in its dying fall ... "[51]). The post-Nietzscheans might agree with this claim, presenting, as they think, persuasive reasons why traditional Christianity is no longer plausible, and, further, is dangerous, in a cultural *milieu* concerned with difference. Yet must we be so persuaded that the post-Nietzscheans are correct that we profoundly alter our doctrines and beliefs so that they are able to withstand the recent "postmodern" turn? Is not the result a sort of free-floating project that appeals to neither Scripture nor reason, nor any easily recognizable authority, to support its theological claims, as Janz argues?[52] Is not Reinhard Hütter right, that Milbank's "enemy, postmodern nihilism, dictates the logic of argumentative victory even in the occurrence of its own defeat, and moves like the Trojan horse as *Christian mythos* into the very citadel of Milbank's theology"?[53]

Hütter furthermore points out that, in certain regards, Milbank is not Augustinian enough.[54] This seems like a correct assessment, for the "radical" turn that Milbank takes in understanding our contingent human creativity as the essence of our participation in the divine obscures what Augustine believed to be the heart of participation, namely reconciled relationship with God the Father through the Son and the Holy Spirit.[55] This is the participation that, according to Augustine, enables humans to be reconciled to God and each other, to have their loves reordered and reharmonized, so that they can be united across their differences in the unchanging Good of the Triune God. This picture of participation, in which all of humanity is harmonized into a family, united in their differences by

51. Milbank, *The Word Made Strange*, p. 1.
52. Janz, "Radical Orthodoxy and Obscurantism," esp. pp. 383–384, 386, 388.
53. Reinhard Hütter, "The Church's Peace Beyond the 'Secular': A Postmodern Augustinian's Deconstruction of Secular Modernity and Postmodernity," *Pro Ecclesia* 2 (Winter 1993), p. 116.
54. Ibid.
55. On Milbank's emphasis on human construction, Christopher J. Insole, writes, "It is extraordinary to see such a bold statement of the constructive capacities and responsibilities – God-like even – of the subject" ("Against Radical Orthodoxy: The Dangers of Overcoming Political Liberalism," *Modern Theology* 20, no. 2 [April 2004], p. 222). It may be worth noting that we share little else in common with Insole's evaluation of either Radical Orthodoxy or political liberalism.

God's love and redemption, *must* remain at the center of our theological understanding, even at the center of our theological discussions of difference. If we redefine our theology too much in terms of difference and human construction, if we abandon theological concepts that have long undergirded orthodox theology, if our reconceptions and "radicalization" of Christian ideas are driven more by abstract concepts and linguistics than Scriptural engagement, then we risk losing sight of the very means whereby harmony in the midst of difference becomes possible, namely participation in God through the Holy Spirit and the person of Jesus Christ.[56]

Milbank openly acknowledges that his theological approach involves a decreased focus on Jesus and an increased emphasis on the Kingdom of God, for "the name 'Jesus' does not indicate an identifiable 'character', but is rather the obscure and mysterious hinge which permits shifts from one kind of discourse to another."[57] In his reading, "christological and atonement doctrines are ... theoretically secondary to definitions of the character of the new universal community or Church."[58] Further, Milbank translates Jesus' life, his death on the cross, and his atonement into the language of signs and metaphor, so that they are not to be understood realistically but metaphorically, so that Jesus on the cross is substituted for us because "he becomes totally a sign, here he is transformed into a perfect metaphor of forgiveness," and metaphors of atonement "are *not* to be taken realistically, as approximations to an 'atonement in itself', an invisible eternal transaction between God and humanity. Instead, these metaphors represent the actual *happening* of atonement' as a meaning in language."[59] By such a retranslation of Christology and atonement Milbank believes that he is providing the way forward for the Church; by such a reinterpretation we believe that he is missing the Incarnation of Christ without which no reconciliation between God and humankind, and therefore no reconciled community, is possible. Without the real presence of Jesus Christ on this earth as divine and human, as the mediator between God and fallen humanity, as the Reconciler and

---

56. Cf. R. R. Reno, "The Radical Orthodoxy Project," *First Things* no. 100 (February 2000), pp. 37–44 and Bauerschmidt, "The Word Made Speculative?" pp. 417–432.
57. Milbank, *The Word Made Strange*, p. 149.
58. Ibid., p. 148.
59. Ibid., pp. 160, 161; author's emphasis.

Savior of God's people, Jesus could not be the founder of a new city, the Heavenly City, present in part on this earth as the Church. Milbank's semantic reappraisal of Jesus would have been unthinkable to Augustine, whose Christology is dependent upon Jesus Christ as mediator. Indeed, Milbank's interpretation tends more towards gnosticism than Augustinianism.[60]

Milbank's efforts to rethink theology in order to distance it from modern thought have pushed him to embrace a "postmodern" turn to semantics. Such a turn, however, is not the only option available to contemporary thinkers and theologians. As Alasdair MacIntyre writes, "Some recent philosophers have supposed that semantics is first philosophy, having displaced epistemology from that fundamental position, and have written as if it is at the level of semantic enquiry that philosophical disagreements have to be resolved first, the answer to epistemological, metaphysical, and ethical questions then being derived, at least in part, from the findings of semanticists." But, he continues, "there is no particular reason to believe this."[61] We have not believed this, and have therefore chosen not to follow the semantic trail blazed by certain "postmodern" thinkers, even as we have tried to move beyond certain problematic assumptions of modernity. Rediscovering the relevance of an Augustinian ontology in the face of certain problematic modern and "postmodern" beliefs and practices is possible without so revising aspects of that ontology that it can no longer deliver the very thing that was promised, namely a community marked by harmony of difference. Milbank would presumably not be content with our efforts. He would say both that the ontology we have presented does not adequately shed the more problematic aspects of Christian theology that postmodern philosophy has so decisively rendered suspect and that it leaves in place a space for the "secular." We would clearly disagree with both assessments, sharing with Milbank the concern that theology not underwrite the belief that certain realms and spaces in the social and political world can and should be considered as completely independent of faith, God, and the Church.

This concern over the "secular" provides a helpful way for us to move this discussion from the Heavenly City to the earthly city, as it

---

60. Cf. Janz, "Radical Orthodoxy and Obscurantism," p. 394.
61. MacIntyre, *Whose Justice? Which Rationality?*, p. 371.

were. On one level, at least, we agree with Milbank and Augustine that the only place where difference can be united in a harmony that continues to respect difference is in the Heavenly City. But what happens in the earthly city, in the here and now, in a society in which the majority of people neither claim nor desire citizenship in the Heavenly City? What hope do we have for social and political theories and structures attempting to create and sustain societies in which difference is recognized and respected? On the one hand, very little, if we hope for too much and look to ontologies with expectations and desires that far outweigh their ability to realize them. On the other hand, with our expectations in check and a theological understanding that Jesus Christ is Lord of all, we can hope for a society in which genuine conversation is possible, in which each party of which that society consists can interact with others in the particularity of its identity, practices, and beliefs. To this matter we will return more directly at the end of the chapter. We can only arrive there theologically if we understand the relationship between the Heavenly and earthly cities in the here and now, meaning the Church and the political realm as they exist in the *saeculum*. That is to say, we are not arguing that the earthly city should be turned into the Heavenly City by the efforts of Christians so that our differences can be harmoniously reconciled in our current political societies, nor are we arguing that the Trinitarian underpinnings of the Heavenly City provide a blueprint for life in the earthily city. How, then, do Christians, whose primary citizenship lies in the Heavenly City, think about the earthly city and their relationship to it? How do they make sure that the Church's reminders to political societies that they cannot achieve the full celebration of difference or the unity amidst diversity for which they are longing, because these are only realized through the reconciler of humanity, creation, and God, Jesus Christ, does not lead those in the Church or those outside of the Church to think that Christianity is to take over the political realm in this age?

The Church and the political: Christ is Lord

Any discussion of political life and pluralism must take into account how the faith traditions and ideological communities that coexist in one political society conceive of their relationship to that

political society. And any theological discussion attempting to address issues related to political society and political theory most certainly needs to consider the relationship between the Church and the political, as this section does. It may be worth noting that this is intentionally *not* a consideration of the relationship between the Trinity and the political, for we do not assume that the unity amidst diversity found in the Trinity can be translated into an earthly political system. The Trinity most certainly shapes the life of the Heavenly City, and underlies all of creation, but how directly the Heavenly City and the earthly city, or the Church and the political, are connected is precisely the subject under consideration. We should also note that this is not an effort to find in Christianity the underpinnings or even an endorsement for one political arrangement over another. As we shall see below, we follow Augustine in believing that Christianity can be compatible with, and can contribute to, a variety of societal arrangements.

By the "political," we mean the realm of the earthly city that is primarily responsible for dealing with the structure or affairs of government of the earthly city.[62] By the Church, we mean that part of the eschatological Heavenly City, or the Kingdom of God, that has its instantiation here on earth. As we saw in the previous chapter, Augustine does not conflate the Heavenly City and the Church, believing that the Church contains those who are faithful and those who are unfaithful, or those who are citizens of the Heavenly City and those who, though part of the Church, continue to be citizens of the earthly city. Augustine nevertheless affirms, as Nicholas Healy puts it, an "ontological relation between the City of God and the church."[63] In other words, the Heavenly City is connected to the Church and present within it, even as the Church, as a mixed body in a fallen era, will never attain the perfection of the City of God in this age. The full revelation and realization of the Heavenly City will not occur until the eschaton, so here and now we can and should expect trouble and conflict within the Church. Yet we should also expect to see, experience, and delight in the firstfruits of the

---

62. We use the terms "the political" and the "political realm" to avoid the use of the "state," believing that the rise of a conception of the "state" over against the "church" is a relatively recent phenomenon that occurs with the rise of liberalism (more on this below).

63. Healy, *Church, World and the Christian Life*, p. 55.

Heavenly City in the Church in this *saeculum*, for Christians already participate in God through Jesus Christ and the Holy Spirit. As Miroslav Volf writes, "... participation in the communion of the triune God ... is not only an object of hope for the church, but also its present experience," and, further, "Christ promised to be present in it through his Spirit as the first fruits of the gathering of the whole people of God in the eschatological reign of God."[64]

Any attempt to conceptualize the Heavenly City and the Church will encounter tensions and obstacles, for the Heavenly City is already present and visible, though not yet nearly all that it will be in the age to come, while the Church lives in the present in a state of eschatological anticipation that involves the beginnings of participation in the realities of the Heavenly City, while still being marked by the realities of sin, evil, and conflict. We need to hold tightly to this tension, as unclear as it may be to us in this age when we continue to see as through a glass, dimly, expecting neither too much nor too little from the Church and Christianity in this age. For as eschatological as the Church's hopes are, its experience of the Kingdom of God and eternal life in the here and now cannot be underestimated. As Kathryn Tanner writes,

> At the most fundamental level, eternal life is ours now in union with Christ, as in the future ... This realm of eternal life is not other-worldly, either in the sense of becoming a reality only after our deaths or in the sense of a spiritualized, merely personal attitude to events of this world. Instead, eternal life exists now in competition with another potentially all-embracing structure or pattern of existence marked by futility and hopelessness .... Eternal life infiltrates, then, the present world of suffering and oppression, to bring life, understood as a new pattern or structure of relationships marked by life-giving vitality and renewed purpose.[65]

This is why Christians and churches must take seriously their responsibility in fostering the unified and diverse communities of love that are only even a possibility because of their participation in God's eternal life. It is also why they must think through the relationship between their own *polis*, the Church as it exists in the earthly city, and the political realm of that same earthly city.

---

64. Miroslav Volf, *After our Likeness: The Church as the Image of the Trinity* (Grand Rapids, MI: William B. Eerdmans, 1998), pp. 129, 158.
65. Tanner, *Jesus, Humanity and the Trinity*, pp. 111, 112.

Should the political and the Church be understood as two separate, unrelated spheres, with independent purposes, concerns, and
purviews? Or do they have overlapping areas of interest, so that
each can and should influence the other, even as they remain distinct? Is a strict distinction between them problematic because the
political requires theological grounding for its very sustenance? Or,
going further, does the political act in opposition to the Church
when the two are separated, so that the ontology with which an
"independent" political realm operates is not only incompatible
with but actually hostile to the ontology of Christianity? On the
latter view, the relationship between the two is nothing short of
competitive and antagonistic, while other views leave open the
possibility of a complementary relationship.

This reference to "possibility" draws our attention to a complicat-
ing factor in this discussion, namely the need to differentiate between
possibility and actuality, between what has the potential to be the
case and what actually is the case at different times and in different
places when it comes to the relationship between the Church and the
political. Such a distinction makes it possible for more than one of
the views cursorily presented above to be correct, or at least to be on
to something important and worthwhile, at the same time. This may
become clearer if we look more closely at some of the nuances and
distinctions found in the thought of different theologians as they
discuss the realms of the Church and the political.

We'll begin by again looking to John Milbank, whose concerns in
this area continue to overlap with ours. In Milbank's estimation, to
believe that the political realm exists as a necessary and independent sphere is to allow for an area of life in which Christianity and
the Church are seen as extraneous. As he writes, "Once the political
is seen as a permanent natural sphere, pursuing positive finite ends,
then, inevitably, firm lines of division arise between what is 'secular' and what is 'spiritual'. Tending gardens, building bridges, sow-
ing crops, caring for children, cannot be seen as 'ecclesial' activities,
precisely because these activities are now enclosed within a sphere
dubbed 'political'."[66] For Augustine, Milbank notes, and here our
interpretation agrees with his, "church" and "state" were not
understood as separate, natural spheres with different concerns and

66. Milbank, *Theology and Social Theory*, pp. 407–408.

purviews resulting from God's order of creation. One could say, however, that (coercive) political rule is "natural" after the fall in the sense that it is part of God's remedy for maintaining order in the face of human sinfulness. This is precisely where Milbank finds deep problems in Augustine's thought, because, according to Milbank, this view allows "a curbing of sin by sin, and, in a way, by more serious sin, because more self-deluded in its pride and claims to self-sufficiency."[67] In other words, the earthly city is marked, according to Augustine, by the *libido dominandi*, by lust for glory and power, by conflict and a lack of true virtue, yet out of this city arises, supposedly, the means for curbing these very appetites and this very sinfulness. How can this be?

For Milbank, resignation to the idea of the necessity of a political realm, even if it is understood as nonnatural (in the sense of part of the remedy of the fall rather than part of God's original creative intentions), inevitably involves certain problems. This may be why, at times, he seems to read back into Augustine's writings the idea that the political realm should, ideally, be ever-receding into the Church ("Augustine himself implies that the Christian emperor will make the empire recede into the Church.";[68] "it is abundantly clear from the writings of Ambrose, Augustine and others, that the gradual conversion of Roman citizens and of Roman rulers was expected to have implications for the character of political governance, and indeed [in a manner they found inherently problematic to define] to bring this rule also within the scope of the ecclesial rule"[69]). Yet he also recognizes that, according to Augustine, sin will exist in this world as long as there is time, thereby necessitating the existence of worldly political rule to mitigate the effects of sin.[70] In keeping with the early Church, Augustine viewed the use of coercion as that which marked the political from the ecclesial. It is here, in the details of Augustine's understanding of the role of coercion and punishment, that Milbank locates "Augustine's real mistake," namely an inconsistency which allows some positive role for punishment in accordance with divine will.[71]

---

67. Ibid., p. 406.
68. Ibid., p. 419.
69. Ibid., p. 400.
70. Ibid., pp. 401–402.
71. Ibid., pp. 417–422; see especially pp. 419–420 on this point.

The details of Milbank's argument are not as relevant to our discussion here as his conclusion: that Augustine's account of the
inevitable continued existence of the political in the fallen world
and his commendation of the use of coercion and punishment in
the political realm risk losing sight of the tragic nature of both
politics and coercion. In other words, the separation of the *imperium*
from the *ecclesia*, of the "state" from the Church, is a tragedy, and its
tragic reality should never be lost from sight. The upshot of this
view, for Milbank, is that "one needs to add to Augustine that *all*
punishment, like the political itself, is a tragic risk, and that
Christianity should seek to reduce the sphere of its operation."[72] On
this reading, the ideal scenario is one in which the scope of the
Church is ever increasing so that the tragic political realm can have
less and less of a presence in this world.

   Milbank is right in one sense when he notes that "Augustine
certainly understands that salvation *means* the recession of *dominium*
(of the political, of 'secular order'),"[73] but for Augustine such a
recession would only be realized in the eschaton. Milbank, too,
believes that the counter-polity of the Church is not yet visibly
perfect; though it exists perfectly in the heavenly realm, in this age
we can only "glimpse dimly its perfection within a process of
reconciliation that is but fragmentarily realized."[74] Yet at the same
time Milbank holds the belief that the Church could have been
perfect enough to effectively displace politics. This becomes clear as
he writes about the failures of the medieval Church: the Church
could have "succeeded"; the middle ages, which he calls "the
Christian 'interruption' of history," could have enabled and sustained a way of ruling that did not involve a formal mechanism of
law or politics. "The Church did not succeed in displacing politics,"
however, "and as a result, politics returned." In other words, the
possibility of the Church's success in realizing an alternative *civitas*
in this age was not ruled out *a priori* but could have been realized,
had things gone differently. All of this seems to reveal a certain
tension in his writing, between recognizing that in the *saeculum* we
have to be resigned to a level of *dominium* and believing that "the

72. Ibid., p. 421.
73. Milbank, *Theology and Social Theory*, p. 421.
74. Milbank, *Being Reconciled*, p. 105; see also pp. 42, 133 for glimpses of the
eschatological tension.

Christian counter-ethics ends and subsumes all politics."[75] As Nicholas Lash writes, in reference to Milbank's *Theology and Social Theory*, "There runs, throughout the book, one strand according to which the citizens of God's new *civitas* have simply left the world of politics behind them, and must refuse to be drawn back into its compromises and entanglements."[76] However much Milbank may try to temper his thought by an eschatological vision, he is unable to remain resigned to the existence of the political (as his continuing efforts towards the realization of Christian socialism attest). This leaves the Church ill-equipped to appropriately respond to the realities of violence, politics, and power which citizens of the Heavenly City will encounter and in which they will inevitably participate in this age.

Underlying Milbank's writings on these matters is a concern that believing that the realm of the political can and should be separate from the realm of the Church renders the political a "secular" sphere, thereby preventing many aspects of life from being seen as concerns of the Church, for Church is reduced to "care for the souls." Disquiet over the existence of the "secular" runs throughout Milbank's work, for Milbank believes that theology has acquiesced to problematic aspects of modernity, including certain unquestioned assumptions related to the existence of supposedly neutral secular realms from which theology is excluded ("Once, there was no 'secular'," begins Milbank's first chapter of *Theology and Social Theory*. "And the secular was not latent, waiting to fill more space with the steam of the 'purely human', when the pressure of the sacred was relaxed. Instead there was the single community of Christendom, with its dual aspects of *sacerdotium* and *regnum*... The secular as a domain had to be instituted or *imagined*, both in theory and in practice."[77]). A desire to move beyond the acceptance of this problematic aspect of modernity in which theology becomes "positioned" by other disciplines and discourses is what, in Milbank's estimation, separates his theology from that of other theologies, such as neoorthodoxy, that mark the contemporary theological world. As

75. The former becomes especially clear in a section entitled "Christianity and Coercion," *Theology and Social Theory*, pp. 417–422; for the latter, see ibid., p. 430.
76. Nicholas Lash, "Not Exactly Politics or Power?" *Modern Theology* 8, no. 4 (October 1992), p. 362.
77. Milbank, *Theology and Social Theory*, p. 9.

he writes, "'post-modern theology', in my usage, goes further than 'neo-orthodoxy', because it does not, like the latter, tend to leave unquestioned the 'godless' and autonomous self-enclosure of modernity."[78]

Yet we have been as concerned as Milbank to discern a way in which to question both modernity and the autonomy and supposed neutrality of the secular, and to insist that Christianity is not meant to be compartmentalized or positioned by other discourses. We have rooted this in Augustine's thought, but in many ways our reading of Augustine seems vastly different from Milbank's, which may be contributing to our differing solutions. This is not to say that areas of agreement with Milbank over interpretations of Augustine do not exist. We agree, for example, that Augustine is not the forerunner of liberalism, and that Augustine does not provide theological or pragmatic reasons for the delineation of a separate sphere called the secular. But questions must be raised about Milbank's proposed solution to the "secular problem." Is his view the only way to overcome a problematic separation of Church and "state" that results in the "privatization" of Christianity? Do we need to support the ever-diminishing role of the political in order for Christianity to be true to itself? Prompted by a questioning of whether certain aspects of secular power and knowledge, including absolute state sovereignty, are compatible with Christianity, as well as by a refusal to be resigned to sinful political and economic structures, much of Milbank's earlier work attempts to articulate a Christian socialism.[79] But is such a socialism possible before the eschaton, given the realities of the earthly city on a theological perspective? Milbank seems much more optimistic here than Augustine, much more open to the idea that the Church does not need to be "resigned" to the permanent existence of two cities during the *saeculum*. It is important to notice that Augustine does not just have more space for a political realm (which, we should note,

78. Milbank, *The Word Made Strange*, p. 35. See also John Milbank, Catherine Pickstock and Graham Ward, eds., *Radical Orthodoxy: A New Theology* (London: Routledge, 1999), p. 2.

79. See Milbank, "Letters to the Editor: A Socialist Economic Order," *Theology* 91 (September 1988), pp. 412–415; "The Body By Love Possessed: Christianity and Late Capitalism in Britain," *Modern Theology* 3 (October 1986), pp. 35–65; "Against Secular Order," pp. 199–224. For more recent writings, see "The Politics of Time: Community, Gift and Liturgy," *Telos* no. 113 (1998), pp. 41–69 and *Being Reconciled*, p. 136.

is neither entirely separate from the Church nor "natural") because he is resigned to humanity's sinfulness in this age, but because of his strong, biblically rooted belief that Christ is Lord of all.

How does Augustine help us think about the important question of the relationship between the political and the Church? "Without the slightest doubt," Augustine writes, "the kingdoms of men are established by divine providence"; "in his control are all the kingdoms of the earth."[80] God granted dominion to the Romans, to the Assyrians and the Persians, and to the Israelites. He gave power to Caesar and Augustus and Nero, to the most attractive and to the most ruthless of leaders. In Augustine's view, "we must ascribe to the true God alone the power to grant kingdoms and empires. He it is who gives happiness in the kingdom of heaven only to the good, but grants earthly kingdoms both to the good and to the evil, in accordance with his pleasure, which can never be unjust."[81] In this sense Augustine is in keeping with the spirit of Paul, for whom Christ is above all rule, authority, and power, under whose feet all things have been placed, and in whom "all things in heaven and on earth were created, things visible and invisible, whether thrones or dominions or rulers or powers."[82] With this in mind, even the earthly city and the powers that reign and conflict in the earthly city are somehow to be considered as placed under the victory and rule of Jesus Christ and, indeed, as part of the creation through Christ. In Augustine's view, in which the mechanisms of the earthly city are part of God's means for minimizing disorder after the disruption of the fall, the political realm can clearly be seen under the purview of God's providence without being understood as part of God's original design for creation. That is to say, politics *per se*, as a realm separate from the Church and other spheres of life, is not part of an order of creation which tends towards, as Milbank pointed out, the establishment of "secular" areas to which Christianity is deemed irrelevant. Yet politics does fall under God's providence and Christ's authority, given its provision to deal with the realities of our not yet fully redeemed world.

If the ideal goal is the continual minimilization of the political in the face of the ecclesial, as it is for Milbank, one wonders to what

80. *City of God* V, 1; V, 12.
81. *City of God* V, 21.
82. Eph. 1:20–23; Col. 1:16.

degree the political can be seen as under God's providence and authority. Whence the inherent suspicion toward the city of this world? It must arise, at some deep level, from an inability to recognize the Lordship of Christ over all of created reality. And yet we have seen the degree to which the *libido dominandi*, lust for power and greed, and conflict and contingency dominate the politics of the earthly city. We have seen the degree to which contemporary political theories seeking to shape political life embody ontologies that are inimical to Christianity, not allowing Christianity or the Church to be true to its nature as a social, embodied public reality. Augustine saw that the difference between the Heavenly City and the earthly city, in terms of the Heavenly City knowing only God as its object of worship, would prevent them from sharing common laws of religion, and indeed would result at times in dissension by the Heavenly City and persecution at the hands of the earthly city. And yet in general the Heavenly City "here on earth makes use of the earthly peace and defends and seeks the compromise between human wills in respect of the provisions relevant to the mortal nature of man, so far as may be permitted without detriment to true religion and piety."[83] In short, Augustine exhibits a trust in the mechanisms of the earthly city as they relate to the things of this world, even as he recognizes that at times citizens of the Heavenly City will be faced with things in the earthly city that prevent the worship of their God. He sees those times as periodic, occasional, rather than as endemic to the nature of the political realm, rather than as a reason to be seeking to expand the "political" purview of the Church. And he holds this view even with his thoroughly realistic picture of the fallen nature of the world. Whence arises his trust? His belief in God's providence and order, his understanding that God has established means to minimize the disorder of the fallen world, and that the political realm is one of those means, rather than separate from or opposed to God's workings in this world.

On this view, the political and the ecclesial both fall under the Lordship of Christ and are part of God's remedy for the fallen world, without necessarily being entirely separate, independent realms. On the contrary, as we have seen in Scripture and in Augustine, both

83. *City of God* XIX, 17.

the Heavenly City in its pilgrimage on earth and the earthly city while it continues to exist in the *saeculum* are upheld by God. Romans 13 contains the most commonly, and controversially, referenced passage on the question of the relation between the Church and political authority:

> Let every person be subject to the governing authorities; for there is no authority except from God, and those authorities that exist have been instituted by God. Therefore whoever resists authority resists what God has appointed, and those who resist will incur judgment. For rulers are not a terror to good conduct, but to bad. Do you wish to have no fear of the authority? Then do what is good, and you will receive its approval; for it is God's servant for your good. But if you do what is wrong, you should be afraid, for the authority does not bear the sword in vain! It is the servant of God to execute wrath on the wrongdoer.[84]

The implication of Paul's writing here seems to be that God has appointed political authority to address certain matters of conduct and to be the bearers of force and punishment, working towards some good outside of the *summum bonum* of the Heavenly City, that is to say worship of God through Christ and the Spirit. The political realm will not be marked by the greatest good of the worship of Christ, nor even by a thick common good (for such a common good is only to be found in Christ), but that does not leave it without Christ. If Milbank is right that to have a place for a political realm is to have a realm separate from Christ and the Church and, in that sense, to be secular, then we would have to join him in hoping to see the end of the existence of such a realm. But Milbank is not right, though he may well be picking up on an area of theology that has been underdeveloped, namely the Christological connection between the earthly city and the Heavenly City.

Karl Barth helps us as we think about the relationship between the Church and the political by probing the connection between the justification available to sinful humans through Jesus Christ and the justice of human society and law, or the relationship between divine justification and human justice.[85] He notes that the existence of

---

84. Rom. 13:1–4, NRSV.
85. This discussion of Karl Barth will highlight some of his thinking on the relationship between the church and the political without presenting an exhaustive account of his thought in this area. Neither will it address the internal difficulties and inconsistencies that can be found within his writings.

these two realities was affirmed clearly and powerfully by Reformation writers, but their emphasis tended to be primarily on the idea that the two are not in conflict rather than on what constitutes their connection. Barth identifies a strange gap between what usually and for the most part forms the center of the Reformers' Christian message, namely the gospel of Jesus Christ, and their discussion of the existence of political authority, speaking of this gap as "the lack of a gospel foundation, that is to say, in the strictest sense, of a Christological foundation, for this part of their creed."[86] It is not only not enough, according to Barth, to posit the existence of these two spheres without articulating and understanding the vital connection between them, it is also dangerous, resulting in either the abandonment of concern for human justice by the Church (because it is so concerned with a "purified" divine justification) or the creation of a system of "secular" human justice that invokes "God" but has no real connection to the justification that comes from the Father through the Son and the Spirit (Barth links the former to "Pietistic sterility" and the latter to the sterility of the Enlightenment). How to avoid these dangers? Recognize the Christological connection between all of creation that forms the "inward and vital connection" between the two realms of Church and state. Barth calls us to look again at Romans 13, for such a passage reveals that the God who has instituted and ordained political authority

> cannot be understood apart from the Person and the Work of Christ; He cannot be understood in a general way as Creator and Ruler, as was done in the exposition of the Reformers .... When the New Testament speaks of the State, we are, fundamentally, in the *Christological* sphere; we are on a lower level than when it speaks of the Church, yet, in true accordance with its statements on the Church, we are in the same unique Christological sphere.[87]

Barth presents a picture of the Church as a circle inside the circle of the political, with both circles having Jesus Christ as their center. Christians are part of both circles, living in the inner circle of the

For more on both, see Will Herberg, "The Social Philosophy of Karl Barth," in *Community, State, and Church: Three Essays* (Gloucester, MA: Peter Smith, 1968), pp. 11–67. For more on his political thought, see William Werpehowski, "Karl Barth and Politics," in *The Cambridge Companion to Karl Barth*, ed. John Webster (Cambridge: Cambridge University Press, 2000), pp. 228–242.
86. Karl Barth, "Church and State," in *Community, State, and Church: Three Essays*, ed. Will Herberg (Gloucester, MA: Peter Smith, 1968), p. 104.
87. Barth, "Church and State," p. 120.

Church as well as the outer circle of the state, while Christ is seen as
the source and foundation of both.[88] The state is a remedy for sin
rather than an order of creation as such, but that does not mean that
the state is not a part of a divine ordinance, an instrument of grace
to minimize the chaos that would otherwise have resulted from the
fall, rather than a product of sin. As such,

> it shares both a common origin and a common centre with the
> Christian community. ... It serves to protect man from the inva-
> sion of chaos and therefore to give him time: time for the preaching
> of the gospel; time for repentance; time for faith. ... Its existence is
> not separate from the Kingdom of Jesus Christ; its foundations and
> its influence are not autonomous. It is outside the Church but not
> outside the range of Christ's dominion – it is an exponent of His
> Kingdom.[89]

Indeed, if one denies that the state is operating according to a bene-
volent arrangement of God when it carries out its responsibilities,
whether or not the state knows it, then, according to Eberhard Jüngel,
one "dispenses those ruling and those ruled of their responsibility
before God ... Like every religious deification, every demonisation of
the state is also a thoroughly unchristian undertaking."[90]

In short, the political realm cannot be seen as an area that is
disconnected from Jesus Christ. As Scripture tells us, Jesus Christ
sustains all things by His powerful word; this must include, for the
Christian, the political, even as the Christian recognizes that the
state can easily and often does stand in opposition to its Lord.[91]
Nevertheless, the political remains under the Lordship of Christ,
connected to but a separate entity from the Church until the time of
Christ's return, when the Kingdom of God will be fully realized and
supersede both the Church and the political. The tasks of the
Church and the state are different, so that the Church, while it is
itself political,[92] best serves the state by being the Church, by, in

88. See Karl Barth, "Christian Community and Civil Community," in
Community, State, and Church: Three Essays, ed. Will Herberg (Gloucester, MA:
Peter Smith, 1968), pp. 158–159.
89. Barth, "Christian Community and Civil Community," p. 156.
90. Eberhard Jüngel, *Christ, Justice and Peace: Toward a Theology of the State*, trans.
D. Bruce Hamill and Alan J. Torrance (Edinburgh: T&T Clark, 1992), p. 64.
91. See Heb. 1:3, NRSV. Barth is very clear that the state may become demonic.
See "Christian Community and Civil Community," p. 138.
92. See Barth, "Christian Community and Civil Community," pp. 153–154,
184–185.

other words, preaching, teaching, and administering the sacraments to proclaim the Kingdom of Christ.[93] The state, on the other
hand, is concerned with (fallen) humanity's need for "an external,
relative, and provisional order of law, defended by superior
authority and force," which those in the Church need as much as
those outside of the Church.[94] Perhaps the importance that Barth
places in the separation between the two is best articulated in the
Barmen Declaration, which Barth drafted on behalf of the German
Confessional Churches in the early 1930s. The fifth thesis of the final
version includes the following:

> We reject the false doctrine that beyond its special commission the
> State should and could become the sole and total order of human
> life and so fulfil the vocation of the Church as well.
>
> We reject the false doctrine that beyond its special commission the
> Church should and could take on the nature, tasks and dignity
> which belong to the State and thus become itself an organ of
> the State.[95]

Barth is concerned about the dangers on both sides, of the state
taking on the role of the Church as that which orders and provides
meaning to life and of the Church unwisely taking on the task of the
state. Contemporary theologians such as Stanley Hauerwas and
Oliver O'Donovan share these concerns. For Hauerwas, when the
Church becomes too concerned with the political realm, forgetting
that it is itself its own proper *polis* and that the realm of government
is also under the Lordship of Christ, the way is paved "for what we
Christians must regard as a truly frightening national agenda:
domesticating religious passion, submerging people's energy in the
self-interested pursuit of material comfort, constructing an arrangement in which religion is subordinated to the political order."[96]
This concern is similar to that expressed by O'Donovan, who notes
that "of the two perils identified by the fifth chapter of the Barmen
Declaration, perhaps the church falls rather less into the temptation

93. Ibid., p. 146; see also pp. 131, 154, 157–158, 166.
94. Ibid., p. 154.
95. "The Barmen Theological Declaration: A New Translation" by Douglas
S. Bax, in Eberhard Jüngel, *Christ, Justice and Peace: Toward a Theology of the State*,
trans. D. Bruce Hamill and Alan J. Torrance (Edinburgh: T&T Clark, 1992),
p. xxviii.
96. Stanley Hauerwas, *In Good Company: The Church as Polis* (Notre Dame, IN:
University of Notre Dame Press, 1995), p. 214.

of assuming the state's authority, rather more into that of acquiescing with the state's assumption of its own."[97] The Church must guard against the temptation to allow the articulation and demands of the Gospel to be swayed by the expectations of society.

The conclusion that can be tentatively reached from this discussion of Milbank, Augustine, and Barth is that a way exists for the Church and the political to be seen as separate realms, both under the Lordship of Christ, without maintaining that the Church or Christianity is irrelevant to what happens in the political or any other realm of society. The "secular" does not have to be granted *a priori* status even as we recognize, with Augustine, that significant and irreconcilable differences exist between the Heavenly City and the earthly city. Another way to approach this might be to determine whether one views the difference between the Heavenly and the earthly cities positively or negatively. Barth represents the former, in that he recognizes that Christians have their citizenship in the Heavenly City, which makes them pilgrims of the earthly city, but, as he writes, "if they are 'strangers and pilgrims' here it is because this city constitutes below their faith and their hope – and not because they see the imperfections or even the perversions of the states of this age and this work! It is not resentment, but a positive sentiment, through which, in contradistinction to non-Christians, it comes about, that they have no 'continuing city' here."[98] Milbank could represent the latter, the "negative" view, for his discussion of the need for the Church to be ever-increasing in the face of the political seems to be almost entirely framed in terms of the perversions of the earthly city, and its concomitant philosophies and ontologies. Yet Milbank is aware of certain dynamics operative within modern political liberalism's characterization of "church and state" that make him wary, dynamics that seem to have escaped the notice of Barth.

Barth denies that the state has any right to make an inward claim upon its subjects and citizens or to impose upon them a particular philosophy of life.[99] He claims that the civil community, as opposed to the church community, has no message of its own to deliver, no

---

97. O'Donovan, *Desire of the Nations*, p. 224. This is not intended to obscure the considerable differences between Hauerwas and O'Donovan.
98. Barth, "Church and State," p. 123.
99. Ibid., p. 143.

creed or gospel to proclaim. "As members of the civil community they can only ask, as Pilate asked: What is truth? since every answer to the question abolishes the presuppositions of the very existence of the civil community."[100] Political liberalism would agree with this, claiming that it can be, to use Rawls' language, political without being metaphysical. This is the very claim that our second chapter called into question, for we noted that at every level the political theories of Rawls and Rorty invoke deep presuppositions about the nature of truth, reality, and human being despite their claims to the contrary. And, as we discussed in our third chapter, the taken-for-granted understandings of truth, reality, and human being in a given society are shaped by those with the power and ability to define those understandings; according to the post-Nietz-scheans, this power and ability have for too long been claimed by the all-too-exclusive political liberals, despite the fact that their efforts have been hidden and veiled under a rhetoric of neutrality. Barth seems to believe that the state could exist neutrally, which is why he feels free to use the term "state," whereas Milbank views the adoption of such a term as too complicitous with theologies and counter-ontologies that articulate and maintain a strict separation between church and state.[101] (Here we side with Milbank, who seems more aware than Barth that such terminology may be problematic in the assumptions and presumptions it brings along with it.)

In drawing these thoughts together, perhaps we can say that ideally the political realm would offer no competing account of truth, no antagonistic gospel to proclaim, but that in reality such an accomplishment is impossible. If this is the way to frame the matter, then Milbank has been helpful in opening our eyes to the nature of the ontologies undergirding the political realm and their potential to usurp and diminish the purview of Christianity. And Barth has, despite a certain naïveté,[102] provided a helpful corrective,

100. Barth, "Christian Community and Civil Community," p. 151; see also p. 158.
101. See Milbank, *Theology and Social Theory*, pp. 406–408.
102. I am wary of accusing Barth of being naïve, for in his post-Nazi Germany context he must have been more aware than most of the dangers associated with the political realm. Yet he does seem to believe that it is possible for the political realm to be entirely neutral on matters of truth, which, to the credit of post-Nietzschean philosophy, is difficult to believe today. At the least we need to follow Augustine in recognizing that the earthly city is always marked

reminding us of the Christological connection between the political and the ecclesial that enables us to, like Augustine, be wary of the political in its inability to share a common object of worship with the Church while still allowing the political to exist as part of God's design to minimize disorder, as part of that which has been placed under Christ's feet and continues to be upheld by the word of Christ, and as that which can be abided by the Church despite their different ends. The goods of the Heavenly City and the earthly city, of the differing ontologies that guide them, can at times overlap. Even when they do not, the earthly city, despite its fallen nature, can through God's providence be used to provide order and overlap between humans and institutions that would otherwise be help-lessly overrun by the *libido dominandi*.

At the same time, reminders that the earthly city is neither neu-tral nor indifferent towards questions of the good and the true cannot be heard often enough. As Augustine shows us, there are limits to what citizens of the Heavenly City can abide in the earthly city, for at times the laws of religion of the earthly city will be in conflict with those of the Heavenly City. Citizens of the Heavenly City are free to follow the customs, laws, and institutions of the earthly city up to the point that they hinder their worship of God.[103] To apply this line of thinking to our contemporary situation, what is it about political liberalism that might be hindering the worship of the Triune God of Christianity? What is it that has Milbank so convinced that the political is opposed to the ecclesial under mod-ern liberal thought? What is it that prompts Milbank to suggest that we need to limit the modern sovereign state by opting instead for a form of "complex space" that consists of small local groups, overlapping boundaries, and plural membership in multiple inter-mediate associations?[104]

In sum, we have now considered how to conceive of the rela-tionship between the political realm and the Church, and we have concluded that, from a theological perspective, the two are neither independent from each other nor equivalent to each other. Because

---

by the *libido dominandi* and can therefore never be free from conflict over power and glory, even as it falls under God's providence.
103. *City of God*, XIX, 17.
104. See Milbank, *Theology and Social Theory*, pp. 407–408 and "On Complex Space," chap. 12 in *The Word Made Strange*, pp. 268–292.

Jesus Christ is Lord of both, they can exist at the same time, connected, under God's providence, with different but not entirely incompatible ends. The political is supposed to play a role within a fallen, disordered world, and some of its good are shared by those in the Church, and some in the Church are called to contribute to the pursuit of those goods. Nevertheless, the political realm is not capable of being neutral, and it is not supposed to have or capable of having the same ends as the Heavenly City, so inevitably times will arise when the political and the Church are in conflict. Is now such a time? Does today's political liberalism hinder the ability of the Church to be respected in its particularity just as so many other particularities fail to receive public acknowledgement? In this next section we will probe what it looks like for the Church to be faithful to its identity within contemporary society and how this faithfulness is impacted or restricted by liberalism. This, concomitantly and seemingly ironically, should open ways for other constituencies to picture how they can be true to the fullness of their identities within our current political arrangements.

Christianity public or private?

Now that we know that the Church does not want to take over the political realm, we need to ask the question in the other direction: what does the political want of the Church? And what does the Church, and the other particularities in our pluralistic society, need to prevent it, and them, from being taken over or substantially altered by the political? To begin to answer these questions, we need to look at the contemporary configuration of the church-state relationship, which has much to do with the story of the rise of liberalism.

In the traditional story, Christianity had to become private and learn to tolerate differing interpretations of its key doctrines to avoid the bloodshed and conflict that inevitably arise when Christianity, or one strand of it, attempts to lay claim to being public. In our initial discussion of liberalism we were introduced to the idea that liberalism emerged out of the religious diversity of post-Reformation Europe and the religious wars of the sixteenth and seventeenth century, which raised the question of how the relationship between groups with different interpretations of Christianity

should be configured and negotiated. Toleration was offered as the answer, understood as the best way to move beyond the antagonism and bloodshed that were afflicting the differing strands of Christianity. John Rawls, as we learned, affirms this view, writing that "the historical origin of political liberalism (and of liberalism more generally) is the Reformation and its aftermath, with the long controversies over religious toleration in the sixteenth and seventeenth centuries."[105] Indeed, Rawls views his own project as the continuation of this liberalism; in his estimation, if his particular configuration of the answer were to be successfully accepted, "it would complete and extend the movement of thought that began three centuries ago with the gradual acceptance of the principle of toleration and led to the nonconfessional state and equal liberty of conscience."[106]

Recently, however, some scholarship has emerged to challenge the story that presents the rise of liberalism as the solution to religious conflict. Pierre Manent, writing what he terms an intellectual history of liberalism, argues that liberalism was motivated more by a desire to escape from the institution of the Church than by the attempt to provide a way out of religious conflict. In this view, modern liberal thinkers were essentially trying to escape the political power of revealed religion and the institutionalized Church, and looked to the theory of those whom we now see as the founders of liberalism for the intellectual resources to make this move.[107] Manent argues that a concomitant part of this escape was the effort to move political questions away from conceptions of the good, because questions of the good clearly and easily fell under the purview of the Church; as Manent writes, "in order to escape decisively from the power of the singular religious institutions of the Church, one had to renounce thinking about human life in terms of its good or end, which would always be vulnerable to the Church's 'trump.' "[108] In short, part of the reason for the liberal move to prioritize the right over the good lies in the desire to move political questions outside of the sphere of the Church. In other words, liberalism arose less because of the need for a solution to

---

105. Rawls, *Political Liberalism*, p. xxvi.
106. Ibid., p. 154.
107. Pierre Manent, *An Intellectual History of Liberalism*, trans. Rebecca Balinski (Princeton, NJ: Princeton University Press, 1994), esp. pp. viii, xvii, 114, 116.
108. Ibid., p. 114.

religious conflict and more because of its own ideological commitments that were in conflict with revealed and institutionalized
religion.

Manent's larger argument is echoed and extended by the more
recent scholarship of William Cavanaugh, whose overarching concern is how Christianity came to be translated from a public,
embodied social institution into a set of private beliefs and values.
In Cavanaugh's estimation, the so-called Wars of Religion did not
necessitate the birth of the modern State as a way out of insur-
mountable religious disagreement; on the contrary, these wars
"were in fact themselves the birthpangs of the State ... fought largely for the aggrandizement of the emerging State over the decaying
remnants of the medieval ecclesial order."[109] To reinforce his
argument he goes back to the history of the time period in question,
noting that it is much more complex and nuanced than is normally
perceived to be the case; the idea that civil authority could outweigh
the Church predates the "Wars of Religion," for example, while
those involved in instigating and sustaining the wars were often
motivated more by the desire for power as it related to the emergence or defeat of a centralized State than they were by theological
or ecclesiological conviction.[110] Yet for Cavanaugh, the issue goes
deeper than the personal religious motivations of the major players
of the time. He wants to question the very creation of the category
of "religion," understood as a set of beliefs related to personal
conviction rather than public loyalty to the State and embodied
ecclesial practice.[111] For with this understanding of "religion,"
Christianity comes to be seen as a set of beliefs that can be separated
from their particular embodiment in the social space of the Church
and as but one manifestation of a universal religious impulse. In
Cavanaugh's reading of the situation, the creation of "religion" as a
universal category separated from its particular instantiations and
communal embodiments leads to religions being treated as
"domesticated belief systems which are, insofar as it is possible,
to be manipulated by the sovereign for the benefit of the State.

---

109. Cavanaugh, "A Fire Strong Enough to Consume the House," p. 398.
110. Ibid., pp. 398–403.
111. In his most recent work, William Connolly also draws attention to the
study of "religion" and the ways in which such study problematically
separates belief from practice and ritual. He is particularly concerned with the
implications of this for Islam today. See Connolly, *Pluralism*, pp. 55–59.

Religion is no longer a matter of certain bodily practices within the Body of Christ, but is limited to the realm of the 'soul,' and the body is handed over to the State."[112]

What is problematic about this? Liberalism presents us with a picture in which the neutral liberal state steps in to end the bloodshed and wars that are concomitant with the competitive and irreconcilable nature of absolute religious truth claims, yet the nineteenth and twentieth centuries saw an increase rather than a decrease in the amount of bloodshed and warfare in the world. The state was supposed to be the peacemaker, enabling us to overcome violence committed in the name of religion. In the Western world, we may no longer see violence undertaken on behalf of religion, but violence itself has not come to an end. Bloodshed, now committed by the state in the name of democracy and freedom, is as common today as it has been throughout the centuries. The call of liberalism, according to Cavanaugh, was merely a call to transfer loyalties from the Church to the State, which embodies a particular set of goods and a soteriology that are at odds with those of the Church, and which, furthermore, has failed to deliver on its promises of peace and harmony. Tolerance, in this reading, was not the solution to conflict and bloodshed but was, and remains, the tool through which the State divided and conquered the Church, while the State continues to be involved in violence and warfare.[113]

Cavanaugh is clearly akin to Milbank in his assessment of the antagonistic relationship between the Church and the State, at least the modern state. Though Christians may not fully agree with this assessment, it would be wise for them to learn from Cavanaugh to take more heed than they often have of the complexity surrounding the rise of the modern political liberal state.[114] This is not to deny that such thinkers as Jean Jacques Rousseau and John Locke genuinely thought that a new way forward was needed to overcome the conflicts they saw arising from Christianity and post-Reformation religious differences, but it is to say that the solutions they proffered were driven by their own beliefs and ideologies and had significant

112. Ibid., p. 405.
113. Ibid., esp. pp. 399, 408–409, 407. See also William T. Cavanaugh, "The City: Beyond Secular Parodies," in *Radical Orthodoxy*, ed. John Milbank, Catherine Pickstock and Graham Ward (London: Routledge, 1999), pp. 182–200.
114. Cf. Jean Bethke Elshtain, *New Wine and Old Bottles: International Politics and Ethical Discourse* (Notre Dame, IN: University of Notre Dame Press, 1998), p. 15.

theological and ecclesiastical consequences. For both Rousseau and
Locke, the danger of Christianity was precisely its potential to divide
allegiances, to limit citizens' loyalty to the political system in which
they lived in favor of loyalty to an ecclesiastical system. This is why
tolerance can be extended only to those who are willing to limit
their Christianity to beliefs that do not interfere with their primary
allegiance to the state; this, in short, is why Roman Catholics, who
retained a more explicit understanding of the universal nature
of the Church and their allegiance to the papacy, were not to be
tolerated. Indeed, according to Michael Walzer, the reason that
toleration works in countries like the United States is that "the
expanding toleration regime tended to protestantize the groups that
it included. American Catholics and Jews gradually came to look less
and less like Catholics and Jews in other countries: communal
controls weakened; clerics spoke with less authority; individuals
asserted their religious independence, drifted away from the community, and intermarried."[115] In short, communities of faith that
formerly would have been unable to imagine themselves as indivi-
dualized, privatized belief systems became just that.

One can hardly fail to see the differences that emerge between
Christianity understood as a matter of private belief, subject primarily to the realm of individual choice and conscience, and
Augustine's picture of Christianity as belief that is necessarily concomitant with a different identity, loyalty, allegiance, and practice.
For Augustine, as we have well seen by now, a Christian is primarily
a citizen of the Heavenly City, and only secondarily a pilgrim in the
political society in which he or she happens to live. It would have
been inconceivable for Augustine to divorce Christianity from the
life of the Church or to view it as anything but a public, social ethic.
Indeed, the very categories of public and private that go hand in
hand with liberalism are foreign to Augustine. As Elshtain notes,
Augustine does not bifurcate "the earthly sphere into rigidly
demarcated public and private realms";[116] instead, as we saw in
the previous chapter , Augustine sees a continuum in which the
peace of a person, of the household, and of the city are all connected. In contrast to Aristotelian thought, in which the city and the

115. Walzer, *On Toleration*, p. 67.
116. Elshtain, *Public Man, Private Woman*, p. 70.

household, or the *polis* and the *oikos*, are markedly opposed, with the latter being significantly devalued in comparison to the former, in Augustine's thought, as Elshtain writes, "the household and city, public and private, do not diverge as types or 'in kind'; rather, aspects of the whole are born into the parts, and the integrity and meaning of the part carries forward to become an *integral part* of the whole."[117] Elshtain uses Augustine's thought as an example of the moral revolution inaugurated by Christianity in which prevailing images of public and private were dramatically transformed.[118] Cavanaugh and Hütter reach similar conclusions in their respective discussions of Ephesians 2:19, in which Paul writes to the Ephesians as "fellow citizens with God's people and members of God's household," thereby transcending the usual distinction between the *polis* and the *oikos*.[119] This issue of "public," as it is conceived and pictured differently by the Church and the contemporary liberal state, may take us to the heart of the matters we have been discussing throughout this work.

As we think about how "public" is used and restricted within our current political configurations, we will see one significant way in which the particularity of some constituencies is being limited. By definition, "public" need not refer only to a nation or a state, or to the explicitly political realm of nations and states; it can also refer to a community or a group of people united by a common interest or good, say, for example, worship of God, the highest and most unchanging good. A people united together through worship of God can be considered a public just as much as a people united together through a common national allegiance. To return to Ephesians 2:19, to be a Christian is to be a citizen of the Kingdom of God and a member of God's family. This identity is a matter of truth and belief, but this truth and belief call forth a response and an ethic that are visible and tangible, embodied in the collective life and practices of the Church. Christianity is at heart a communal and public enterprise: the Church is comprised of a group of people sharing the common interest of worship of God and love of neighbor. Liturgy

117. Ibid.
118. Ibid., p. 56.
119. See Reinhard Hütter, *Suffering Divine Things: Theology as Church Practice*, trans. Doug Stott (Grand Rapids, MI: William B. Eerdmans, 2000), pp. 163–164; William T. Cavanaugh, "Is Public Theology Really Public?" *Annual of the Society of Christian Ethics* 21 (2001), pp. 116–117.

itself is, by definition, public; more precisely it is the public worship of God that belongs to the people. As such, as Cavanaugh writes, "the liturgy does more than generate interior motivations to be better citizens. The liturgy generates a body, the Body of Christ – the Eucharist makes the church, in Henri de Lubac's words – which is itself a *sui generis* social body, a public presence irreducible to a voluntary association of civil society."[120] Augustine similarly reminds us that through participation in the Church and its sacraments, citizens of the Heavenly City are united around the communal and unchanging good of God, their collective *summum bonum*. As Robert Jenson notes, "what must always be in our vision when thinking of Augustine's City of God is the Eucharist, a public space where the one God gives himself to his community, and where in consequence all sorts and conditions of humanity drink from one cup and eat of one loaf."[121]

This emphasis on the public nature of the Church is different from that with which most proponents of "public theology" operate, for our concern is less to provide legitimacy for theological and ecclesiastical contributions to the public square and more to rethink the very conceptions of public and private that have come to be taken-for-granted within contemporary liberal society.[122] As Cavanaugh notes in his discussion of recent Catholic attempts to articulate a "public theology," such approaches accept the notion of public as defined by the liberal nation-state and then try to present Christianity as a set of values or a type of voluntary association that, because it has a contribution to make to civil society and/or political citizenship, should be allowed in the public square.[123] Missing from their discussion is any of the Augustinian notion that membership in the Heavenly City might have priority over membership in civil

120. Cavanaugh, "Public Theology," p. 116. Cf. Catherine Pickstock, "Liturgy and Modernity," *Telos* 30, no. 113 (fall 1998), pp. 19–40.
121. Robert W. Jenson, "Eschatology," in *The Blackwell Companion to Political Theology*, edited by Peter Scott and William T. Cavanaugh (Oxford: Blackwell, 2004), p. 413.
122. For examples of the former type of public theology, see Richard John Neuhaus, *The Naked Public Square: Religion and Democracy in America* (Grand Rapids, MI: William B. Eerdmans, 1984) and Ronald F. Thiemann, *Constructing a Public Theology: The Church in a Pluralistic Culture* (Louisville, KY: Westminster/John Knox, 1991).
123. He has in mind John Courtney Murray, Richard John Neuhaus, Michael and Kenneth Himes, and other work based in John Boyte's thoughts on civil society.

and political society, indeed that the Church is its own *res publica*.[124] This is integral to Augustine's picture of the Heavenly City, as we have well seen by now.[125]

Indeed, Williams argues that Augustine's main purpose in *City of God*, and particularly in book XIX, is not only to show that the Church is its own public but to redefine the very understanding of what is truly public and political: "he is engaged in a *redefinition* of the public itself, designed to show that it is life outside the Christian community which fails to be truly public, authentically political."[126] On this reading, for something to be truly public it must provide common ends around which people can be united, common purposes around which shared life can take shape, a common good that is unchanging; such ends and purposes, such a common good cannot be found outside of Jesus Christ and His Body, the Church. It must, furthermore, address the truest human needs, which according to Augustine are, of course, related to God. Human beings, who were created for communion with and enjoyment of God, cannot have their deepest needs addressed outside of a restored relationship with God or the community of those who have been similarly restored. While a social or political unit united around certain aims that do not include enjoyment of God "may be empirically an intelligibly unified body, it is constantly undermining its own communal character, since its common goals are not and cannot be those abiding values which answer to the truest human needs."[127] Such societies cannot, ultimately, cohere, because they fail to be united around the only true source of coherence; "their character and structure are inimical to the very nature of an ordered unity in plurality, a genuine *res publica*."[128]

Augustine's belief that at the heart of sin lies a turn away from the common good to the self, from that which is public and shared to that which is private, is integrally related to this discussion. On this view, a commonwealth, a society that is truly concerned with the common good, is not possible outside of redemption and restoration, for humans need some way to be transformed so that they can

124. Cavanaugh, "Public Theology," p. 116.
125. Cf. Gray, "Two Liberalisms of Fear," p. 17.
126. Williams, "Politics and the Soul," p. 58.
127. Ibid., p. 60.
128. Ibid.

move out of their preoccupation with themselves and into their greatest good, namely the enjoyment of God and love for others which constitute their proper end. To be concerned primarily with what is private and personal is, in fact, a loss for humanity, for, as Augustine notes, "private" is "a word clearly suggesting loss rather than gain in value; every privation, after all, spells diminution."[129] This is why, for Augustine, the Heavenly City is that which is truly public and political: it restores the proper end to humanity and provides the place in which common goals and goods serve to unify its people. If, in other words, a *polis* is understood as Alasdair MacIntyre defines it, "as the form of social order whose shared mode of life already expresses the collective answer or answers of its citizens to the question 'What is the best mode of life for human beings?' ", and if concomitant with that answer are certain goods and systematic forms of activity related to those goods, then Christianity is as much a *polis* as the *polis* of liberal democratic society.[130]

This discussion is not meant to deny a place or a role for the political realm, but it is supposed to raise questions about how we understand what is meant by "public" and what is allowed to be public and enter the so-called public square in contemporary liberalism. We are not disputing the claim ably represented by Elshtain that some distinction between public and private is necessary for politics to exist, nor are we disagreeing with the idea that important and significant areas of life can best flourish when left outside of the direct purview of an all-embracing public (as in political) imperative.[131] We are, however, like Elshtain, wondering how different conceptions of public and private and, here differently than Elshtain, an expanded space for overlapping "publics," might help expand our current political and theological imagination. From a theological perspective, we must be wary of accepting definitions that undermine the essence of Christianity as an embodied, social public, united around the common interest of love of God. We must be careful to prevent the Church from grafting into its self-understanding ways of thinking that do not allow it to be seen

---

129. "The Literal Meaning of Genesis" XI, 19.
130. MacIntyre, *Whose Justice? Which Rationality?* p. 133.
131. See Elshtain, *Public Man, Private Woman*, pp. 201, 351. On the importance of the private sphere, see also Duncan B. Forrester, *Beliefs, Values and Policies: Conviction Politics in a Secular Age* (Oxford: Clarendon, 1998), pp. 7–8.

as the site of the true common good around which people can be united in shared purpose, as the commonwealth in which justice and peace are actual possibilities, through the mediating and redeeming work of Jesus Christ.

If we understand politics as a human mode of association, Christianity and liberalism (and post-Nietzschean political theory for that matter) present vastly different pictures of the humans in that association and of the association itself. This is just as we would expect, given the differences in the ontologies that underlie their respective political and social thought, but these differences have often been occluded as Christianity has accepted reigning paradigms of thought in order to be included in the current conversation. Such inclusion should not need to come at the expense of Christianity's identity as communal and public; it should not need to require Christianity to compromise its integrity by distancing itself from its social, public, and institutionalized home so that it becomes a privatized system of beliefs with relevance only for the "life of the soul." In short, a way should exist for Christianity to be public without taking over what we commonly understand as the public square or ceasing to abide by the rule of law established by the larger political society. All of this is to say that Christianity, in an Augustinian vein, cannot remain content with the way it has let itself be positioned by contemporary political liberalism. Nor can other communal constituencies currently residing in Western societies.[132]

To look at this from another perspective, let us briefly follow the argument of Reinhard Hütter as he considers the concept of public. Whereas our contemporary understanding of public legitimizes only the public of liberal political society, Hütter offers a vision of "a structural concept of public" that allows for "a whole multiplicity of different publics that overlap and complement one another and yet also are able to relate to one another from within positions of serious, fundamental tension."[133] Why is this important? Because if the Church is not understood fundamentally and explicitly as its own public, then it is defined and positioned "from the perspective of the normative public of modern, differentiated liberal society that promptly effects the Church's eclipse *as*

132. Connolly begins to discuss this in relation to Islam in *Pluralism*, pp. 55–59.
133. Hütter, *Suffering Divine Things*, p. 159.

a public."[134] When the Church loses its sense of itself as public, it begins to be defined and to define itself by an alien logic, by the logic of, for example, contemporary liberalism, thereby losing its ability to stand alongside, apart from, or in critical relationship to the public of modern society.[135] This could, in fact, be what so often leads the (Protestant) Church to align itself with the purposes of the nation-state: "this eclipse of the Protestant church as public might be one reason it is susceptible to becoming the bearer of national and other identities and projects, securing for itself thus as a national or civil religion a measure of public relevance within the framework of the public arena of society at large."[136] This eclipse of the Church as a public, then, affects not only the Church's self-understanding, but also its ability to stand as a critical or prophetic voice in the larger society.

That is to say, just as one of the strengths of post-Nietzschean political theory is that it allows a questioning of the definitions and configurations of political society established by political liberalism, one of the dangers of allowing "public" to remain synonymous with the political realm as defined by contemporary political theory and practice is that it limits the critical abilities of other constituencies within political society. By creating space for multiple publics, overlapping yet each marked by its own telos, doctrine, and practices, we open the possibility of critical interaction between these publics, and between these publics and the political society of the time. Such intercourse between publics would, furthermore, avoid the prioritization of the individual that is concomitant with much liberal theory, something which Connolly's political theory tries unsuccessfully to escape. Those who view themselves primarily as individuals and who place their identity first and foremost in the public of political liberal society continue to be welcome to do so, but those who find in other publics their more formative identities and allegiances can be given the space to operate from within those publics in interaction with the public of political society, which will continue to supply the overarching rule of law. This does not mean that it will always be easy to negotiate the different identities and allegiances that may come from the different publics and the

134. Ibid., p. 169.
135. See ibid., p. 171.
136. Ibid., p. 11.

political society of which citizens are a part, but it does mean that it is worth allowing space for these tensions to arise. Michael J. Sandel's effort to articulate a renewed version of republicanism for our time similarly seeks to allow such space. Recognizing that "most of us organize our lives around smaller solidarities," Sandel writes that whatever political vision we adopt "will have to enable us to live with multiple, overlapping, sometimes contending moral and political loyalties. It must equip us to live – this is the difficult part – with the tensions to which multiply-situated and multiply-encumbered selves are prone."[137]

The discussion we have been having up to this point leaves us with conclusions that are not far afield, in some respects, from those of Stanley Hauerwas.[138] For Hauerwas, Christian beliefs cannot be divorced from the kind of community the Church is and should be. Christian discipleship both creates and is a polity: to be a Christian is to be in a community formed around the obedience of Jesus Christ to the cross.[139] Theology cannot be conceived as merely a set of ideas or interior beliefs. It must be rooted in practices and disciplines that constitute the Church through time; in other words, Christianity is ecclesiology.[140] Yet Christianity, in Hauerwas' opinion, has let itself become privatized, allowing democracy to become primary while it has become subordinate to democratic political arrangements.[141] When Christianity is separated from its embodied social form, when it comes to be seen first and foremost as a set of private beliefs or values, it not only ceases to be understood as public, it also allows for the emergence of a "public" space in which a vague national or civil "religion" comes to be seen and embraced as that which is common to all citizens. Such a national "religion" is, however, deeply at odds with a Christianity that is understood as, at heart, public and with a Church that is seen as,

---

137. Michael J. Sandel, "The Politics of Public Identity," *The Hedgehog Review* 2, no. 1 (Spring 2000), p. 87.
138. A full articulation of Hauerwas' thought is well beyond the purview of this work. For an impressively thorough and articulate account of much of Hauerwas' thinking, see Arne Rasmusson, *The Church as Polis: From Political Theology to Theological Politics as Exemplified by Jürgen Moltmann and Stanley Hauerwas* (Notre Dame, IN: University of Notre Dame Press, 1995), esp. pp. 174–230 and 248–302.
139. Stanley Hauerwas, *A Community of Character: Toward a Constructive Christian Social Ethic* (Notre Dame, IN: University of Notre Dame Press, 1981), pp. 1, 49.
140. Hauerwas, *In Good Company*, p. 58.
141. Ibid., p. 201

fundamentally, its own *polis*.[142] Furthermore Christianity is deeply
at odds with liberalism, as evident in everything from their differing
understandings of the "individual" to their conceptions of freedom,
justice, and truth. For Hauerwas, Christians have failed to see the
profound differences between the politics of liberal democracy
and the politics of the Church, and have thereby assumed that by
serving the secular polity they have been advancing the Gospel.
Christians, for example, believe that they should be engaged in
politics to help secure a more nearly just society, while failing to see
that the justice of Christianity is profoundly different from that of
political society. Whereas liberal political societies have focused on
the just distribution of desires and goods, the Church's political task
is the development of virtuous people, formed in a society built on
trust rather than fear, who are equipped with skills of discrimination that enable its members to perceive and interpret the larger
society (and its limitations) in which they find themselves. This
happens only as Christians are uninvolved in the politics of that
larger society and involved in the polity that is the Church.[143]

The latter condition is not one promulgated by Augustine, who
believes that Christians can and should accept involvement in the
political realm. We will return to this matter shortly, as it is a significant one. For now, however, let us notice the considerable
agreement between Hauerwas and Augustine on the importance of
recognizing that one's primary identity is as a citizen in the Kingdom of God, which is itself a polity with its own distinct ends and
means. Hauerwas is right to remind Christians that the language
and presuppositions of liberalism are often at odds with those of
Christianity, and that Christians need to acquire skills of discernment and the virtues and practices that enable them to distinguish
between, for example, the justice of liberalism and the justice of
Christ. In other words, the Word of God in Christ needs to define the
words and practices of the Church; the words by which Christians
live and in which Christians believe must have their source in the
Word made flesh. As Alan Torrance asks,

> How far does the specific and concrete Word of God to humankind
> in Christ require a revision of our intuitive interpretations of the

---

142. Ibid., p. 210.
143. Hauerwas, *Community of Character*, pp. 73–74.

nature and function of the state and of its obligations and responsibilities for justice, peace and freedom? How far does the Word,
as the impetus and warrant for God-talk within the political
domain, involve a semantic reconstruction of these terms
reorienting their meaning rather than simply endorsing their
everyday language?[144]

His answer: "to the extent that Christ is the Logos of God he stands
as the Counter-logos to our preconceived social, cultural, political,
and religious conceptualities. As such he radically revises and reorders the prior blueprints with which we intuitively desire to shape
our world and interpret our experience."[145]

All of this is to say, the language and definitions that are used and
given are of profound importance to the discussion of issues related
to pluralism and the political realm (as our post-Nietzscheans
helped us to see in chapter three). Indeed, one of the most fundamental tasks for the Church to consider is who defines its language:
what understandings are invoked in descriptions of the Church's
ends or the tasks undertaken by Christians? How far does the
Church want to go, for example, in explaining what Christians are
doing when they love their neighbor as "helping civil society"
rather than as being faithful to the Christian calling? How much do
Christians want to enable themselves to be part of liberal political
society by accepting that their Christianity is a matter merely of
private belief, when that goes against the grain of the history and
tradition of the Church and the writings of the earliest Church
fathers and Holy Scripture? How far does the Church go in choosing
to view itself as one of a number of "voluntary associations,"
thereby enabling itself to be part of the "public realm," when that
comes at the cost of an understanding of Christianity as that which
is authentically public, providing the only real source of commonality, goodness, peace, justice, and right? Or are Christians willing to
view themselves as members of a *polis* that takes primacy over the
political societies of which they happen to be a part, and to have
their involvement in that *polis* serve, to some degree, as a reminder
that certain goals will never be attained in the earthly city?

144. Alan J. Torrance, "Introductory Essay," in Eberhard Jüngel, *Christ,
Justice and Peace: Toward a Theology of the State,* trans. D. Bruce Hamill and
Alan J. Torrance (Edinburgh: T&T Clark, 1992), p. x.
145. Torrance, "Introductory Essay," p. xiii.

At the same time, despite the critical distance this reading fosters in Christians towards the earthly city, they also need to be willing to participate in it, even in its current liberal configuration, bringing to it contributions, criticisms, and challenges that can help further certain of its goods and goals. For, as Robert Song writes, "liberal society as much as any other social order may be sacralized, and stands in as great a need of challenging and, if necessary at times, changing."[146] Such challenging and changing may at times be fostered by the Church's prophetic role, and it may also be aided by direct involvement of members of the Church in political society. In short, Christians may be called to serve in the social and political institutions and arrangements of the earthly city. When called, they should undertake their service with humility and charity, pursuing the goods of the earthly city as those who both share some of these goods and desire the best in this age for their neighbors who are not, or are not yet, part of the Church. For love of their neighbors must surely involve the pursuit of earthly justice and earthly peace from which these neighbors can and will benefit, even as the pursuit is undertaken with the knowledge that earthly justice and peace are not comparable to heavenly justice and peace. And this pursuit cannot require that citizens of the Heavenly City distance themselves from their citizenship in the Heavenly Kingdom as they seek to contribute to and serve the earthly city.

When some in a political society consider their identity as members of other communities more formative than their identity as political citizens, in what manner should they be able to be involved in that political society? Does their involvement in political life require them to see themselves first as citizens and then as members of another public? We remember from the last chapter Augustine's conviction that not only should Christians be involved in the earthly political society but that they should be involved *as Christians*. In his writings on the role of Christians in different aspects of the earthly city's legal and political structures, Augustine always places the Christian identity of those whom he is addressing or discussing at the forefront. A pilgrim, for example, who is called to be a judge is to approach being a judge *as*, rather than separate from his identity as, a Christian. Such a Christian judge is called to remember his own guilt

146. Robert Song, *Christianity and Liberal Society* (Oxford: Clarendon, 1997), p. 229.

and his need of God's generous grace, so that he judges in mercy and love with, as Dodaro puts it, "the love born in the interior recognition of a moral symmetry between himself and the other."[147] In the case of Christian rulers, Augustine writes that "there is no happier situation for mankind than that they, by God's mercy, should wield power;"[148] he says this not because he thinks Christian rulers can and should make Christian empires or nations, for he is far too realistic about the *libido dominandi* of the earthly city and its citizens to think that the political realm could itself embody the justice and peace of Christ. He says this because, in his view, only a Christian ruler can escape the lust for power and self-glorification that generally marks the earthly city. Such rulers rule with justice rather than pride, they submit their power to God rather than to their own desires for aggrandizement (remember that for Augustine power is rightly subsumed under justice), they are slow to punish and eager to pardon, they restrain their self-indulgent appetites, and they are motivated by love of God rather than the desire for empty glory.[149] They remember, in short, that even "the loftiest summit of power ... is nothing but a passing mist."[150]

For Augustine, the Christian brings to political involvement a right understanding of the provisionality and contingency of contemporary arrangements, a proper source for humility, the grace to counter the lust for power that dominates the earthly city, and a knowledge of the God-intended order of the universe that provides a point of critique and challenge. Even as Christians share in the life and peace of the earthly city, even as they are open to participation in its political structures, they remember with each step that they are first and foremost citizens of the Heavenly City. The primary task of Christians is to be citizens of the Heavenly City, defining themselves and their actions in light of the Christian narrative, and only secondarily is their task to be part of and to work towards the goods of the earthly city. In light of this claim, what can Christians expect of the earthly city? Perhaps to not demand so much of its

147. Robert Dodaro, "Loose Canons: Augustine and Derrida on Their Selves," in *God, the Gift, and Postmodernism*, eds. John D. Caputo and Michael J. Scanlon (Bloomington, IN: Indiana University Press, 1999), p. 95. See also pp. 91–93 and 99.
148. *City of God* V, 19.
149. Ibid., 24.
150. Ibid., 26 (drawing on James 4:14).

members that the particularity of what they view as their primary identity, and what members of other faith communities may view as their primary identities, is not undermined. Perhaps to give space for these members to practice their identities and their faiths publicly and as publics, so that they might be "publicly" respected and even mutually appreciated.

This returns us again to the question of what a political arrangement that allows the public recognition of particularity might look like. Benjamin Gregg has recently articulated a position that looks more promising than other ones we have considered thus far. He is in search of a way to have a political realm marked not by "normative consensus" but by the more realistic goal of "accommodation." Instead of presupposing or searching for "fundamentally shared principles," he offers space for a variety of "thick" moralities as embodied in different political, social, and cultural groups and individuals. His proposal of "thick moralities, thin politics" allows for the presence of different, coexisting moralities, so long as those groups agree to work within the bounds of law. In other words, "no one of these groups has the right to impose its position on another, unless those positions 'win' in terms of legislation or judicial interpretation."[151] And if they don't win? They "retain the right to maintain their contrarian viewpoints and to continue to advocate them."[152] In short, "the politics of thick norms must expect constant disagreement at the moral level, but it seeks political cooperation in the face of enduring disagreement."[153]

This seems to be a very promising way forward, but Gregg also grafts some problematic assumptions into his thinking. While claiming that his proposal "does not elide differences among normatively thick groups or standpoints", he continues to insist that, as citizens in debate, they be required to share their viewpoints and attempt to persuade the other side using only "thin terms," meaning terms which are potentially acceptable to that other side.[154] In other words, "one must be prepared to place (in the public sphere, on matters of public policy) one's faith in rational deliberation above one's own moral commitments, when those commitments are not

151. Gregg, *Thick Moralities, Thin Politics*, p. 5.
152. Ibid.
153. Ibid., pp. 5–6.
154. Ibid., p. 6.

sustained by rational deliberation or rational process in the public sphere."[155] Leaving aside the point, well made in our second chapter, that asking groups and individuals to prioritize "rational debate" over their own commitments and beliefs fails to truly respect the depth and particularity of those commitments, we might be tempted to agree that the wisest course for one side of a debate to follow is that of attempting to use language and reasoning with which it expects the other side could concur. Yet we might also consider that the other side could be open to hearing many or all of the reasons behind its opponent's position, even if it doesn't yet find them persuasive. It might be that both sides could learn from being exposed to the particularity and the thickness that underlie, shape, and inspire the other, and that "public" debate is and should be a place that provides the forum for a deep exchange of ideas that has the potential to alter and change the positions of both sides, at thin and thick levels.

This is a crucial point of consideration, for contemporary liberal political society does not allow for the type of debate and interaction that would enable real questions about the good and the true to be engaged. According to the diagnosis of MacIntyre, "liberal individualism" operates with a conception of the good that supposes, ironically, that there is no overriding good. This means that the public arena it facilitates is a site for the exchange of "preferences" and "choices" rather than a place of debate about the human good or between rival conceptions of the good.[156] And yet, while not allowing explicit debate over questions of the good, liberalism implicitly suggests certain answers (for every law embodies some idea of the good and every ruling discloses a normative stance) while preventing others from having public presence. As we have seen, liberalism is afraid of the divisiveness that might emerge were questions of the good to be engaged publicly; this fear stems from liberalism's origins in the religious wars of previous centuries. Yet other scholars, such as Philip Quinn, wonder whether this fear still needs to be such a driving force in limiting what we can publicly engage.[157] And others, such as our agonistic political theorists, fear

155. Ibid., p. 8.
156. See MacIntyre, *Whose Justice? Which Rationality?* pp. 336–339.
157. See Philip Quinn, "Religious Diversity and Religious Toleration," *International Journal for Philosophy of Religion* 50 (2001), p. 59. See also Sandel, *Democracy's Discontent*, p. 64.

that by not engaging such differences publicly, we leave them no choice but to make themselves known violently. Of course, these differences need to be engaged not only publicly, according to liberalism's definition, but also in the reality of daily living, as interactions between people and groups with different ontologies inevitably occur within a pluralist society. How can individuals, groups, and faiths meet together from within their substantially different goods, beliefs, and practices? What could this coming together of particularities look like? And how should Christians engage in these efforts to find unity amidst our diversity in the earthly city?

Conversation, rich and deep

We began this book asking how we are to live together in the midst of our differences. We have now listened to some of the voices that are trying to answer this question and we have tried to imagine the solutions they are offering. In one case, we sensed that the vision of political unity proffered came at the expense of much of the diversity found within our society. In another, we concluded that the commitment to difference problematically came at the expense of achieving any harmony between those differences. And in a third voice we heard that unity amidst our diversity could only be realized in the Heavenly City, in which people are reunited and reconciled through Jesus Christ. None of these three voices seems altogether helpful in providing a satisfying answer to the original question. Is there any hope that we might find a way to come together within this earthly city, without leaving either our differences or our need for some level of harmony behind? A renewed picture of conversation, one that recovers lost aspects of conversation's historical and biblical definition, may help us in our search.

This effort to offer a picture of different particularities coming together within political society needs to be undertaken with two caveats in mind. First, this does not represent an attempt to create a picture of an "ideal" political society or to articulate a theory that would sufficiently undergird the political realm of the earthly city. We remember Augustine, who thought that citizens of the Heavenly City could contribute to the earthly city, but certainly did not prescribe, nor think it possible for Christianity to prescribe, an ideal

city or political regime this side of the eschaton. Christians can give what they are able to their current political situation, but they must not think they can find a solution that will answer all of its problems, for many of its problems cannot be fully resolved in the earthly city. Our current political situation is one marked by rich pluralism, and so the picture we offer arises in response to that context. This leads to our second caveat, namely that what is articulated here is not suggested in an attempt to achieve the reconciliation and the celebration of unity and diversity that are only possible in the Heavenly City. In the Heavenly City alone can differences come together in love, as its citizens offer each other and delight together in the humility, generosity, hospitality, and grace they have by virtue of their participation in their Triune God. And yet, precisely because of this participation, which yields its firstfruits in the lives of Christians and the Church in the here and now, we can move from a picture of reconciliation and celebration in the Heavenly City to one in which we see what the resources and perspectives of the Christian ontology might contribute to the earthly city in the *saeculum*. This could perhaps be seen as our version of William Connolly's ethos of critical responsiveness, our articulation of ways in which differences can come together with humility and generosity, grounded in a Christian rather than a post-Nietzschean ontology.

This last point is important to keep in mind. The hope of this discussion is to provide a picture of rich conversation between the different constituencies of contemporary society. This picture may seem most relevant or convincing to those who are already persuaded by the truths of Christianity, just as Connolly's ethos seems most applicable to those who already accept the beliefs that underlie it. Nevertheless, those with differing ontologies can learn from the pictures offered by ontologies different than their own. Indeed, this belief in our ability to learn from each other in the midst of our differences lies at the heart of the picture of conversation we are here trying to present. As we draw this picture, it will be clear that much of our discussion is given from the viewpoint of the Church and of those who adhere, however differently in the details, to the overall truths of the Christian faith. As our post-Nietzscheans have helpfully and clearly reminded us, no theory can divorce itself from its ontological presuppositions, even should it so

desire. This work of Christian theology has neither the aspiration nor the expertise to provide pictures of engagement with others that do not flow from an understanding of the narratives, practices, and beliefs of the Christian faith. And yet, if our presuppositions are correct, this will not preclude other faiths, practices, and "publics" from learning from the picture we offer.

Conversation lies at the center of this picture. This is not conversation restricted to verbal communication but conversation that includes interaction between ways and manners of life. Both scripturally and historically, conversation has more often been associated with this broader picture of interaction. Indeed, "conversation" is never used in Scripture to mean verbal communication from one to another; instead, it generally refers to the "goings out and in of social intercourse."[158] Likewise, the earliest references to conversation as cited in *The Oxford English Dictionary* have to do with "the action of living"; "the action of consorting or having dealings with others; living together; commerce, intercourse, society, intimacy"; and "manner of conducting oneself in the world or in society; behaviour, mode, or course of life."[159] These are the richer conceptions of conversation to which our account appeals, ones that involve both verbal exchange and interaction between different manners of life. It is as identities are embodied and practiced, as narratives are incarnated and lived out, and as people live together and engage with one another from within the embodiment of their differing narratives that the possibility of true conversation exists. In this type of conversation, each party speaks from within the particularity and fullness of its own identity and beliefs and operates with a trust in what can be learned and accomplished through interaction, debate, and deliberation. Each party is open to being persuaded by the other, to changing its convictions and practices, in small and large ways, and even to being converted to different beliefs and manners of life.

Let us pause for a moment to notice how different this is from the theory put forward by John Rawls. For Rawls, public conversation should only consist of reasons and arguments that all reasonable

---

158. See M. G. Easton, *Illustrated Bible Dictionary*, 3d. ed. (New York: Thomas Nelson, 1897).
159. *The Oxford English Dictionary*, vol. 3, 2d. ed., eds. J. A. Simpson and E. S. C. Weiner (Oxford: Clarendon, 1989).

people can be expected to understand. As with Gregg's proposal, one can sense the immediate appeal of such a view, yet underlying it is a disbelief in the ability of people to learn from each other and to change their opinions and ways of thinking and living in light of being introduced to ideas that are fundamentally different from their own. The site of the political may not be a place where we can all get along; it may instead be a forum for airing some of our most deep-seated differences and conflicts and learning (how) to live with them. Yet in that airing something crucial may take place: a level of openness, honesty, and critical engagement with "the other" that brings forth empathy and understanding, that enables genuine, appreciative, respectful relationship with "the other," and that opens up the possibility of change in opinion, belief, and manner of life may be attained. What assumption drives the view that we can only come together in the name of or for the sake of an overlapping consensus? Why must we hide the differences that underlie our incompatible viewpoints instead of hoping that we can learn from each other in the midst of our differences? Why must we believe that respect for persons depends upon conversing only in terms and reasons that all have in common rather than also involving the sharing of our differences and our particularity?[160] Why must we build a political theory that, instead of encouraging people to keep and pursue their identities and beliefs, relies on their "comprehensive doctrines" not being comprehensive? For Rawls' theory depends for its success on the very thing that we have here been decrying, namely the alteration of comprehensive doctrines in the name of and for the sake of political principles that have, without people realizing it, won their primary allegiance. We are here searching for a way for comprehensive doctrines to come together, to interact as publics and publicly, in ways that do not involve such covert manipulation.

The picture of conversation we are offering also differs from that recently described by Jeffrey Stout in *Democracy & Tradition*. Stout shares the concern that Rawls' vision of public discourse unnecessarily restricts the role of religious reasoning and commitments,

---

160. See Christopher J. Eberle, *Religious Conviction in Liberal Politics* (Cambridge: Cambridge University Press, 2002), pp. 11–13 and Jeffrey Stout, *Democracy & Tradition* (Princeton, NJ: Princeton University Press, 2004), pp. 72–73, 85.

and he commends "conversation" as a way for citizens to engage in discourse that freely draws upon whatever premises and beliefs provide support for their respective positions. He writes of conversation as "an exchange of views in which the respective parties express their premises in as much detail as they see fit and in whatever idiom they wish, try to make sense of each other's perspectives, and expose their own commitments to the possibility of criticism."[161] While this certainly overlaps with the picture of conversation being drawn here, Stout limits the application of his concept of conversation to the exchange of ideas about issues that are of concern to the body politic.[162] We would like to put forward a picture of conversation that also applies to interactions between people with different beliefs and ways of life as they *live* together in our pluralist society; in this sense, it is more of an ethos permeating our involvements with one another than an idea that pertains only when we are engaged in explicitly political dialogue.

Perhaps one further comparison would be instructive, with a political theory that is centered around discourse and seeks to enlarge our vision of the public forum. The deliberative democracy articulated by Seyla Benhabib proposes a picture of democratic discourse that does not limit the content or range of dialogue that can occur between citizens.[163] It "permits maximal cultural contestation within the public sphere"[164] and it does "not prescribe the content of moral argument through thought experiments or definitional boundary drawings between the public and the private."[165] Rather, her version of deliberative democracy encourages discourse about the lines that separate the public from the private.[166] She seeks to broaden how the public sphere is understood, from its usual association with the official institutions of the political realm to a "decentered public sphere [that] consists of mutually overlapping networks and associations of opinion-forming as well as decisional bodies. Within these multiple and overlapping networks

161. Stout, *Democracy & Tradition*, pp. 10–11.
162. Ibid., p. 64.
163. This treatment will obviously be cursory, not least because it will not engage any of the deeper philosophical and ontological differences underlying our respective positions.
164. Benhabib, *Claims of Culture*, p. ix.
165. Ibid., p. 13.
166. Ibid., p. 109.

of publicity, different logics of reason giving, greeting, storytelling, and embedded speech can flourish."[167]

To summarize and compare, Benhabib's picture of discourse is similar to ours in that she would also like to see deliberation that does not restrict which reasons, stories, ways of thinking, or beliefs people can employ. Furthermore, she is concerned that such discourse engage the organizations and associations of civil society as much as those of the political culture. Yet it is precisely by viewing civil society as the site where "normative dialogue" takes place, by seeing "the free public sphere of civil society as the principal arena for the articulation, contestation, and resolution of normative discourses,"[168] that Benhabib's evaluation of the current situation differs from the one offered here. Our point has been that the public realm has been almost entirely eclipsed by the political; we cannot just look to current civil society to be the place where unrestricted conversation takes place because the institutions and associations that supposedly inhabit civil society have been severely restricted and diminished, albeit often by their own acquiescence, by historical and contemporary conceptions of political liberalism. What we need is to reimagine our understanding of public to such an extent that new spaces begin to exist for multiple publics that can overlap and interact, publics that are richer and more identity-constitutive than what we now consider voluntary associations and yet are different from the political realm as such. The resulting conversation would be between these publics, or between the individuals who constitute them and individuals who claim participation in no particular public, and the substance of such conversation would be both political issues and the rest of life. We are less concerned, here, with articulating a means of discourse that results in political decisions than with offering a picture of conversation that can help engage the current realities of pluralism on numerous levels and help foster a hospitable ethos of interaction.

For this to happen, engagement between different identities and publics needs to occur not only in words but also in practices. As Cavanaugh, writing with the Church in mind, comments, "the most fruitful way to dialogue with those outside of the church ... is

167. Ibid., p. 139; pp. 21, 106.
168. Ibid., p. 115.

through *concrete practices* that do not need translation into some putatively 'neutral' language to be understood."[169] This is integrally related to the need to understand Christianity as more than a set of private beliefs that pertain only to one's values, for Christianity takes shape as an embodied narrative, defined by practices, disciplines, and sacraments that are rightfully and authentically public. To reiterate, we need to discern a way to allow other publics to exist and interact alongside the "public" of political liberalism, which has become the only public we recognize as such.

Such a reconfiguration of public and private may be particularly timely in light of recent diagnoses regarding the disappearance of the public spaces of contemporary liberal politics. One could appeal to works on the decline of civil society such as Robert Putnam's *Bowling Alone* or to the more drastic diagnosis of the neo-Marxists Michael Hardt and Antonio Negri.[170] Hardt and Negri argue that under the conditions of postmodernity public space has been privatized to such a large degree (they cite the transition from common squares and public encounter to gated communities and the closed space of shopping malls) that the spaces of modern liberal politics no longer exist. With the loss of the clear distinction between the private world of the household and the public world outside the home, they maintain that not only has the place of politics been de-actualized, but a deficit of the political has arisen.[171] We are here reminded of the diagnosis of post-Nietzschean theorists who likewise notice a loss of the political, although they tend to blame this on political liberalism itself rather than on the conditions of postmodernity. Either way, a clear concern exists for the need of a return of the public argumentation and interaction that mark genuine politics, for the need of space for communication and conversation between people, groups, and forces that are, at times, antagonistic.

Perhaps the first thing to come to mind when words such as "debate" and "conversation" are used is a formal setting in which agreed participants verbally exchange ideas and share beliefs. This is, of course, one obvious and necessary way for such interaction to take place, particularly when we think of "public" dialogue and

---

169. Cavanaugh, "Public Theology," p. 120; emphasis added.
170. Robert D. Putnam, *Bowling Alone: The Collapse and Revival of American Community* (New York: Simon & Schuster, 2000); Hardt and Negri, *Empire*.
171. See Hardt and Negri, *Empire*, pp. 186–190, esp. p. 188.

"public" reason as defined by political liberalism. When we expand our understanding of public, however, and see multiple "publics" and various forms of "public" presence, we also open the way for acknowledgement of different types of interaction. The embodiment of ideas, beliefs, and narratives in practices, traditions, and communities means that conversation occurs through incarnated interaction rather than merely verbal exchange. Nicholas Healy offers a picture of debates which "occur not only at the level of ideas, but in their communal embodiment, within and between religious and non-religious bodies whose concrete identities conflict internally and with one another."[172] Likewise Cavanaugh, as we saw above, thinks that the most fruitful kinds of dialogue happen through the interaction of concrete practices. This happens eachday in a pluralist society, as different people and communities interact with each other. It needs no formal setting to take place, although it can certainly be augmented by "official" forums and discussions. But we must not forget that "the real public realm," as Alistair McFadyen writes, "has to do with communication between different frames of thought."[173] That is to say, the public realm is defined not by what is considered the "public square" by political liberalism but by places and conversations marked by communication between different ways of thinking and living.

What does this communication look like? It does not look like the effort to discover consensus and harmony at the cost of the recognition of genuine particularity and difference. We are careful to avoid the language of "dialogue," which too often operates with the assumption that the differences that emerge in dialogue can be subsumed under larger universal and unifying categories.[174] We prefer the language of "conversation," in which people and groups interact with one another verbally and through their ways of life. Through such interaction and conversation different participants have the opportunity to learn from each other and to change their

172. Healy, *Church, World and the Christian Life*, p. 106.
173. Alistair McFadyen, "Truth as Mission: The Christian Claim to Universal Truth in a Pluralist Public World," *Scottish Journal of Theology* 46, no. 4 (1993), p. 445.
174. For a particularly strong, and at times refreshingly honest, response to such dialogue, see John Milbank, "The End of Dialogue," in *Christian Uniqueness Reconsidered: The Myth of a Pluralistic Theology of Religions*, ed. Gavin D'Costa (Maryknoll, NY: Orbis, 1990), pp. 174–191.

beliefs, practices, or stories in large and small ways. The desired goal is not discussion or engagement over that which participants already have in common, agree on, or can "reasonably" be expected to understand and accept. While trying to find areas of agreement and commonality is not undesirable, it is also worthwhile to try to understand others in their differences and particularity. Underlying this picture of conversation is a belief that such attempts at understanding and interacting have some positive good, that people can learn from each other, that groups can and should be open to such learning and to change.

Yes, genuine differences exist within contemporary Western society, but we need not be driven by fear when we contemplate interaction between these differences. We need not assume that the only way to secure stability and justice within a pluralist political society is to find language and arguments upon which we can all agree. As the post-Nietzscheans have reminded us, the element of the "political" can never be ignored. The realities of conflict and power are deep and pervasive. Everyone may not fit easily and neatly into a political society. But perhaps in this current *milieu*, we should be more afraid of ignoring differences than of what will happen when we attempt to engage them. Political liberalism seems fearful of what will happen if we enter into debate and deliberation from within our particularity. We, like the post-Nietzscheans, are more afraid of what will happen if we do not allow for such forms of interaction. The culture wars of the eighties and nineties and the more recent terrorism and suspicions of the Muslim world towards Western society involve the deepest ontological differences; they stem from underlying divergent views of the nature of reality and human being and all the beliefs, embodiments, and positions that flow from those divergent views. Engaging with those differences, in formal and informal ways, is no longer the "conversation-stopper." Without such engagement, no conversation can even begin, never mind be "stopped."

Indeed, as Charles T. Mathewes persuasively argues, religion is not the "conversation-stopper" that many (such as Rorty) have assumed it to be.[175] The idea that religious belief is more intrinsically connected to intolerance than many forms of secular belief

175. See also Stout, *Democracy & Tradition*, pp. 85–91.

(Mathewes thinks of Nazism, communism, and liberalism) is more a reflection of the cultural mythology of our "liberal" society than intrinsically true. That is to say, all theories, philosophies, and ideologies, not just those that are explicitly "religious," involve deep and controversial views that have the potential to foster intolerance towards those who hold different views. Furthermore, Mathewes argues that religious discourse provides positive insights that are unavailable outside of explicitly religious language and that to demand the use of "neutral" language inevitably weakens religious convictions because of language's influential role in shaping experience and identity.[176] This is clearly a different ideal than that held by Rawls, who, while later allowing for nonshared reasons and beliefs to be used in public discourse, and even acknowledging the contribution different traditions have made to democratic life, still speaks of this only as a *proviso* rather than a positive good. We would be more inclined to follow Mathewes and others, such as Paul Brink, who view our traditions and committed positions not as things to be ignored or retreated into, but as sources of strength and insight, as means of fostering relationships and mutuality, as avenues for learning and change.[177]

This returns us again to the importance of the embodiment and practice of Christianity. The Christian narrative must be matched by its enactment in Christian practice, the Christian story is inseparable from its embodiment in a Christian *polis*, and Christian truth is only public as mission, as the communication and action that occur in witness to the faith and hope of Christianity's eschatological vision, or so McFadyen argues.[178] Importantly, McFadyen reminds us that the "publicness of Christian truth cannot be a matter of communicating a fully known truth to an audience; it is also the process of *becoming* the community we claim to be."[179] As Christians communicate, it is not as those who fully possess and incarnate the truth of which they speak, but as those who are trying to become

176. See Charles T. Mathewes, *A Theology of Public Life During the World* (forthcoming), esp. introduction, chap. 5.
177. See Paul A. Brink, "Selves in Relation: Theories of Community and the *Imago Dei* Doctrine," in *The Re-Enchantment of Political Science: Christian Scholars Engage Their Discipline*, ed. Thomas W. Heilke and Ashley Woodiwiss (Lanham, MD: Lexington Books, 2001), p. 114. Cf. Eberle, *Religious Conviction in Liberal Politics*.
178. McFadyen, "Truth as Mission," p. 453.
179. Ibid., p. 455.

the communal embodiment of what they believe. As citizens of the Heavenly City attempt to live into the gospel story that they believe in faith, their lives and communities should offer, partial and sinful yet nevertheless graceful, reflections of that gospel story. It is in this embodied communication that the genuine interaction and conversation that we've been discussing happen. "Another way of putting this," as Trevor Hart writes,

> is simply to say that the way in which the Christian community "interprets" its gospel is not limited to intellectual accounts and explanations of the story itself, ... but extends to the entirety of the forms of thought and activity adopted by Christian people in the world. The Church's attempts to be the people of God in the world, that is to say, to continue the story, provide the most poignant commentary on the meaning of the gospel which it has to share with others.[180]

This picture of Christian interaction and mission as lying fundamentally in the embodiment of Christian *praxis*, rather than, for example, in universalizable, propositional statements, reveals an understanding of truth that relies more on faith and hope than "knowledge in the strict sense," as McFadyen puts it.[181] It takes into account the epistemic humility engendered by post-Enlightenment thought, avoiding the problematic ingrafting of Enlightenment optimism about human access to universal truth into the heart of Christianity. And yet it does not entail the abandonment of universal truth itself as a category and reality, even as it limits our claims to have unequivocal access to it. As Hart argues, there is a way to recognize the partiality of our perspectives, to acknowledge that we stand within particular traditions and fiduciary commitments, and yet to continue to think it important to find the account of things that offers the most satisfactory approach to reality. Though we can never be absolutely certain that what we know, believe, and practice corresponds to reality, it should be acceptable to say that we believe we have identified a truer or more satisfactory outlook than others currently known, while accepting the possibility that a more adequate outlook may exist or be discovered.[182]

180. Trevor Hart, *Faith Thinking: The Dynamics of Christian Theology* (London: SPCK, 1995), p.184.
181. McFadyen, "Truth as Mission," p.448.
182. See Hart, *Faith Thinking*, esp. pp.66–67, 222–225.

With this understanding, the Christian is open to learning from others who stand in the particularity of their perspectives and faith commitments even as he or she stands from within the faith, tradition, and disciplines of Christianity.[183]

Healy's description of what he terms "theodramatic debate" offers a similar picture of participants operating from within the particularity of their traditions as they seek answers to the question of truth. When participants operate with an understanding that they seek rather than possess truth, they are open to learning from each other. When this is combined with the belief that the Holy Spirit is active in people, religious bodies, and nonreligious bodies who are not explicitly Christian, Christian participants have the sources they need to engage in conversation with humility and openness. Yet this humility towards and openness to learn from others does not come at the cost of bold and tenacious witness to the truth as they perceive and comprehend it. In such a picture, participants in debate stand within the particularity of their own traditions and beliefs, either as individuals or as representatives of communal bodies, learning from the other participants, at times changing or adapting their beliefs and practices as they come to see them as untrue or sinful, at times standing firm in witness to the truth as they perceive it and believe it has been revealed to them. The Church, within this picture, views truth not as something that it possesses or knows in full, but as something that is received, through Scripture, tradition, and engagement with views and ways of life different from its own.[184] The Church is, in short,

> the communal embodiment of the search for truthful witness and discipleship within the theodrama. It is a religious body which knows that truth cannot be possessed, but must be continually received, and with due humility in face of its sinfulness and finitude. It is a religious body that knows that the gift of truth is essentially dependent upon genuine engagement with both the divine Other and human others.[185]

Interaction between differences requires humility, towards others and towards one's grasp of the truth. This is not a new insight, not

---

183. Cf. William Placher, *Unapologetic Theology: A Christian Voice in a Pluralistic Conversation* (Louisville, KY: Westminster/John Knox, 1989), esp. pp. 147–149.
184. See Healy, *Church, World and the Christian Life*, pp. 105–108.
185. Ibid., pp. 107–108.

even within Christianity. Despite some prevailing conceptions of Augustine, for example, humility, recognition that truth is received as a gift, and desire for genuine engagement with others are all marks of his life and thought. Because of his own weakness, Augustine believes in the need to proceed carefully in his theological tasks ("From now on I will be attempting to say things that cannot altogether be said as they are thought by a man – or at least as they are thought by me ... For I am as keenly aware of my weakness as of my willingness").[186] Because of common human weakness, Augustine believes that we need to be more gentle with each other than we might otherwise be.[187] Because of the nature of truth, which belongs not to any one individual but is shared by all as a public possession and gift, given by God who *is* truth,[188] it is possible to be in conversation with others about and pursue the truth of the matter. Indeed, Augustine's belief in the importance and efficacy of such conversation is evident throughout his writings, many of whose origins lie precisely in the perceived need to discuss and search for truth as it related to particular matters. Such writings are marked by a desire to proceed with humility and openness towards his intended audience. As he writes in one letter,

> I have given you an exposition of my considered opinion on this issue, and of my deepest wishes. I admit that I do not know what is hidden in the plan of God: I am only human. However, I am absolutely certain that whatever it is, it is just and wise by comparison with any human mind, and very firmly established in incomparable excellence.[189]

And another example, from *The Trinity*:

> if anyone reads this work and says, "I understand what is being said, but it is not true," he is at liberty to affirm his own conviction as much as he likes and refute mine if he can. If he succeeds in doing so charitably and truthfully, and also takes the trouble to let me

186. *The Trinity* V, 1.
187. See Letter 153 in *Augustine: Political Writings*, pp. 71–88.
188. *Confessions* XII, xxv (34), (35).
189. Augustine to Nectarius, Letter 104, 11 in *Augustine: Political Writings* (p. 17). See also Augustine to Emeritus, Letter 87, 1. N.B. Dodaro provides a thorough account of what is happening in the correspondence between Augustine and Nectarius, with special reference to Connolly's critiques of Augustine, in "Augustine's Secular City," pp. 231–259.

> know (if I am still alive), then that will be the choicest plum that
> could fall to me from these labors of mine.[190]

Even if Augustine's conception of conversation is not quite as rich as
the one we have here been articulating, we can agree with Mathewes that "Augustine's system can affirm what Augustine himself
may never have admitted, that the Christian church can in fact
engage in genuine conversation with others, in a way which leads to
a deeper understanding for all parties involved."[191]

All of this points to some very different reasons for entering into
conversation with others than those offered by the political theorists
of our earlier chapters. Such differences do not come together merely
because of the fact of pluralism, nor because of a recognition of
universal irony. Their forbearance towards those who are different
involves a recognition that they are inextricably linked to others in
contemporary society, not because of the irreducible contingency
and inevitable paradoxicality of their identities and beliefs, but
because of their common humanity and sinfulness. They are humble,
patient, and open to learning from and being changed by the differences they encounter not because they believe that truth is a
harmful concept and that life is a chaotic whirlwind that exceeds all
of our abilities to capture it, but because truth and life are gifts from
God that exceed in capacity, mystery, and grandeur the ability of any
person or group to know them in full. To the concept of a "radical
and plural democracy" Christians offer a radical love for the other, a
radical hospitality and generosity towards those who are different,
guided not by their own strength but by participation in the God
whose very life was given freely and without violence for those who
considered themselves God's enemy. They reject exclusion and
choose to embrace those not like themselves not, as Volf writes,
"because of a contingent preference for a certain kind of society" but
because "the prophets, evangelists, and apostles tell [them] that it is a
wrong way to treat human beings, any human being, anywhere."[192]

If the Heavenly City on earth is being faithful to embodying its
own narratives, it will be marked not by conflict, coercion, or

---

190. *The Trinity* I, 5. Note also his humility towards interpretation of Scripture
and his belief that a diversity of truths can be found within a given passage or
story. See, for example, *Confessions* XII, xxxi (42); *On Christian Doctrine* XXVII, XLI.
191. Mathewes, "Pluralism," pp. 89–90.
192. Volf, *Exclusion and Embrace*, p. 68.

intolerance, but by love, humility, hospitality, and grace. This is
not a claim that Christians have always been guided by love, nor
that they have not misconstrued calls to "make disciples of all
nations"[193] as justification for taking matters of conversion into
their own hands, or mistakenly placing it into the hands of civil
authorities. Conversion itself, rightly conceived, is the work of God,
not the work of the Church or the Christian. Christians are called to
love and serve each other while they obey and trust that the same
God who they believe created the earth; established a covenant with
Abraham; called and gathered the people of Israel; became flesh,
lived, died, and rose again to reconcile humanity to Godself; and
continues to sustain in being all that is, is always already at work in
the world. For according to the biblical witness, it is God who
reveals, calls, and reconciles, working through people without
depending upon them for the realization of God's saving love and
purposes. This involves a deep belief that the Holy Spirit is present
and active, sustaining and working through those who know God
as Father through Jesus Christ, and sustaining and working in those
who do not yet participate in this communion or recognize themselves as sons and daughters in God's richly diverse and unified
family. Because of this belief, the Church can view itself as responsible not for imposing its faith and practices onto others but for
being the community in which the narratives of Christianity are
embodied and practiced.

As citizens of the Heavenly City answer the call to be and live as
the people of God, as they come together united around the common love of God and neighbor, and as they reside as pilgrims in the
earthly city without abandoning the public of the Church, they can
enter from their own particularity into conversation with others in
their particularity. Such conversation, rich and deep, occurring in
word and practice, in formal and informal ways, does not abandon
the hope that together we can seek after truth, guided by humility
and love. Neither does it naïvely search for easy common ground
and consensus over the most potentially divisive issues. It maintains
that within this conversation one can be persuaded by another, by
their manner of life or their words, their practices or their speech,
and this persuasion may well result in a change of position, belief,

193. Jesus' parting words to His disciples according to Matthew 28:19, NRSV.

way of life, and even ontology. Such change does not happen easily or quickly, through one interaction or a handful of verbal exchanges, but its possibility must always remain open. For without such a possibility, how are we ever to learn and grow from each other as we, in our differences and our particularities, seek to think and live more generously and gracefully with each other in a markedly pluralist society?

A brief conclusion

Perhaps, after all of this discussion, the response that we offer to the question of how to live together in the midst of difference is not very grand. Instead of an all-encompassing political theory, we offer a picture in which differences come together in rich conversation in a pluralist society. We expand the backdrop of this picture to include not only verbal exchanges that address explicitly "public" questions but the interactions of groups and individuals in various realms of life, across the variety of circumstances and issues that constitute the many publics of our political society. This is not to say that our political life will not be guided by a theory or practice that relies upon some ontology, and that this ontology will not be at odds with many others currently in existence within our culture. It is to recognize that we cannot look to any one ontology to provide a political theory that will enable all of the different ontologies and all of the particularities of the earthly city to be respected, reconciled, and celebrated. The desire for recognition of particularity and difference is genuine and good, but it can quickly become dangerous when those promoting it fail to recognize that the hopes and dreams that guide them cannot be fulfilled in the *saeculum*.

We need to rediscover Augustine's Heavenly City as the place in which unity and diversity, harmony and plurality can come together in ways that are not possible outside of participation in the Triune God. This does not mean that the Heavenly City is to take over or be instituted in the earthly city, nor does it mean that the picture of life together in the Trinity translates into an earthly political system. Citizens of the Heavenly City wait in hope for the day when God will bring the full reconciliation of which they now taste the firstfruits. They live in faith that Christ is Lord of all, including the political realms of which they are a part while they are on pilgrimage in this

age. Their concern is not to take over the political realm but to serve in it, when called, while retaining their primary citizenship in the *polis* of the Church. Perhaps the most they ask today is that whatever political theory is in place does not limit their ability to be the embodied community of faith that God calls them to be. Then other communities and ideologies would also find more space to live out their beliefs and practices. And then deep conversation would be possible between the individuals, communities, and publics that constitute contemporary pluralist society, conversation that does not limit, alter, or hide the particularity of these different constituencies even as it leaves open the possibility that they may learn from and be changed by one another.

6

Conclusion

We have now reached the end of a rather long journey, one that has wound its way through different theories, practices, and ontologies in an effort to explore some of the pictures and possibilities available to a pluralist society composed of a multitude of differences. This journey has carried us from liberal tolerance to a post-Nietzschean celebration of difference to a Christian hope for the harmonization of differences in the Heavenly City. It has taken us from theory determined to avoid reliance on controversial assumptions to theory that draws attention to the ontological assumptions at play within every position to theology that offers its own contestable ontology as one that might help the Church navigate the tricky waters of pluralism, tolerance, and difference at the same time as it helps to augment our current political imagination. For our imagination today is impoverished, as indicated by the limited success we have had in picturing how to move beyond liberal tolerance, so that the particularity of differences can be recognized, and beyond the agonistic veneration of difference, so that differences can be harmonized without being muted or silenced.

Every theory relies upon an ontology that is held as a matter of faith, either implicitly or explicitly invoking deep beliefs about the nature of reality and human being. Political liberalism is undergirded by an ontology that prioritizes the universal over the particular, post-Nietzschean political theory and radical democracy by an ontology that celebrates diversity at the cost of unity. The ontologies informing these main voices within political theory today have yet to provide persuasive pictures of the relationships between

differences in our political community, leaving us with the need to entertain other ontologies and their concomitant pictures of unity and diversity. Having uncovered this need along our journey, we immersed ourselves in the thought of Augustine, exploring the ontology that shaped his voice and how this ontology might contribute to our current conversation.

What contribution does Augustine make to this conversation? Perhaps most importantly, he reminds us that we need to limit what we can expect from this earthly city and political theory concerned therewith. Unity is a worthy desire, as is a longing for differences to be recognized, respected, and celebrated, but neither of these desires can be truly fulfilled in a *polis* that is marked by disordered desires and confused loves. It is possible for unity and diversity to come together within a political society, but the only *polis* in which they can be genuinely reconciled is the Heavenly City, through participation in the Triune God. This participation alone can provide a sufficient basis from which to engage with and respect others, for, as Augustine shows us, fallen humanity needs its loves to be re-ordered so that it can look to others not out of its own neediness but for the sake of God, so that it can love with humility and grace rather than pride and selfishness, so that it can prioritize justice and peace over power and domination. Augustine reminds us that outside of the redemption and transformation that the mediating work of Jesus Christ enables, humanity has no way to overcome the division that comes with each person seeking his or her own private, independent, and varying goods and no means by which to be re-united around the one truly public, common, and unchanging good, that is, God.

Political liberalism recognizes the division and the competing private interests and goods that mark individuals and communities. In response, it offers a way to unite divided citizens within a single political society that depends heavily upon the idea and inculcation of tolerance. As we have seen, post-Enlightenment versions of liberalism, recognizing the fact of pluralism, give tolerance ever more prominence within their theories, and yet as they do so they fail to recognize their role in defining both what toleration entails and to whom it extends. The result is that their "tolerant" political societies, rather than giving space to those doctrines and persons of whom they morally disapprove, actually exclude many significant

constituencies of contemporary society from participation before they even begin. Those who are included must emphasize the commonalities they share with others within that political society rather than their own particularities. How can the tolerance of political liberalism, which calls for differences to be either excluded or ignored, be considered tolerant at all? If political liberalism is relying on tolerance as the means to attain a unified political society in the midst of pluralism, then it offers us little help today.

If, on the other hand, post-Nietzschean political theorists and proponents of radical democracy are searching for a way to move beyond liberal tolerance to an acceptance or embrace of difference, their own ontologies fail to provide the resources to sustain such a move. If power and conflict are as pervasive as they think they are, surely we need something beyond the strength garnered by the recognition that our relationships, identities, and political societies are contingent and paradoxical to sustain the celebration and recognition of difference for which they call. On an Augustinian view, the only political community in which this move beyond tolerance is possible is the one that arises through participation in Jesus Christ, who enables reconciliation between and within humanity and God. Out of this participation in God flows an ethic along the lines of that sought by the agonists. In this ethic, people and groups are slow to judge and quick to love, unwilling to coerce and eager to respect, because they recognize the kinship they share with all of creation, a kinship of createdness and of sinfulness that simultaneously engenders care and humility. Furthermore, through participation in God their own loves and desires are reordered so that they can love generously and rightly, giving each person and virtue its proper due. Finally, as they participate in God, they become a part of the God who loved humanity and creation to such an extent that no price was considered too large to pay to restore relationality with those from whom God was estranged. This self-giving and self-donating should be a mark not only of the Triune God but of those who participate in this Triune God.

We want to admit straightaway that the Church as it exists on earth has not often visibly displayed the unity, the humility, the love, the generosity, or the grace which we have here described. On the contrary, as Kathryn Tanner comments, "probably more often than not over the course of Western history, Christians have used

beliefs about God and the world to undergird attitudes and actions with a highly problematic political import."[1] And yet, as Tanner herself attempts to show, Christian beliefs are not necessarily and inherently linked to repressive, intolerant, and otherwise dangerous sociopolitical practices.[2] This has much to do with the eschatological nature of the Heavenly City, for even though the Kingdom of God manifests itself in part as the Church in the *saeculum*, the full realization of God's promises to His people will not occur until He ushers in a new age. This new age will occur in God's timing, not humanity's, and it does not depend upon the work of humans for its arrival. That is to say, the role of citizens of the Heavenly City as they live as members of the Church and as pilgrims in the earthly city is *not* to inaugurate the eschatological City of God, even as they embody and delight in the firstfruits of being part of this City, and even as they pray that God's Kingdom will be present on earth as it is in heaven. This Kingdom, while a *polis*, is vastly different from the *polis* of the earthly city, so much so that it positions the earthly city without needing to take it over.

What does this mean? It means, on one level, that entering into citizenship in the Heavenly City enables one to realize that the political societies and identities of the earthly city are neither ultimate nor unquestionable. Unlike liberal political theory, which, according to John Gray, relies upon the sovereign nation-state as its "great unexamined assumption,"[3] and unlike agonistic political thought, which opens our eyes to the contingencies and dangers of nation-states and national identities without providing an alternative community, an Augustinian understanding of the Heavenly City invites us to participate in a truly universal society while still residing in our respective earthly cities, which remain important while no longer being seen as ultimate. We need, as Oliver O'Donovan writes, "the disclosure of a universal society, a Kingdom of Heaven, a new identity capable of weaning us from dependence upon our varied identities. Without it we cannot envisage those identities in sober clarity, as grounds neither of boasting nor

1. Kathryn Tanner, *The Politics of God: Christian Theologies and Social Justice* (Minneapolis, MN: Fortress, 1992), p. 1.
2. See Tanner, *Politics of God*, pp. 193–223. Cf. Stephen Toulmin, *Cosmopolis: The Hidden Agenda of Modernity* (Chicago, IL: The University of Chicago Press, 1992), pp. 135–136, 144.
3. Gray, *Two Faces*, p. 123.

shame." Such a universal society cannot be the product of mere imagination; instead, as he continues, "we must become actual members of a real community constituted by the real and present image of God as uniquely lord, and the real and present image of mankind as subject uniquely to God. Jesus Christ, very God and very man, is the double representative around whom such a community has come into being."[4] The Heavenly City, through the Church as it exists on earth, provides a community in which people from all countries and various identities can come together, united through Christ in such a way that their differences do not become ultimate nor their political identities decisive, even as both can be and are recognized. Does this not provide a way between the Scylla of liberalism's "unifying" universalism and the Charybdis of post-Nietzschean difference?

On another level, the difference between the Heavenly City and the earthly city means that to some degree they are operating on two different planes, so that the Heavenly City need not and should not attempt to take over the earthly city or its political institutions. The Heavenly City calls people out of their earthly cities to be joined together in the City of God, but in this *saeculum* this means neither that their earthly cities are abandoned nor that they are called to impose the *polis* of the Heavenly City on the earthly city. Instead, they are to see the political realm as part of God's providential provision for the fallen world, a way for God to minimize the disorder and domination that would otherwise take over every aspect of fallen life together. This does not mean that the political realm is neutral, a place in which citizens of the Heavenly City can blithely play a role as they rest in their belief that it is part of God's provision for their security and welfare. As Augustine clearly demonstrates, the earthly city is always marked by the *libido dominandi* and by loves that are private and personal rather than those that seek the highest and greatest good for all. And yet Christians believe that even these disordered loves, even the powers and principalities of the fallen world, have been placed under the authority of Jesus Christ. This may not be visible this side of the eschaton, but it does engender a patient trust in the Lordship of Christ that prevents citizens of the Heavenly City from thinking that they have to take the political

4. O'Donovan, *Common Objects of Love*, p. 44.

realm of the earthly city into their own hands and through their own efforts place it into the hands of God.

Citizens of the Heavenly City must not look to the earthly city to be the site of the realization of God's promises or to be the place in which the community and people of God are primarily located. If they are going to dedicate themselves and their lives to one *polis*, it should be that of the City of God. If, however, their citizenship in the Heavenly City is firmly in place, if through their participation in God they have had their loves and goods reprioritized so that they can appreciate the earthly city without making it their final good, then they may have a very helpful role indeed to play in the earthly city. For what does the earthly city need more than people who can both recognize a degree of contingency in its arrangements and draw upon a source of love and humility, a standard of community and grace, a picture of peace that involves flourishing and delight between God, humanity, and all of creation, as they seek to question current political arrangements and further certain political goods? As Augustine notes, while on pilgrimage in this earthly city citizens of the Heavenly City share some goods with citizens of the earthly city, so they have reason to contribute to earthly peace and justice. And they further contribute because they desire earthly peace and justice for the sake of their neighbors who do not yet have knowledge of the greater peace and justice that could be theirs through Christ.

What might this contribution look like? It will take different forms at different times, depending on the political and social situations currently in existence in the various earthly cities of which these citizens are a part. Christianity does not translate directly into any one political theory, for reasons that should well be clear by now. It can and does coincide with a variety of earthly cities, political institutions, and social arrangements, even as it attempts to be its own *polis* within these. Perhaps the most that we can say in our current *milieu* is that whatever political theory is used in the common places ("politics" in a popular way) to justify common practices would, ideally, accommodate a deep conversation of communal religious practices.[5] In other words, given contemporary conditions of pluralism, the political realm needs to leave space for

---

5. I owe this sentence to Keith Starkenburg, who helpfully put my own conclusion in these words.

its members to garner their primary identities from other sources and to come together in political society from within the particularity of those identities in formal and informal ways. This is precisely what is precluded in political liberalism, for its ontology requires too much of its members as it either commandeers or neuters their other identities. Veiled in the guise of "neutrality" and drawing upon such seemingly universal concepts as "reasonableness" and "overlapping consensus," this liberalism in actuality asks the constituents of contemporary pluralist society to considerably change their beliefs, practices, and identities before it will consider them "reasonable" and thereby allow them to be a part of the political society as it searches for an "overlapping consensus." Once they are included, they are still precluded from being publicly present as the particular constituencies that they are, as are all members of a society governed by a political liberalism that emphasizes "public" unity and "private" difference.

Here, in its conception of "public" and "private," is precisely where we need to ask significant questions of contemporary liberalism. For, as Jean Bethke Elshtain notes, "images of public and private are necessarily, if implicitly, tied to views of moral agency; evaluations of human capacities and activities, virtues, and excellence; assessments of the purposes and aims of alternative modes of social organization."[6] This means that when we think about public and private, and ponder ways of reimagining how they might be conceptualized, "if we are to avoid the presumptuous and the abstracted, we are thinking about a multiplicity of moral claims and about competing human values concerning what an ideal way of life ought to be."[7] When political liberalism delineates its strict separation between public and private, and defines public as that which pertains to "constitutional essentials" and "basic justice," when it separates the public political forum, as a place in which citizens can come together to discuss political matters independent of their "private" comprehensive philosophical doctrines, from the rest of the "background culture," it enforces its own deep beliefs and assumptions about, among other things, the relationship between the political realm and other components of political

6. Elshtain, *Public Man, Private Woman*, p. 4.
7. Ibid., p. 123.

society and the relationship between citizens and the beliefs and practices of their faith communities. These beliefs and assumptions have become so taken-for-granted that they receive scant attention, while the conception of public and private that they undergird has become the only conceivable one, even as people long for more public recognition of particularity and difference.

What if this recognition is not possible outside of a reconceptualization of public and private, a reimagining of how we conceive of public and its relation to other facets of life? For liberalism is problematic in its failure to provide the space and the means for interactions between the different particularities that coincide in contemporary political society, and this applies to the particularity that is Christianity as much as to any other particularity. Yet Christians themselves have acquiesced to the definitions and parameters provided to them by liberalism. By allowing themselves to be positioned and trained by the language and practices of liberalism, they have lost the imaginative power to picture other possibilities that are rooted in the language and practices of Christianity. What theological resources might offer an alternative to the hegemonic control of "public" held by political liberalism? Here again we return to Augustine, for whom Christianity was nothing if not a public, social ethic embodied in the life of the Church (not, we are careful to note, embodied in the political realm of the earthly city). This reminder of the one-time public nature of the Church can help us pause for a moment to remember that, by definition, "public" can refer to any community or group of people united by a common interest or good. It need not refer only to a nation or a state, or to the explicitly political realm of nations and states. This means, for example, that a people united by worship of God can be considered a public just as much as a people united by a common national allegiance. Throughout its history and tradition, Christianity has been conceived, by both its participants and its opponents, as communal, social, and public at its very core. It is only recently, under liberalism, that it has distanced itself from its communal embodiment to become more a matter of private faith and belief. Such a transformation has surely impacted not only Christianity but many other constituencies within western liberal societies who have reduced their communal claims in order to exist as "private" entities, coming together in the public realm of liberalism as almost

anonymous entities. Might there be a way for Christianity and other components of political society to exist as publics without this meaning that they want to take over what we commonly understand as the public square? By creating space for multiple publics that overlap and yet are marked by their own telos, doctrine, and practices, might we open the possibility of critical and fruitful interaction between these publics? And might this offer us a glimpse of an alternative picture of political arrangements, one in which multiple publics and different individuals can come together in rich and deep conversation?

This alternative picture relies on an historical understanding of conversation that involves both exchange of words and interaction between different manners of life. As people converse, they are to speak from within the particularity and fullness of their identities, beliefs, and practices, for it is as identities are embodied, as narratives are incarnated, and as people live together and engage with one another from within the embodiment of their differing narratives, that true conversation occurs. Such conversation operates with a trust in what can be learned and accomplished through interaction, debate, and deliberation. This means that each party in the conversation is open to being persuaded by the other, to changing its convictions and practices, in small and large ways, and even to being converted to different beliefs and manners of life. For without keeping open the possibility of being persuaded and changed through our interactions with each other, how are we ever to learn and grow as we seek to think and live more generously and gracefully with each other in a decidedly pluralist society? Such honest conversation, which is as eager to understand others in their differences as it is to find places of agreement and commonality, will find significant points of divergence and dissimilarity. Should we be afraid of raising these differences? Perhaps, in our contemporary *milieu*, we need to be more afraid of ignoring them than of what will happen when we attempt to engage them. Such engagement may only be possible if we considerably rethink our conceptions of public and private, so that the public square is thought of not as the forum in which debate over political and constitutional matters takes place but as the communication and interaction that occurs between different ways of thinking and living, between the different groups and individuals that together constitute contemporary political society.

Is this picture of conversation probable or realistic? To some degree, such conversation already happens as these different constituencies reside side-by-side in daily life. In other ways, we are far from a society in which rich, deep, honest conversation of practices and words occurs in either formal or informal ways, and much more needs to be developed before such a picture could take root in our current political imagination. And yet offering this preliminary picture may be a worthwhile beginning, even if at the end of this discussion we realize that we are far from a place in which this picture can be accepted and embraced. Even William Connolly acknowledges that his "ethos of deep pluralism" is not a probable achievement, although the actual diversity in contemporary society raises the need for just such an ethos. He offers his contribution because he believes that "political and cultural theory should focus first and foremost on possibilities that speak to pressing needs of the time. Concentration on probabilities alone can be left to bureaucrats and consultants."[8] This project represents our effort to respond to those same pressing needs, even as our discernment of those needs and our proposed answers are rooted in Christian theology rather than a post-Nietzschean ontology. We might say that what is offered here is an "ethos of gospel participation," and it is certainly more a work of theology than political theory. In the end, it seeks to offer not a comprehensive political theory that will provide all the answers to our contemporary questions (for such a theory is well beyond the bounds of a theology whose primary concern is to point to the *polis* of the Heavenly City rather than the earthly one), but a picture that represents one way in which differences might come together more richly and honestly than either political liberal or agonistic pictures allow. This picture is my offering to both the Church and our contemporary political and pluralist imagination.

Such a picture provides a way to recognize particularity that goes well beyond what is possible, and deemed desirable, in political liberalism. And it provides a way out of the hopeless, contingency-based, conflict-ridden alternative offered by agonistic political theorists. Other contemporary thinkers are likewise drawing attention to the need that has arisen in a post-Enlightenment context to offer alternatives to those, like the post-Nietzscheans, who most

8. Connolly, *Neuropolitics*, pp. 136-137.

radically try to move beyond Enlightenment certainties. Among these thinkers are Slavoj Zizek and Alain Badiou, who in their work are responding, as Zizek puts it, to "the absent centre of political ontology." They are trying to provide an alternative to "postmodern" acceptance of radical contingency and metaphysical uncertainty by resuscitating a politics of universal Truth that takes into account contemporary awareness of multiplicity and contingency.[9] And yet they assume, along with post-Nietzscheans, that the time in which Christianity could make a direct contribution towards these efforts has long since passed. We have argued, on the contrary, that Christianity has a considerable contribution to make to political theory, most importantly by reminding us that many of the goals that we currently hold for the political realm cannot be realized outside of participation in the Triune God who reigns in the Heavenly City.

It is only in the Triune God of grace that the desire for a true recognition of difference that moves beyond tolerance to celebrate both unity and diversity can be met. If we look for this desire to be fulfilled through liberal or post-Nietzschean political societies, it will always remain unquenched, but if we look to Christ, we need never know this thirst again. And yet we have reason to seek and hope for more recognition of particularity within the earthly city than either political liberalism or post-Nietzschean political thought has thus far delivered. If we draw on theology to help us reimagine our received conceptions of both "public" and "conversation," we can see a picture in which the different particularities of our pluralist society come together to interact through their words and their practices, through their communal identities and their individual concerns, in ways that keep open the possibility of honest learning, growth, change, and conversion. Moving beyond liberal tolerance and agonistic difference may, in a seemingly ironic twist, become more possible as we move towards rather than away from Christianity, towards, that is to say, an imagination informed by Christian faith, a practice informed by Christian belief, and an ontology informed by Christian theology.

9. See Zizek, *Ticklish Subject*; Alain Badiou, *Saint Paul: The Foundation of Universalism* (Stanford, CA: Stanford University Press, 1997).

Bibliography

Allen, Barry. "Foucault and Modern Political Philosophy." In *The Later Foucault: Politics and Philosophy*, edited by Jeremy Moss, 164–198. London: Sage, 1998.

Anderson, Benedict. *Imagined Communities: Reflections on the Origin and Spread of Nationalism*. Rev. ed. London: Verso, 1983.

Arendt, Hannah. *Love and Saint Augustine*, edited by Joanna Vecchiarelli Scott and Judith Chelius Stark. Chicago: The University of Chicago Press, 1996.

Audi, Robert and Nicholas Wolterstorff. *Religion in the Public Square: The Place of Religious Convictions in Political Debate*. Lanham, MD: Rowman & Littlefield, 1997.

St. Augustine. *On Music*. Translated by Robert Catesby Taliaferro. Vol. 4, The Fathers of the Church. New York: Fathers of the Church, 1947.

"The Nature of the Good." In *Augustine: Earlier Writings*. Translated by John H. S. Burleigh. London: SCM, 1953.

"Of True Religion." In *Augustine: Earlier Writings*. Translated by John H. S. Burleigh. London: SCM, 1953.

On Christian Doctrine. Translated by D. W. Robertson, Jr. Indianapolis, IN: Bobbs-Merrill, 1958.

Contra academicos. De beata vita. De ordine. Edited by William M. Green and Klaus D. Daur. Turnholti: Typographi Brepols, 1970.

Concerning the City of God Against the Pagans. Translated by Henry Bettenson. Harmondsworth, England: Penguin, 1972.

Confessions. Translated by Henry Chadwick. Oxford: Oxford University Press, 1991.

The Trinity. Translated by Edmund Hill, O. P. Edited by John E. Rotelle, O.S.A. Brooklyn, NY: New City, 1991.

The Augustine Catechism: The Enchiridion on Faith, Hope, and Love. Translated by Bruce Harbert. Edited by John E. Rotelle, O.S.A. Hyde Park, NY: New City, 1999.

Augustine: Political Writings. Edited by E. M. Atkins and R. J. Dodaro. Cambridge: Cambridge University Press, 2001.

Letters 1–99. Translated by Roland Teske, S. J. Edited by John E. Rotelle, O.S.A. Hyde Park, NY: New City, 2001.

Bibliography

"The Literal Meaning of Genesis." In *On Genesis*. Translated by Edmund Hill, O.P. Edited by John E. Rotelle, O.S.A. Hyde Park, NY: New City, 2002.

Ayres, Lewis. "The Fundamental Grammar of Augustine's Trinitarian Theology." In *Augustine and His Critics*, edited by Robert Dodaro and George Lawless, 51–76. London: Routledge, 2000.

Badiou, Alain. *Saint Paul: The Foundation of Universalism*. Stanford, CA: Stanford University Press, 1997.

Ethics: An Essay on the Understanding of Evil. Translated by Peter Hallward. London: Verso, 2001.

Barber, Benjamin R. "Liberal Democracy and the Costs of Consent." In *Liberalism and the Moral Life*, edited by Nancy L. Rosenblum, 54–68. Cambridge, MA: Harvard University Press, 1989.

Barry, Brian. *Culture and Equality: An Egalitarian Critique of Multiculturalism*. Cambridge: Polity, 2001.

Barth, Karl. "Church and State." In *Community, State, and Church: Three Essays*, edited by Will Herberg, 101–148. Gloucester, MA: Peter Smith, 1968.

"Christian Community and Civil Community." In *Community, State, and Church: Three Essays*, edited by Will Herberg, 149–189. Gloucester, MA: Peter Smith, 1968.

Bauerschmidt, Frederick Christian. "The Word Made Speculative? John Milbank's Christological Poetics." *Modern Theology* 15, no. 4 (October 1999): 417–432.

Benhabib, Seyla. "Liberal Dialogue Versus a Critical Theory of Discursive Legitimation." In *Liberalism and the Moral Life*, edited by Nancy L. Rosenblum, 143–156. Cambridge, MA: Harvard University Press, 1989.

The Claims of Culture: Equality and Diversity in the Global Era. Princeton, NJ: Princeton University Press, 2002.

Bonner, Gerald. "Christ, God and Man in the Thought of St. Augustine." *Angelicum* 61 (1984): 268–294.

"Augustine's Concept of Deification." *Journal of Theological Studies* 37 (1986): 369–386.

Brink, Paul A. "Selves in Relation: Theories of Community and the *Imago Dei* Doctrine." In *The Re-Enchantment of Political Science: Christian Scholars Engage Their Discipline*, edited by Thomas W. Heilke and Ashley Woodiwiss, 85–120. Lanham, MD: Lexington, 2001.

Brown, P. R. L. "Political Society." In *Augustine: A Collection of Critical Essays*, edited by R. A. Markus, 311–335. New York: Doubleday, 1972.

"The Limits of Intolerance." In *Authority and the Sacred: Aspects of the Christianisation of the Roman World*, 27–54. Cambridge: Cambridge University Press, 1995.

Augustine of Hippo: A Biography. Berkeley, CA: University of California Press, 2000.

Brueggemann, Walter. *The Bible and Postmodern Imagination: Texts Under Negotiation*. London: SCM, 1993.

Budziszewski, J. *True Tolerance: Liberalism and the Necessity of Judgement*. New Brunswick, NJ: Transaction, 1992.

Burnaby, John. *Amor Dei: A Study of the Religion of St. Augustine*. London: Hodder & Stoughton, 1938.

Burnell, Peter J. "The Status of Politics in St. Augustine's *City of God.*" *History of Political Thought* 13, no. 1 (Spring 1992): 13–29.

"The Problem of Service to Unjust Regimes in Augustine's *City of God.*" In *The City of God: A Collection of Critical Essays*, edited by Dorothy F. Donnelly, 37–49. New York: Peter Lang, 1995.

Castiglione, Dario and Catriona McKinnon. "Introduction: Beyond Toleration?" *Res Publica* 7, no. 3 (2001): 223–230.

Cavanaugh, William T. "'A Fire Strong Enough to Consume the House:' The Wars of Religion and the Rise of the State." *Modern Theology* 11, no. 4 (October 1995): 397–420.

"The City: Beyond Secular Parodies." In *Radical Orthodoxy*, edited by John Milbank, Catherine Pickstock and Graham Ward, 182–200. London: Routledge, 1999.

"The World in a Wafer: A Geography of the Eucharist as Resistance to Globalization." *Modern Theology* 15, no. 2 (April 1999): 181–196.

"Is Public Theology Really Public?" *Annual of the Society of Christian Ethics* 21 (2001): 105–123.

Theopolitical Imagination. London: T&T Clark, 2002.

Chadwick, Henry. *Augustine.* Oxford: Oxford University Press, 1986.

Cochrane, Charles Norris. *Christianity and Classical Culture: A Study of Thought and Action from Augustus to Augustine.* Oxford: Clarendon, 1940.

Coles, Romand. *Self/Power/Other: Political Theory and Diaological Ethics.* Ithaca, NY: Cornell University Press, 1992.

Rethinking Generosity: Critical Theory and the Politics of Caritas. Ithaca, NY: Cornell University Press, 1997.

Connolly, William E. *Identity\Difference: Democratic Negotiations of Political Paradox.* Ithaca, NY: Cornell University Press, 1991.

The Augustinian Imperative: A Reflection on the Politics of Morality. Newbury Park, CA: Sage, 1993.

The Ethos of Pluralization. Minneapolis, MN: University of Minnesota Press, 1995.

"Beyond Good and Evil: The Ethical Sensibility of Michel Foucault." In *The Later Foucault: Politics and Philosophy*, edited by Jeremy Moss, 108–128. London: Sage, 1998.

Why I am Not a Secularist. Minneapolis, MN: University of Minnesota Press, 1999.

"Cross-State Citizen Networks: A Response to Dallmayr." *Millennium: Journal of International Studies* 30, no. 2 (2001): 349–355.

"Confessing Identity\Belonging to Difference." In *Identity\Difference: Democratic Negotiations of Political Paradox*, xiii–xxxi. Expanded ed. Minneapolis, MN: University of Minnesota Press, 2002.

Neuropolitics: Thinking, Culture, Speed. Minneapolis, MN: University of Minnesota Press, 2002.

"Preface to the New Edition: The Pluralization of Religiosity." *The Augustinian Imperative*, xvii–xxv. Lanham, MD: Rowman & Littlefield, 2002.

Pluralism. Durham, NC: Duke University Press, 2005.

Conyers, A. J., *The Long Truce: How Toleration Made the World Safe for Power and Profit.* Dallas, TX: Spence, 2001.

Corlett, William. *Community without Unity: A Politics of Derridian Extravagance.*
    Durham, NC: Duke University Press, 1989.
Crouse, Robert. "*Paucis Mutatis Verbis*: St. Augustine's Platonism." In *Augustine
    and His Critics*, edited by Robert Dodaro and George Lawless, 37–50.
    London: Routledge, 2000.
Deane, Herbert A. "Augustine and the State: The Return of Order Upon
    Disorder." In *The City of God: A Collection of Critical Essays*, edited by
    Dorothy F. Donnelly, 51–73. New York: Peter Lang, 1995.
Dees, Richard H. "Establishing Toleration." *Political Theory* 27 (October 1999):
    667–693.
Dietz, Mary G. "Merely Combating the Phrases of This World: Recent
    Democratic Theory." *Political Theory* 26, no. 1 (February 1998): 112–139.
Dodaro, Robert. "Loose Canons: Augustine and Derrida on Their Selves." In
    God, the Gift, and Postmodernism, edited by John D. Caputo and Michael
    J. Scanlon, 79–111. Bloomington, IN: Indiana University Press, 1999.
    "Augustine's Secular City." In *Augustine and His Critics*, edited by Robert
    Dodaro and George Lawless, 231–259. London: Routledge, 2000.
    Christ and the Just Society in the Thought of Augustine. Cambridge: Cambridge
    University Press, 2004.
Dombrowski, Daniel A. *Rawls and Religion the Case for Political Liberalism.* Albany,
    NY: State University of New York Press, 2001.
Easton, M. G. *Illustrated Bible Dictionary*, 3d. ed. New York: Thomas Nelson, 1987.
Eberle, Christopher J. *Religious Conviction in Liberal Politics.* Cambridge: Cambridge
    University Press, 2002.
Elshtain, Jean Bethke. *Public Man, Private Woman: Women in Social and Political
    Thought.* Oxford: Martin Robertson, 1981.
    Augustine and the Limits of Politics. Notre Dame, IN: University of Notre Dame
    Press, 1995.
    New Wine and Old Bottles: International Politics and Ethical Discourse. Notre Dame,
    IN: University of Notre Dame Press, 1998.
    "Response to Panel Papers." *Annual of the Society of Christian Ethics* 21 (2001):
    151–154.
Fergusson, David. *Community, Liberalism and Christian Ethics.* Cambridge:
    Cambridge University Press, 1998.
Fish, Stanley. *The Trouble with Principle.* Cambridge, MA: Harvard University
    Press, 1999.
Forrester, Duncan B. *Beliefs, Values and Policies: Conviction Politics in a Secular Age.*
    Oxford: Clarendon, 1998.
Foucault, Michel. "Politics and Ethics: An Interview." In *The Foucault Reader*,
    edited by Paul Rabinow, 373–380. New York: Pantheon, 1984.
Fukuyama, Francis. "*The Return of the Political* (book review)." *Foreign Affairs* 73,
    no. 5 (September/October 1994): 144.
Galeotti, Anna Elisabetta. "Do We Need Toleration as a Moral Virtue?" *Res
    Publica* 7, no. 3 (2001): 273–292.
Galston, William A. *Liberal Purposes: Goods, Virtues, and Diversity in the Liberal State.*
    Cambridge: Cambridge University Press, 1991.
    *Liberal Pluralism: The Implications of Value Pluralism for Political Theory and
    Practice.* Cambridge: Cambridge University Press, 2002.

Geuss, Raymond. "Liberalism and its Discontents." *Political Theory* 30, no. 3 (June 2002): 320–338.

Gray, John. *Enlightenment's Wake: Politics and Culture at the Close of the Modern Age.* London: Routledge, 1995.

   Two Faces of Liberalism. New York: The New Press, 2000.

   "Two Liberalisms of Fear." *The Hedgehog Review* 2, no. 1 (Spring 2000): 9–23.

Gregg, Benjamin. *Thick Moralities, Thin Politics: Social Integration Across Communities of Belief.* Durham, NC: Duke University Press, 2003.

Gregory, Eric Sean. "Love and Citizenship: Augustine and the Ethics of Liberalism." Ph.D. dissertation, Yale University, 2002.

Gunton, Colin. *The One, the Three, and the Many: God, Creation and the Culture of Modernity.* Cambridge: Cambridge University Press, 1993.

Gutmann, Amy. "Communitarian Critiques of Liberalism." *Philosophy and Public Affairs* 14, no. 3 (Summer 1985): 308–322.

Habermas, Jürgen. "Reconciliation Through the Public Use of Reason: Remarks on John Rawls's *Political Liberalism.*" *The Journal of Philosophy* 92, no. 3 (March 1995): 109–131.

Hampton, Jean. "The Common Faith of Liberalism." *Pacific Philosophical Quarterly* 75 (1994): 186–216.

Hanby, Michael. "Desire: Augustine Beyond Western Subjectivity." In *Radical Orthodoxy: A New Theology,* edited by John Milbank, Catherine Pickstock, and Graham Ward, 109–126. London: Routledge, 1999.

Augustine and Modernity. London: Routledge, 2003.

Hankey, Wayne J. *"Theoria versus Poesis:* Neoplatonism and Trinitarian Difference in Aquinas, John Milbank, Jean-Luc Marion, and John Zizioulas." *Modern Theology* 15, no. 4 (October 1999): 387–415.

Hardt, Michael and Antonio Negri. *Empire.* Cambridge, MA: Harvard University Press, 2000.

Harrison, Carol. *Augustine: Christian Truth and Fractured Humanity.* Oxford: Oxford University Press, 2000.

Hart, Trevor. *Faith Thinking: The Dynamics of Christian Theology.* London: SPCK, 1995.

Harvey, Barry. *"Why I am Not a Secularist* (book review)." *Journal of Church and State* 43 (Winter 2001): 141.

Hauerwas, Stanley. *A Community of Character: Toward a Constructive Christian Social Ethic.* Notre Dame, IN: University of Notre Dame Press, 1981.

   In Good Company: The Church as Polis. Notre Dame, IN: University of Notre Dame Press, 1995.

   Wilderness Wanderings: Probing Twentieth-century Theology and Philosophy. Boulder, CO: Westview, 1997.

Healy, Nicholas M. *Church, World and the Christian Life: Practical-Prophetic Ecclesiology.* Cambridge: Cambridge University Press, 2000.

Herberg, Will. "The Social Philosophy of Karl Barth." Introduction to *Community, State, and Church: Three Essays,* edited by Will Herberg, 11–67. Gloucester, MA: Peter Smith, 1968.

Heyd, David, ed. *Toleration: An Elusive Virtue.* Princeton, NJ: Princeton University Press, 1996.

Heywood, Andrew. *Political Theory: An Introduction*. 2d. ed. Hampshire: Palgrave, 1999.

Hoekema, David A. "Liberalism Revisited: Religion, Reason, Diversity. A Review of John Rawls's *Political Liberalism*." *The Christian Century* 111, no. 29 (October 19, 1994): 957–964.

Hollenbach, David. "Religion and Political Life." *Theological Studies* 52, no. 1 (March 1991): 87–106.

Honig, Bonnie. *Political Theory and the Displacement of Politics*. Ithaca, NY: Cornell University Press, 1993.

Hunter, James Davison. *The Death of Character: Moral Education in an Age Without Good or Evil*. New York: Basic, 2000.

Hurd, Heidi M. "*Political Liberalism* (book review)." *Yale Law Journal* 105, no. 3 (December 1995): 795–824.

Hütter, Reinhard. "The Church's Peace Beyond the 'Secular': A Postmodern Augustinian's Deconstruction of Secular Modernity and Postmodernity." *Pro Ecclesia* 2 (Winter 1993): 106–116.

    Suffering Divine Things: Theology as Church Practice. Translated by Doug Stott. Grand Rapids, MI: William B. Eerdmans, 2000.

Insole, Christopher J. "Against Radical Orthodoxy: The Dangers of Overcoming Political Liberalism." *Modern Theology* 20, no. 2 (April 2004): 213–241.

Janz, Paul D. "Radical Orthodoxy and the New Culture of Obscurantism." *Modern Theology* 20, no. 3 (July 2004): 363–405.

Jenson, Robert W. *Systematic Theology*. Vol. 2, The Works of God. New York: Oxford University Press, 1999.

    "Eschatology." In *The Blackwell Companion to Political Theology*, edited by Peter Scott and William T. Cavanaugh, 407–420. Oxford: Blackwell, 2004.

Jüngel, Eberhard. *Christ, Justice and Peace: Toward a Theology of the State*. Translated by D. Bruce Hamill and Alan J. Torrance. Edinburgh: T&T Clark, 1992.

Kautz, Steven. "Liberalism and the Idea of Toleration." *American Journal of Political Science* 37, no. 2 (May 1993): 610–632.

Knight, W. F. Jackson. *St. Augustine's De Musica: A Synopsis*. London: The Orthological Institute, 1949.

Kymlicka, Will. *Contemporary Political Philosophy: An Introduction*. 2d. ed. Oxford: Oxford University Press, 2002.

Laclau, Ernesto and Chantal Mouffe. *Hegemony and Socialist Strategy: Towards a Radical Democratic Politics*. London: Verso, 1985.

Langerak, Edward. "Theism and Toleration." In *A Companion to Philosophy of Religion*, edited by Philip L. Quinn and Charles Taliaferro, 514–521. Cambridge, MA: Blackwell, 1997.

Larmore, Charles. *Patterns of Moral Complexity*. Cambridge: Cambridge University Press, 1987.

    "Political Liberalism." *Political Theory* 18, no. 3 (August 1990): 339–360.

    "Pluralism and Reasonable Disagreement." *Social Philosophy & Policy* 11, no. 1 (Winter 1994): 61–70.

Lash, Nicholas. "Not Exactly Politics or Power?" *Modern Theology* 8, no. 4 (October 1992): 353–364.

Laursen, John Christian and Cary J. Nederman, eds. *Beyond the Persecuting Society: Religious Toleration Before the Enlightenment.* Philadelphia, PA: University of Pennsylvania Press, 1998.

Locke, John. *A Letter Concerning Toleration*, edited by Mario Montuori. The Hague: Martinus Nijhoff, 1963.

MacIntyre, Alasdair. *After Virtue: A Study in Moral Theory.* 2d. ed. Notre Dame, IN: University of Notre Dame Press, 1984.

Whose Justice? Which Rationality? Notre Dame, IN: University of Notre Dame Press, 1988.

Three Rival Versions of Moral Enquiry: Encyclopaedia, Genealogy and Tradition. Notre Dame, IN: University of Notre Dame Press, 1990.

Manent, Pierre. *An Intellectual History of Liberalism.* Translated by Rebecca Balinski. Princeton, NJ: Princeton University Press, 1994.

Markham, Ian S. *Plurality and Christian Ethics.* Cambridge: Cambridge University Press, 1994.

Markus, R. A. *Saeculum: History and Society in the Theology of St Augustine.* London: Cambridge University Press, 1970.

Mathewes, Charles T. "Pluralism, Otherness, and the Augustinian Tradition." *Modern Theology* 14, no. 1 (January 1998): 83–112.

"Faith, Hope, and Agony: Christian Political Participation Beyond Liberalism." *Annual of the Society of Christian Ethics* 21 (2001): 125–150.

A Theology of Public Life During the World. Forthcoming.

McCarthy, Thomas. "Kantian Constructivism and Reconstructivism: Rawls and Habermas in Dialogue." *Ethics* 105 (October 1994): 44–63.

McClelland, J. S. *A History of Western Political Thought.* London: Routledge, 1996.

McClure, Kirstie M. "Difference, Diversity, and the Limits of Toleration." *Political Theory* 18, no. 3 (August 1990): 361–391.

McFadyen, Alistair. "Truth as Mission: The Christian Claim to Universal Truth in a Pluralist Public World." *Scottish Journal of Theology* 46, no. 4 (1993): 437–456.

Meckled-Garcia, Saladin. "Toleration and Neutrality: Incompatible Ideals?" *Res Publica* 7, no. 3 (2001): 296–297.

Mendus, Susan. *Toleration and the Limits of Liberalism.* Atlantic Highlands, NJ: Humanities, 1989.

ed. *Justifying Toleration: Conceptual and Historical Perspectives.* Cambridge: Cambridge University Press, 1988.

ed. *The Politics of Toleration: Tolerance and Intolerance in Modern Life.* Edinburgh: Edinburgh University Press, 1999.

Milbank, John. "The Body by Love Possessed: Christianity and Late Capitalism in Britain." *Modern Theology* 3 (October 1986): 35–65.

"An Essay Against Secular Order." *Journal of Religious Ethics* 15 (Fall 1987): 199–224.

"Letters to the Editor: A Socialist Economic Order." *Theology* 91 (September 1988): 412–415.

"The End of Dialogue." In *Christian Uniqueness Reconsidered: The Myth of a Pluralistic Theology of Religions*, edited by Gavin D'Costa, 174–191. Maryknoll, NY: Orbis, 1990.

"The End of Enlightenment: Post-modern or Post-secular?" In *The Debate on Modernity*, edited by Claude Geffré and Jean Pierre Jossua, 39–48. London: SCM, 1992.

"Problematizing the Secular: The Post-Postmodern Agenda." In *Shadow of Spirit: Postmodernism and Religion*, edited by Philippa Berry and Andrew Wernick, 30–44. London: Routledge, 1992.

Theology and Social Theory: Beyond Secular Reason. Oxford: Blackwell, 1993.

"Can a Gift be Given?: Prolegomena to a Future Trinitarian Metaphysic." *Modern Theology* 11 (January 1995): 119–161.

"The Midwinter Sacrifice: A Sequel to 'Can Morality be Christian?' " *Studies in Christian Ethics* 10, no. 2 (1997): 13–38.

"Postmodern Critical Augustinianism: A Short *Summa* in Forty-two Responses to Unasked Questions." In *The Postmodern God*, edited by Graham Ward, 265–278. Oxford: Blackwell, 1997.

"Sacred Triads: Augustine and the Indo-European Soul." *Modern Theology* 13, no. 4 (1997): 451–475.

The Word Made Strange: Theology, Language, Culture. Oxford: Blackwell, 1997.

"The Politics of Time: Community, Gift and Liturgy." *Telos* no. 113 (1998): 41–69.

Being Reconciled: Ontology and Pardon. London: Routledge, 2003.

Milbank, John, Catherine Pickstock, and Graham Ward, eds. *Radical Orthodoxy: A New Theology*. London: Routledge, 1999.

Mitchell, Joshua. "The Uses of Augustine, After 1989." *Political Theory* 27, no. 5 (October 1999): 694–705.

Moss, Jeremy, ed. *The Later Foucault: Politics and Philosophy*. London: Sage, 1998.

Mouffe, Chantal. *The Return of the Political*. London: Verso, 1993.

ed. *The Challenge of Carl Schmitt*. London: Verso, 1999.

The Democratic Paradox. London: Verso, 2000.

Mulhall, Stephen and Adam Swift. *Liberals and Communitarians*. Oxford: Blackwell, 1992.

Murphy, Andrew R. *Conscience and Community: Revisiting Toleration and Religious Dissent in Early Modern England and America*. University Park, PA: The Pennsylvania State University Press, 2001.

"Rawls and a Shrinking Liberty of Conscience." *Review of Politics* 60 (1998): 247–276.

"Tolerance, Toleration, and the Liberal Tradition." *Polity* 29 (1997): 593–623.

Nederman, Cary J. *Worlds of Difference: European Discourses of Toleration, C. 1100–C. 1550*. University Park, PA.: The Pennsylvania State University Press, 2000.

Nederman, Cary J. and John Christian Laursen, eds. *Difference and Dissent: Theories of Toleration in Medieval and Early Modern Europe*. Lanham, MD: Rowman & Littlefield, 1996.

Neuhaus, Richard John. *The Naked Public Square: Religion and Democracy in America*, Grand Rapids, MI: William B. Eerdmans, 1984.

Newey, Glen. "Is Democratic Toleration a Rubber Duck?" *Res Publica* 7, no. 3 (2001): 315–336.

Norton, Anne. "*Identity\Difference* (book review)." *Journal of Politics* 54, no. 3 (August 1992): 918–920.

O'Daly, Gerard. *Augustine's City of God: A Reader's Guide*. Oxford: Clarendon, 1999.

O'Donovan, Oliver. *The Problem of Self-Love in St. Augustine.* New Haven, CT: Yale University Press, 1980.

———. "Augustine's *City of God* XIX and Western Political Thought." In *The City of God: A Collection of Critical Essays,* edited by Dorothy F. Donnelly, 135–149. New York: Peter Lang, 1995.

———. *The Desire of the Nations: Rediscovering the Roots of Political Theology.* Cambridge: Cambridge University Press, 1996.

———. *Common Objects of Love: Moral Reflection and the Shaping of Community.* Grand Rapids, MI: William B. Eerdmans, 2002.

O'Neill, Onora. "Political Liberalism and Public Reason: A Critical Notice of John Rawls, Political Liberalism." *The Philosophical Review* 106, no. 3 (July 1997): 411–428.

Owen, J. Judd. *Religion and the Demise of Liberal Rationalism: The Foundational Crisis of the Separation of Church and State.* Chicago: University of Chicago Press, 2001.

Pangle, Thomas L. *The Ennobling of Democracy: The Challenge of the Postmodern Age.* Baltimore, MD: The Johns Hopkins University Press, 1992.

Pickett, Brent L. "Foucault and the Politics of Resistance." *Polity* 28, no. 4 (Summer 1996): 445–466.

Pickstock, Catherine. *After Writing: On the Liturgical Consummation of Philosophy.* Oxford: Blackwell Publishers, 1998.

———. "Liturgy and Modernity." *Telos* 30, no. 113 (fall 1998): 19–40.

Placher, William. *Unapologetic Theology: A Christian Voice in a Pluralistic Conversation.* Louisville, KY: Westminster/John Knox Press, 1989.

Prusak, Bernard G. "Politics, Religion & the Public Good: An Interview with Philosopher John Rawls." *Commonweal* 125, no. 16 (1998): 12–18.

Putnam, Robert D. *Bowling Alone: The Collapse and Revival of American Community.* New York: Simon & Schuster, 2000.

Quinn, Philip. "Religious Diversity and Religious Toleration." *International Journal for Philosophy of Religion* 50 (2001): 57–80.

Rabinow, Paul, ed. *The Foucault Reader.* London: Penguin Books, 1984.

Rasmusson, Arne. *The Church as Polis: From Political Theology to Theological Politics as Exemplified by Jürgen Moltmann and Stanley Hauerwas.* Notre Dame, IN: University of Notre Dame Press, 1995.

Rawls, John. *Political Liberalism.* Paperback ed. New York: Columbia University Press, 1993.

———. "The Idea of Public Reason Revisited." In *The Law of Peoples,* 129–180. Cambridge, MA: Harvard University Press, 1999.

———. *A Theory of Justice.* Rev. ed. Oxford: Oxford University Press, 1999.

———. *Justice as Fairness: A Restatement,* edited by Erin Kelly. Cambridge, MA: Belknap Press, 2001.

Rengger, N. J. "*Identity\Difference* (book review)." *Millennium: Journal of International Studies* 20, no. 3 (Winter 1991): 531–534.

———. *Political Theory, Modernity and Postmodernity: Beyond Enlightenment and Critique.* Oxford: Blackwell, 1995.

Reno, R. R "The Radical Orthodoxy Project." *First Things* no. 100 (February 2000): 37–44.

Rorty, Richard. *Contingency, Irony, and Solidarity.* Cambridge: Cambridge University Press, 1989.

"The Priority of Democracy to Philosophy." In *Objectivity, Relativism, and Truth: Philosophical Papers.* Vol. 1, 175–196. Cambridge: Cambridge University Press, 1991.

"Postmodernist Bourgeois Liberalism." In *Objectivity, Relativism, and Truth: Philosophical Papers.* Vol. 1, 197–202. Cambridge: Cambridge University Press, 1991.

"On Ethnocentrism: A Reply to Clifford Geertz." In *Objectivity, Relativism, and Truth: Philosophical Papers.* Vol. 1, 203–210. Cambridge: Cambridge University Press, 1991.

"Moral Identity and Private Autonomy: The Case of Foucault." In *Essays on Heidegger and Others: Philosophical Papers.* Vol. 2, 193–198. Cambridge: Cambridge University Press, 1991.

"Religion as Conversation-Stopper." *Common Knowledge* 3, no. 1 (Winter 1997):1–6.

Achieving our Country: Leftist Thought in Twentieth-century America. Cambridge, MA: Harvard University Press, 1999.

Rosenblum, Nancy L., ed. *Liberalism and the Moral Life.* Cambridge, MA: Harvard University Press, 1989.

ed. "Pluralism and Self-Defense." In *Liberalism and the Moral Life*, edited by Nancy L. Rosenblum, 207–226. Cambridge, MA: Harvard University Press, 1989.

Obligations of Citizenship and Demands of Faith: Religious Accommodation in Pluralist Democracies. Princeton, NJ: Princeton University Press, 2000.

Rubenstein, Diane. "The Four Discourses and the Four Volumes." *Journal of Politics* 56, no. 4 (November 1994): 1119–1132.

Sandel, Michael. *Liberalism and the Limits of Justice.* Cambridge: Cambridge University Press, 1982.

Democracy's Discontent: America in Search of a Public Philosophy. Cambridge, MA: Belknap Press, 1996.

"The Politics of Public Identity." *The Hedgehog Review* 2, no. 1 (Spring 2000): 72–88.

Sardar, Ziauddin. *Postmodernism and the Other: The New Imperialism of Western Culture.* London: Pluto, 1998.

Scarry, Elaine. *On Beauty and Being Just.* Princeton, NJ: Princeton University Press, 1999.

Schwartz, Joseph M. "*Ethos of Pluralization* (book review)." *Journal of Politics* 59, no. 2 (May 1997): 616–618.

Seligman, Adam. *The Idea of Civil Society.* Princeton, NJ: Princeton University Press, 1992.

Shklar, Judith N. "The Liberalism of Fear." In *Liberalism and the Moral Life*, edited by Nancy L. Rosenblum, 21–38. Cambridge, MA: Harvard University Press, 1989.

Skerrett, K. Roberts. "The Indispensable Rival: William Connolly's Engagement with Augustine of Hippo." *Journal of the American Academy of Religion* 72, no. 2 (June 2004): 487–506.

Skinner, Quentin. *The Foundations of Modern Political Thought*. Vol. 2, The Age of Reformation. Cambridge: Cambridge University Press, 1978.

Song, Robert. *Christianity and Liberal Society*. Oxford: Clarendon, 1997.

Spinner-Halev, Jeff. *Surviving Diversity: Religion and Democratic Citizenship*. Baltimore, MD: The Johns Hopkins University Press, 2000.

Stout, Jeffrey. *Democracy & Tradition*. Princeton, NJ: Princeton University Press, 2004.

Strong, Tracy B. "*Identity\Difference* (book review)." *Ethics* 102, no. 4 (July 1992): 863–865.

Tanner, Kathryn. *The Politics of God: Christian Theologies and Social Justice*. Minneapolis, MN: Fortress, 1992.

    Jesus, Humanity and the Trinity: A Brief Systematic Theology. Edinburgh: T&T Clark, 2001.

Taylor, Charles. *Philosophy and the Human Sciences: Philosophical Papers*, Vol. 2. Cambridge: Cambridge University Press, 1985.

    Sources of the Self: The Making of the Modern Identity. Cambridge, MA: Harvard University Press, 1989.

    Multiculturalism: Examining the Politics of Recognition, edited by Amy Gutmann, 25–73. Princeton, NJ: Princeton University Press, 1994.

TeSelle, Eugene. *Augustine the Theologian*. London: Burns & Oates, 1970.

    "Towards an Augustinian Politics." *The Journal of Religious Ethics* 16 (1988): 87–108.

Thiemann, Ronald F. *Constructing a Public Theology: The Church in a Pluralistic Culture*. Louisville, KY: Westminster/John Knox, 1991.

Topper, Keith. "Richard Rorty, Liberalism, and the Politics of Redescription." *The American Political Science Review* 89, no. 4 (December 1995): 954–965.

Torrance, Alan J. "Introductory Essay." In Eberhard Jüngel, *Christ, Justice and Peace: Toward a Theology of the State*. Translated by D. Bruce Hamill and Alan J. Torrance, ix–xx. Edinburgh: T&T Clark, 1992.

Toulmin, Stephen. *Cosmopolis: The Hidden Agenda of Modernity* Chicago, IL: The University of Chicago Press, 1992.

Volf, Miroslav. *Exclusion and Embrace: A Theological Exploration of Identity, Otherness, and Reconciliation*. Nashville: Abingdon, 1996.

    After Our Likeness: The Church as the Image of the Trinity. Grand Rapids, MI: William B. Eerdmans, 1998.

Von Balthasar, Hans Urs. *The Glory of the Lord: A Theological Aesthetics*. Vol. 2, Studies in Theological Style: Clerical Styles. Translated by Andrew Louth, Francis McDonagh, and Brian McNeil, C. R.V. Edited by John Riches. San Francisco, CA: Ignatius Press, 1998.

Wallach, John R. "*The Ethos of Pluralization* (book review)." *Political Theory* 25, no. 6 (December 1997): 886–893.

Walzer, Michael. *Spheres of Justice: A Defense of Pluralism and Equality*. Oxford: Blackwell, 1983.

    On Toleration. New Haven, CT: Yale University Press, 1997.

Ward, Graham, ed. *The Postmodern God: A Theological Reader*. Oxford: Blackwell , 1997.

Wenar, Leif. "*Political Liberalism*: An Internal Critique." *Ethics* 106, no. 1 (1995): 32–62.

Werpehowski, William. "Karl Barth and Politics." In *The Cambridge Companion to Karl Barth*, edited by John Webster, 228–242. Cambridge: Cambridge University Press, 2000.

Wetzel, James. "Snares of Truth: Augustine on Free Will and Predestination." In *Augustine and His Critics*, edited by Robert Dodaro and George Lawless, 124–141. London: Routledge, 2000.

White, Stephen K. *Sustaining Affirmation: The Strengths of Weak Ontology in Political Theory.* Princeton, NJ: Princeton University Press, 2000.

——— "Pluralism, Platitudes, and Paradoxes: Fifty Years of Western Political Thought." *Political Theory* 30, no. 4 (August 2002): 472–481.

Williams, Bernard. "Tolerance: An Impossible Virtue?" In *Toleration: An Elusive Virtue*, edited by David Heyd, 18–27. Princeton, NJ: Princeton University Press, 1996.

Williams, Rowan. "Politics and the Soul: A Reading of the *City of God*." *Milltown Studies* no. 19/20 (1987): 55–72.

——— "*Sapienta* and the Trinity: Reflections on the *De trinitate*." In *Collectanea Augustiniana: Mélanges T. J. Van Bavel.* Vol. 1. Edited by B. Bruning, M. Lamberigts, and J. Van Houtem, 317–332. Leuven: Augustinian Historical Institute, 1990.

——— " 'Know Thyself': What Kind of an Injunction?" In *Philosophy, Religion and the Spiritual Life*, edited by Michael McGhee, 211–227. Cambridge: Cambridge University Press, 1992.

——— "Between Politics and Metaphysics: Reflections in the Wake of Gillian Rose." *Modern Theology* 11, no. 1 (January 1995): 3–22.

Wills, Garry. *Saint Augustine.* New York: Viking, 1999.

Wilson-Kastner, Patricia. "Grace as Participation in the Divine Life in the Theology of Augustine of Hippo." *Augustinian Studies* 7 (1976): 135–152.

Wolff, Robert Paul, Barrington Moore, Jr., and Herbert Marcuse. *A Critique of Pure Tolerance.* Boston, MA: Beacon Press, 1969.

Wolterstorff, Nicholas. *John Locke and the Ethics of Belief.* Cambridge: Cambridge University Press, 1996.

——— "Religious Reasons, Liberal Theory and Coercion." Unpublished paper.

Zizek, Slavoj. *The Ticklish Subject: The Absent Centre of Political Ontology.* London: Verso, 1999.

Index

agonistic political theory 3, 20–22, 24,
83, 84–139, 140, 143, 179, 182, 183, 185,
193, 213, 225, 232, 239, 241, 250, 252,
259
Allen, Barry 128
Ambrose 202
Anderson, Benedict 22
Arendt, Hannah 85, 86, 120
Augustine 22, 25, 140–173, 174, 175,
176–179, 180, 186, 199, 201, 205, 212,
214, 219, 222–223, 227, 229–230, 233,
245, 248, 251, 254, 257 see also
Connolly, William
Church 159, 179
Cicero 165
coercion 164, 202
creation 145, 150, 177
deification see participation
earthly city, city of man 142, 152,
161–173, 178
evil 152
fall see sin
goods, ordering of goods 146, 164
government, politics 148, 170
harmony see order
Heavenly City, City of God 142, 148,
152, 159, 161–173, 176, 178, 181
human self 155–157
Jesus Christ 147, 158, 163
justice 162–169, 179
libido dominandi, lust for dominion
142, 148, 153, 162, 170, 202, 230,
254–255
love, loves 153, 161, 177, 254–255
order 144–149, 152, 153, 159, 164,
177
participation 159, 160, 172, 177
peace 143, 149, 166–169, 179

pilgrims, pilgrimage 159, 161, 170, 172,
178, 208
Platonic, Neoplatonic 147, 159
power 162–165
private 148, 152, 154, 155, 159,
161
saeculum 142, 168, 177
sin 147, 148, 151, 155, 183
Trinity 150, 157, 177, 179, 195

Badiou, Alain 134, 260
Barber, Benjamin 125
Barry, Brian 8
Barth, Karl 26, 175, 208–214
Bauerschmidt, Frederick 193
Benhabib, Seyla 27, 63, 120, 237–238
Blumenberg, Hans 120
Brink, Paul 242
Brown, Peter 141, 150
Brueggemann 23
Burnaby, John 154

Cavanaugh, William 23, 26, 217–218,
220, 221, 238, 240
Christianity 4, 5, 22, 26, 109, 134, 175,
183, 184, 185, 198, 215, 217, 219–228,
242, 255, 257, 260
church and state see state
Church, the 4, 12, 26, 175, 196, 199, 215,
216, 219–229, 234, 244, 250, 252, 257
see also Augustine
civil society 49, 73, 228, 238, 239
Cochrane, Charles Norris 142, 169
Coles, Romand 63
common good 35, 152, 155, 159, 161, 181,
208, 220, 222, 224